The great merger movement in American business, 1895–1904

Between 1895 and 1904 a great wave of mergers swept through the manufacturing sector of the U.S. economy. More than 1,800 firms disappeared into horizontal combinations, at least a third of which controlled more than 70 percent of the markets in which they operated. In *The Great Merger Movement in American Business,* Naomi Lamoreaux explores the causes of the mergers, concluding that there was nothing natural or inevitable about turn-of-the-century combinations.

With the aid of a formal model, Lamoreaux demonstrates that the merger wave was the product of a particular historical combination of circumstances: the development of capital-intensive production techniques; a spurt of rapid growth in a number of heavy industries in the late 1880s and early 1890s; and the panic and depression of 1893. Together, this sequence of events produced an episode of abnormally severe price competition that manufacturers finally turned to consolidation to alleviate.

Despite her conclusion that the mergers were not inevitable, Lamoreaux does not accept the opposing view that they were necessarily a threat to competition. She shows that most of the consolidations formed at the turn of the century were less efficient than the new rivals that appeared almost immediately, and that as a result the combines quickly lost their positions of market dominance. Moreover, in those few cases where consolidations proved to be more efficient, the nation was better off for their formation. Exceptions to these generalizations occurred, however, in a few industries where the new giant firms succeeded in erecting barriers to future competition. There, Lamoreaux argues, was where antitrust policy had a significant role to play. Unfortunately, the peculiar division of power and authority that characterizes our federal system of government prevented an effective policy from emerging. Limits on the national government's ability to regulate the activities of state-chartered corporations handicapped the enforcement of antitrust policy against those firms large enough to erect barriers to entry by purely internal means. Ironically, antitrust policy proved much more effective against small firms in relatively competitive industries than against large firms in oligopolistic ones.

Naomi Lamoreaux is Assistant Professor of History at Brown University. She received her Ph.D. from Johns Hopkins University.

The great merger movement in American business, 1895–1904

Naomi R. Lamoreaux
Brown University

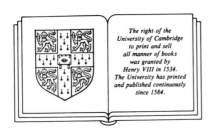

The right of the
University of Cambridge
to print and sell
all manner of books
was granted by
Henry VIII in 1534.
The University has printed
and published continuously
since 1584.

Cambridge University Press

Cambridge
New York   Port Chester
Melbourne   Sydney

Published by the Press Syndicate of the University of Cambridge
The Pitt Building, Trumpington Street, Cambridge CB2 1RP
40 West 20th Street, New York, NY 10011, USA
10 Stamford Road, Oakleigh, Melbourne 3166, Australia

First published 1985
Reprinted 1987, 1989
First paperback edition 1988

Printed in the United States of America

Library of Congress Cataloging in Publication Data
Lamoreaux, Naomi R.
The great merger movement in American business,
1895–1904.
Bibliography: p.
1. Consolidation and merger of corporations – United
States – History. I. Title.
HD2785.L36   1984   338.8'3'0973   84–16983

ISBN 0 521 26755 2 hardcovers
ISBN 0 521 35765 9 paperback

To Marguerite, Sol,
David, Nathan, Asher, Adley,
Sara, and Dara

Contents

Acknowledgments	*page*	ix
List of tables and figures		xi
1.	Introduction	1
2.	Product differentiation, mass production, and the urge to merge: competitive strategies and collusion in the late nineteenth century	14
3.	High fixed costs and rapid expansion: a model of price warfare and two examples	46
4.	Quantitative and qualitative evidence on the great merger movement	87
5.	What changed? The impact of consolidations on competitive behavior	118
6.	The great merger movement and antitrust policy	159
7.	Conclusion	187
Bibliographical essay		195
Index		203

Acknowledgments

Many scholars have contributed to the preparation of this book with their careful readings and helpful suggestions. I would especially like to thank Louis Galambos, Robert E. Gallman, Mark Lawrence Kornbluh, David Lamoreaux, James T. Patterson, and Peter Temin for their close scrutiny of the entire manuscript—some of them more than once. At the risk of overlooking some important contributors, I would also like to express my appreciation to Alan D. Anderson, Shannon Brown, Carl F. Christ, Heywood Fleisig, Robert Forster, Mary Gluck, Rhett Jones, Jacob Klerman, Peter Lindert, Charles W. McCurdy, William G. McLoughlin, Alan Olmstead, Glenn Porter, David G. Raboy, Barbara Rosen, Richard Rubinson, Steven Sass, John L. Thomas, Christopher L. Tomlins, David Underdown, and members of the Johns Hopkins University Economic History Seminar, the Smithsonian Institution's Washington Area Seminar in Economic History and the History of Technology, and Brown University's Social History Workshop, Second Year Graduate Workshop, and Junior Honors Seminar. Ralph L. Nelson was kind enough to supply me with the complete list of consolidations he compiled for his study *Merger Movements in American Industry*. I am also grateful for the help of Florence Bartoshesky and Marjorie A. Kierstead of the Manuscripts and Archives Department of the Harvard University Business School's Baker Library, T. Gedosch, Jerry N. Hess, and Lane Moore of the National Archives and Record Service, Janet Draper of Brown University's Rockefeller Library, and numerous librarians at Brown, Johns Hopkins, the Library of Congress, the University of Pittsburgh, the Carnegie Library of Pittsburgh, and Cornell University. Finally, thanks to Paul Wilson for his help with the econometrics computer package Shazam.

Tables and figures

Tables

1.1 Number of consolidations formed per year in the
    manufacturing sector   *page* 2
1.2 Market shares of consolidations   3
2.1 Size classification of Eastern newsprint mills, 1892 and
    1900   43
3.1 Production of wire and cut nails   64
3.2 Changes in the numbers and capacities of wire-nail
    firms   65
3.3 Trends in per-unit and total gross profits in the
    wire-nail industry   72
3.4 Production of Bessemer steel rails   77
4.1 Difference-of-means test using proxies for high fixed
    costs and rapid growth   90
4.2 Difference-of-means test: additional variables   92
4.3 Logit estimation 1 (maximum-likelihood method)   95
4.4 Logit estimation 2 (maximum-likelihood method)   96
4.5 Results of discriminant analysis   113
5.1 Changes in numbers and capacities of independent
    Eastern newsprint firms   128
5.2 Changes in numbers and capacities of independent
    tin-plate firms   150
5.3 Changes in numbers and capacities of independent
    wire-rod firms   151
6.1 Rates of return by size of firm and concentration ratio   185

Figures

2.1 Transactions in no. 1 foundry pig iron, Pittsburgh
    market, by weeks, 1891–4   20

2.2   Transactions in Bessemer pig iron, Pittsburgh market, by weeks, 1891–4   21
3.1   Cost and revenue curves for the firm   48
3.2   Cost and revenue curves for the industry   49
3.3   Cost and revenue curves for a firm with high fixed costs   51
3.4   Real price of 8-d wire nails, by months, 1890–9   66
3.5   Margin between price of wire nails and cost of raw materials, by months, 1891–8   68
3.6   Nominal and real prices of steel rails, 1890–9   79
5.1   Dominant-firm strategy   120
5.2   Cost curves for an independent firm   122
5.3   Effect of a decline in demand on the dominant-firm strategy   125
5.4   Prices of tin plate and wire nails, by months, 1901–8   137
5.5   Price ratios for steel outputs and inputs, 1891–1910   148

1. Introduction

Between 1895 and 1904 a great wave of mergers swept through the manufacturing sector. Nothing like it had ever been seen before, or has been seen since. Although subsequent waves of mergers have occurred, they have typically involved the acquisition of one or more small firms by a larger competitor or, more recently, by a firm in a completely different industry. By contrast, among turn-of-the-century mergers, the predominant process was horizontal consolidation – the simultaneous merger of many or all competitors in an industry into a single, giant enterprise.[1]

Although some manufacturers had previously organized consolidations, there had never been so many in such a short time. The formation in 1882 of the Standard Oil Trust, the first consolidation, had stimulated a few imitations in the sugar, whiskey, lead, cordage, cottonseed-oil, and linseed-oil industries. New Jersey's passage in 1888 of a general incorporation law for holding companies gave the merger movement another shot in the arm, but it was not until the late 1890s that the idea of consolidation really caught on. In 1895, four consolidations were organized; in 1897, there were six. Then, in 1898, the number of new combines suddenly rose to sixteen, and, in 1899, to a high of sixty-three. By the next year the movement began to taper off. Twenty-one consolidations were formed in 1901, seventeen in 1902, and a scant three in 1904 (Table 1.1).[2]

[1] From 1895 to 1904, 75 percent of the firms that disappeared into mergers joined consolidations of five or more enterprises. During the next wave of mergers, 1915-20, this figure fell to 14 percent. Ralph L. Nelson, *Merger Movements in American Industry, 1895-1956* (Princeton University Press, 1959), p. 53; for a general description of the turn-of-the-century merger wave, see pp. 33-70.

[2] This time series is based on the unpublished list of mergers Nelson compiled for his study *Merger Movements in American Industry*. I included in the series only horizontal consolidations of at least five previously competing firms. According to Hans Thorelli, who also compiled a list of mergers, 57 consolidations were organized from 1890 to 1893, 27 from 1894 to 1897, 186 from 1898 to 1901, and 34 from 1902 to 1903. However, Thorelli's list, especially for the early years, includes many firms that would not meet my criteria – firms such as Atlas Tack, Colorado Fuel and Iron, and Wheeling Steel and Iron, which involved mergers but were not true consolidations. Hans B. Thorelli, *The Federal Antitrust Policy: Origination of an*

Table 1.1. *Number of consolidations formed per year in the manufacturing sector*

Year	Number	Year	Number
1895	4	1900	21
1896	3	1901	19
1897	6	1902	17
1898	16	1903	5
1899	63	1904	3

Source: See Note 2.

Brief as the merger movement was, it threatened to make radical changes in the competitive structure of American industry. All told, more than 1,800 firms disappeared into consolidations, many of which acquired substantial shares of the markets in which they operated. Of the ninety-three consolidations whose market shares I have been able to trace, seventy-two controlled at least 40 percent of their industries and forty-two at least 70 percent. Even assuming that none of the remaining mergers achieved significant market power, this still means that more than half of the consolidations absorbed over 40 percent of their industries, and nearly a third absorbed in excess of 70 percent (Table 1.2).[3] Moreover, though some of the consolidations

American Tradition (Baltimore: Johns Hopkins Press, 1955), pp. 294-303. See also Alfred D. Chandler, Jr., *The Visible Hand: The Managerial Revolution in American Business* (Cambridge: Harvard University Press, 1977), pp. 320-34.

[3] Market shares are for dates as close as possible to the formation of the consolidations, with the term "consolidation" defined as in Note 2. My main source for these figures is John Moody, *The Truth About Trusts: A Description and Analysis of the American Trust Movement* (New York: Moody Publishing, 1904). Moody's own sources are not clear, but it is likely that he relied heavily on the statements of promoters. In order to correct for possible exaggeration in Moody's estimates, I used broad numerical categories and checked Moody's findings against other sources whenever possible (see citations that follow). I also introduced some downward biases in my figures. For example, I placed U.S. Steel in the 40-70 percent category, based on its share of crude steel production. U.S. Steel, however, was a consolidation of consolidations, and many of its constituents had encompassed more than 90 percent of their markets. My results differ strikingly from those of Jesse Markham, mainly because Markham included numerous small mergers in his calculations. Jesse W. Markham, "Survey of the Evidence and Findings on Mergers," *Business Concentration and Price Policy,* Universities-National Bureau Committee for Economic Research Conference (Princeton University Press, 1955), pp. 158-62; George W. Stocking, "Comment," *ibid.,* pp. 196-9; Nelson, *Merger Movements in American*

Table 1.2. *Market shares of consolidations*

Consolidations with < 40%	Consolidations with ≥ 40% but < 70%	Consolidations with ≥ 70%
Amalgamated Copper	American Bicycle	American Brake Shoe & Foundry
American Cigar	American Brass	American Can
Cleveland & Sandusky Brewing Co.	American Car & Foundry	American Chicle
Dayton Breweries	American Felt	American Fork & Hoe
Empire Steel & Iron	American Fisheries	American Hide & Leather
Independent Glass	American Linseed	American Ice
Maryland Brewing	American Malting	American Locomotive
Massachusetts Breweries	American Sewer Pipe	American School Furniture
New Orleans Brewing	American Shipbuilding	American Seeding Machine
New York & Kentucky	American Smelting & Refining	American Snuff
Pacific Coast Biscuit	American Stove	American Stogie
Pennsylvania Central Brewing	American Thread	American Window Glass
Pittsburgh Brewing	American Woolen	American Writing Paper
Providence Ice	California Fruit Canners Assoc.	Casein Co. of America
Pure Oil	General Chemical	Central Foundry
Republic Iron & Steel	International Salt	Chicago Pneumatic Tool
Standard Shoe Machinery	International Silver	Continental Tobacco
Susquehanna Iron & Steel	National Biscuit	Corn Products
United Breweries	National Candy	Crucible Steel
U.S. Flour Milling	National Enameling & Stamping	Distilling Co. of America
Virginia Iron, Coal & Coke	National Fireproofing	DuPont
	National Glass	Eastman Kodak
	New England Cotton Yarn	General Aristo
	Royal Baking Powder	Harbison-Walker Refractories
	Rubber Goods Mfg. Co.	International Harvester
	Standard Table Oil Cloth	International Paper
	United States Cotton Duck	International Steam Pump
	United States Shipbuilding	Mississippi Wire Glass
	United States Steel	National Asphalt
	Virginia-Carolina Chemical	National Carbon
		National Novelty
		Otis Elevator
		Pittsburgh Plate Glass
		Railway Steel Spring
		Standard Sanitary Mfg.
		Union Bag & Paper
		United Box Board & Paper

Table 1.2 (*cont.*)

Consolidations with < 40%	Consolidations with ≥ 40% but < 70%	Consolidations with ≥ 70%
		United Shoe Machinery
		United States Bobbin & Shuttle
		United States Cast Iron Pipe & Foundry
		United States Envelope
		United States Gypsum

Source: See Note 3. This list of consolidations differs from the one that underlies Table 1.1 in that double counting of successive mergers has been eliminated.

Industry, pp. 161-2, and unpublished list of consolidations; G. Warren Nutter and Henry Adler Einhorn, *Enterprise Monopoly in the United States, 1899-1958* (New York: Columbia University Press, 1969), pp. 132-7; Orris C. Herfindahl, *Copper Costs and Prices, 1870-1957* (Baltimore: Johns Hopkins Press, 1959), pp. 80-2; Arthur S. Dewing, *Corporate Promotions and Reorganizations* (Cambridge: Harvard University Press, 1914), pp. 64-71, 95-106, 209-13, 252, 259, 438-9, 526; Chandler, *The Visible Hand,* pp. 387-8, 570; Harry W. Laidler, *Concentration of Control in American Industry* (New York: Crowell, 1931), pp. 191-92, 246-47, 281; James E. Fell, Jr., *Ores to Metals: The Rocky Mountain Smelting Industry* (Lincoln: University of Nebraska Press, 1979); J. W. Jenks, "The Development of the Whisky Trust," *Trusts, Pools and Corporations,* ed. William Z. Ripley (rev. ed.; New York: Ginn & Co., 1916), p. 38; "The Tobacco Monopoly," *ibid.,* pp. 269-83, 314; "The International Harvester Company," *ibid.,* pp. 334-8; Pearce Davis, *The Development of the American Glass Industry* (New York: Russell & Russell-Atheneum, 1970), pp. 130-1, 175-80; Arthur Harrison Cole, *The American Wool Manufacture* (Cambridge: Harvard University Press, 1926), Vol. II, p. 9; David C. Smith, *History of Papermaking in the United States (1691-1969)* (New York: Lockwood Publishing, 1970), pp. 170, 185, 198-201; Myron W. Watkins, *Industrial Combinations and Public Policy: A Study of Combination, Competition, and the Common Welfare* (Boston: Houghton Mifflin, 1927), pp. 184-5; Richard Roe, "The United Shoe Machinery Company," *Journal of Political Economy,* 21 (December 1913), p. 942; Almarin Phillips, *Market Structure, Organization and Performance: An Essay on Price Fixing and Combinations in Restraint of Trade* (Cambridge: Harvard University Press, 1962), pp. 114-15; M. J. Fields, "The International Steam Pump Company: An Episode in American Corporate History," *Journal of Economic and Business History,* IV (1931-2), pp. 637-64; Glenn D. Babcock, *History of the United States Rubber Company: A Case Study in Corporate Management* (Bloomington: Indiana University Graduate School of Business, 1966), p. 73; Whitney Eastman, *The History of the Linseed Oil Industry in the United States* (Minneapolis: T. S. Denison & Co., 1968), p. 32; William G. Lathrop, *The Brass Industry in the United States: A Study of the Origin and the Development of the Brass Industry in the Naugatuck Valley and its Subsequent Extension over the Nation* (rev. ed; Mount Carmel, Conn.: William G. Lathrop, 1926), p. 156; Herman Steen, *Flour Milling in America* (Minneapolis: T. S. Denison & Co., 1963), p. 65; *Paper,* July 14, 1899, pp.

quickly lost their dominant positions, others – including U.S. Steel, DuPont, International Harvester, Pittsburgh Plate Glass, American Can, and American Smelting and Refining – still ranked among the nation's 100 largest corporations half a century later.[4]

Not surprisingly, contemporaries reacted to the great merger movement with alarm – a mood that was reflected in the scholarly literature as well as in the popular press. According to Charles J. Bullock's 1901 survey of the literature on trusts, the number of works devoted to the subject grew, as did public concern, with the number of consolidations. In the 1880s, for example, the spread of the holding company device had elicited "a marked increase of writings dealing with the subject." Between 1887 and 1890 there appeared at least fifteen treatises or reports of official investigations and over thirty-five articles in important periodicals. Over the next six years, interest declined, and only eight books or reports and hardly more than a score of articles were published. Then, as the merger movement gathered strength, scholarly commentary increased. "In 1897 and 1898 at least six books or pamphlets and about thirty articles appeared, foreshadowing an increased interest in the problem of monopoly. And, finally, the last two years have given us not less than twenty-eight books, reports, and pamphlets, together with a flood of periodical articles that will reach probably one hundred and fifty titles when the returns for 1900 have all been received."[5]

1, 6; *Paper Trade Journal,* May 21, 1898, pp. 419-20; July 24, 1902, pp. 99-100; *Iron Age,* July 13, 1899, p. 12; July 5, 1900, p. 20; April 11, 1901, p. 11; U.S. Congress, House, *Hearings before the Committee on Investigation of United States Steel Corporation* (Washington, D.C.: U.S. Government Printing Office, 1912), Vol. II, pp. 825, 829, Vol. III, p. 1753; U.S. Industrial Commission, *Preliminary Report on Trusts and Industrial Combinations,* 56th Cong., 1st Sess., 1900, House Doc. 476, pp. 76-9, 176-8, 1049, and *Report on Trusts and Industrial Combinations,* 57th Cong., 1st Sess., 1901, House Doc. 182, pp. xiii, xli, lviii, lxxxii-lxxxv, 57, 97, 207, 239, 348, 356, 411, 677, 681-2, 684, 691, 719.

[4] Nelson, *Merger Movements in American Industry,* pp. 154-6.

[5] Charles J. Bullock, "Trust Literature: A Survey and a Criticism," *Quarterly Journal of Economics,* 15 (February 1901), pp. 167-8. See also Louis Galambos, *The Public Image of Big Business in America, 1880-1940: A Quantitative Study in Social Change* (Baltimore: Johns Hopkins Press, 1975), pp. 79-156. Galambos analyzed the attitudes toward big business reflected in a selection of work-related middle-class publications. He found that unfavorable references to big business reached an all-time peak in the late 1890s, when the consolidation movement overlapped the depression of that decade, and they remained at a high level for the duration of the wave of mergers, though the return of prosperity somewhat dampened discontent.

In their zeal to understand what was happening around them, turn-of-the-century writers proposed a number of different explanations for the consolidation movement. For some, mergers were the inevitable result of tendencies inherent in the competitive process itself – viewed as the drive for more efficient methods of production or the susceptibility of capital-intensive enterprises to ruinous competition (depending on whether the observer was by temperament an optimist or pessimist). Other scholars saw nothing inevitable in combinations at all. Although they agreed that big enterprises were often more efficient than small ones, they insisted that there were well-defined limits beyond which diseconomies of scale would set in. Formed for the purpose of monopoly control, consolidations were generally too large to be efficient. Only by using their size to unfair advantage could they maintain their dominance – for example, by means of predatory pricing.[6]

Regardless of their positions on the inevitability of consolidations, most scholars accepted the prevailing view that large size carried with it market power and the potential for abuse. They therefore advocated increased government oversight of large corporations. In order to counterbalance the growth of private economic power they proposed a variety of reforms, ranging from state statutes outlawing predatory pricing to new federal regulatory agencies with unprecedented powers to rule on the legality of combinations.[7]

The concern over the abuse of private economic power that underlay these proposals for expansion in governmental activity persisted in the scholarly literature through the 1930s.[8] With the growth in the

[6] See, for examples, John Bates Clark, *The Control of Trusts: An Argument in Favor of Curbing the Power of Monopoly by a Natural Method* (New York: Macmillan, 1905); William M. Collier, *The Trusts: What Can We Do with Them? What Can They Do for Us?* (New York: Baker and Taylor, 1900); Richard T. Ely, *Monopolies and Trusts* (New York: Macmillan, 1900); Ernst von Halle, *Trusts or Industrial Combinations in the United States* (New York: Macmillan, 1899); Jeremiah Whipple Jenks, *The Trust Problem* (New York: McClure, Phillips and Co., 1900).

[7] See the citations in Note 6. Jenks was particularly active in the movement to expand federal authority. He served on the Industrial Commission created by Congress to investigate (among other matters) trusts and industrial combinations. He also helped to draft the Hepburn bill of 1907, which aimed to expand the regulatory powers of the Commissioner of Corporations. See Chapter 6.

[8] For a summary of the literature to 1930, see Paul T. Homan, "Industrial Combination as Surveyed in the Recent Literature," *Quarterly Journal of Economics*, XLIV (February 1930), pp. 345-75. Major studies include Eliot Jones, *The Trust Problem*

size and activities of the federal government as a result of the New Deal, however, the focus of attention shifted – partly because government at that time seemed able to counterbalance the power of big business, but also because big government itself was becoming a source of growing concern. Interest in explaining the turn-of-the-century consolidation movement and assessing its consequences dwindled. Indeed, since World War II, only a handful of pieces have appeared addressing such issues, and even these mark a noticeable shift away from the problem that most agitated earlier scholars: monopoly power.[9] For example, in his article "The Beginnings of 'Big Business' in American Industry," Alfred D. Chandler, Jr., claimed that mergers for the purpose of market control could account for the rise of large-scale enterprises only in several types of industries: finished producer goods and those consumer goods industries in which transport improvements had suddenly brought local firms into competition in a national market. In most other cases, Chandler argued, large-scale mergers aimed either to improve efficiency or to guarantee access to raw-material supplies.[10] Although Ralph L. Nelson, in his study *Merger Movements in American Industry*, refused to eliminate the market control motive as a possible cause of the consolidation movement, he attached more explanatory importance to developments in the stock market, in particular to fluctuations in securities prices and the volume of trading.[11] In a more extreme position, Jesse W. Markham, in "Survey of the Evidence and Findings on Mergers,"

in the United States (New York: Macmillan, 1921); Watkins, *Industrial Combinations and Public Policy;* and Henry R. Seager and Charles A. Gulick, Jr., *Trust and Corporation Problems* (New York: Harper & Brothers, 1929). During the Great Depression, fear that the crisis had been prolonged by large firms' pricing policies spurred another outpouring of scholarship. For examples, see Arthur Robert Burns, *The Decline of Competition: A Study of the Evolution of American Industry* (New York: McGraw-Hill, 1936); Laidler, *Concentration of Control in American Industry;* Caroline F. Ware and Gardiner Means, *The Modern Economy in Action* (New York: Harcourt, Brace and Company, 1936).

[9] A major exception is Gabriel Kolko, *The Triumph of Conservatism: A Reinterpretation of American History, 1900-1916* (Chicago: Quadrangle Paperbacks, 1967). See also George Bittlingmayer, "Decreasing Average Cost and Competition: A New Look at the Addyston Pipe Case," *Journal of Law and Economics,* XXV (October 1982), pp. 201-79; and Bittlingmayer, "Price-Fixing and the Addyston Pipe Case," *Research in Law and Economics,* V (1983), pp. 57-128.

[10] Alfred D. Chandler, Jr., "The Beginnings of 'Big Business' in American Industry," *Business History Review,* XXXIII (Spring 1959), pp. 1-31.

[11] Nelson, *Merger Movements in American Industry,* pp. 89-126.

concluded that at best only one of five mergers was motivated by a desire for monopoly power. The explanation for the abnormally large volume of mergers at the turn of the century, Markham suggested, was instead a speculative frenzy in stock issues.[12] Finally, Lance Davis has hypothesized that imperfections in U.S. capital markets put small firms at a disadvantage in securing financing, thereby inducing them to form consolidations.[13]

Whereas previously the great merger movement had appeared in the literature as the central transforming event of the modern era, in recent years the significance of its role has been greatly diminished. Thus, Chandler argues in *The Visible Hand* that the crucial transformation involved not horizontal combination but vertical integration – the joining together within one firm of mass distribution and mass production, and the development of managerial systems capable of coordinating the flow of raw materials and output through large multiunit enterprises. According to Chandler, these innovations occurred first in firms such as Swift & Company (meat packing) and the I. M. Singer Company (sewing machines), where creative entrepreneurs faced complex organizational problems. In later years the consolidation movement proved important because it quickly transformed single-unit firms into multiunit giants. But, claims Chandler, consolidations were successful only when managers abandoned their strategy of horizontal combination and followed the example of Singer, Swift, and other pioneers, who integrated their operations from raw materials to final markets and adopted a management structure capable of administering their organizations efficiently.[14]

While Chandler has downplayed the role of the consolidation movement in the rise of the modern, large-scale business enterprise, the so-called New Economic Historians (or Cliometricians), who have dominated the discipline of economic history for the past twenty years, have gone even further. They have devoted virtually no attention to the subject of big business at all, let alone the consolida-

[12] Markham, "Survey of the Evidence and Findings on Mergers," pp. 141-82.
[13] Lance Davis, "The Capital Markets and Industrial Concentration: The U.S. and the U.K., a Comparative Study," *Economic History Review*, Second Series, XIX (August 1966), pp. 255-72.
[14] Chandler, *The Visible Hand*, pp. 285-376.

tion movement. *A New Economic View of American History*, by Susan Previant Lee and Peter Passell, is the most complete survey of this body of literature to date, and the concerns of the discipline are accurately reflected in the organization of their text. Lee and Passell allocate five chapters to the economic history of slavery, sharecropping, and the Civil War. Their lone chapter on "Economic Growth and Institutional Change after the Civil War" discusses Robert Fogel's thesis that railroads were not indispensable to American economic development, as well as the problem of nineteenth-century farmers' discontent. The book contains no discussion at all of the changing organizational structure of American industry.[15]

This neglect cannot be excused by the youthfulness of the field; in twenty years, New Economic Historians have explored a wide range of topics, from economies of scale in river steamboating to the rise of the entire Western world to economic dominance. Nor can it be explained by the inappropriateness of Cliometric techniques to the topic. The hallmark of the New Economic History has been innovative application of economic theory and quantitative analysis to many different kinds of historical problems. Rather, the neglect seems to have resulted from the Cliometricians' belief that the merger movement was not important.[16] New Economic Historians have, for the most part, accepted the current conventional wisdom of the economics profession that the economy is "workably" competitive – that is, that industrial concentration has not resulted in significant deviations from competitive pricing. Thus, when Jeffrey G. Williamson constructed an elaborate two-sector, two-region simulation model of the American economy from 1870 to 1914 – the period of the consolidation movement and the growth of large-scale enterprise in general – he built into his model the assumption of perfect competition and constant returns to scale. In other words, he assumed that the consolidation movement did not alter the competitive structure of

[15] Susan Previant Lee and Peter Passell, *A New Economic View of American History* (New York: W. W. Norton, 1979).
[16] Of course there are exceptions – Lance Davis's work, for example. See also Thomas S. Ulen, "Cartels and Regulation: Late Nineteenth-Century Railroad Collusion and the Creation of the Interstate Commerce Commission" (unpublished Ph.D. dissertation, Stanford University, 1979); Bittlingmayer, "Decreasing Average Cost and Competition;" and "Price Fixing and the Addyston Pipe Case."

American industry and that big business was no more (or less) efficient than small business. Williamson himself recognized the problems that this decision might create: "The changes in economic structure following World War I are much too profound to make our pre-war model useful for understanding the 1920s. Indeed, we may even wish to use our results to suggest how and to what extent the American economy underwent significant structural changes after the mid-1890s should our ability to predict the last decade or so be relatively poor."[17] After subjecting his results to a number of different econometric tests, however, Williamson concluded that no such effort was necessary, that the model adequately reproduced trends in the data that have survived from the period, including the years 1890 to 1914.[18]

Certainly this result is surprising. So, for that matter, is the general scholarly neglect of a phenomenon that transfigured virtually overnight such a major part of the manufacturing sector. My purpose, therefore, is to assess the reasonableness of this neglect by reexamining the turn-of-the-century merger movement, its causes and consequences. Why did so many firms in so many industries suddenly combine into a few large enterprises? What relationship did this phenomenon have to the growth of big business in general? Was consolidation simply, as Chandler has suggested, an alternative route to the modern, vertically integrated, professionally managed corporation? Or did it have unique structural consequences? Is the conventional wisdom of most Cliometricians correct that the economy, despite the merger movement, has been workably competitive? Or did consolidations alter competitive behavior and the functioning of the economy? Certainly the movement provoked a political reaction. How, in turn, did this political response affect economic decision making?

The method I use to answer these questions combines traditional business-history techniques with the theoretical economic reasoning characteristic of the New Economic History. As is common in research in business history, I collected data for detailed case studies, in

---

[17] Jeffrey G. Williamson, *Late Nineteenth-Century American Development: A General Equilibrium History* (Cambridge University Press, 1974), p. 62.
[18] *Ibid.*, pp. 21–91.

this instance for the steel and paper industries. I chose these two industries because they both generated consolidations, but in other respects they differed considerably from each other. Although both industries produced mainly intermediate goods, steel was a durable, relatively high-valued product, whereas paper was a low-valued nondurable. The steel industry was famous for its daring entrepreneurs and robber barons, men such as Andrew Carnegie and J. W. ("Bet-a-Million") Gates; the paper industry, by contrast, produced no similarly prominent figures. Finally, the fates of the consolidations were very different in the two industries. Steel-industry consolidations generally succeeded, whereas mergers in the paper industry had at best a marginal existence.

As is less common in business history, I consciously used economic models to make sense of the data collected for the case studies, to help me decide what story to tell. In order both to test the theories and to gain the most explanatory leverage from them, I derived predictions from the models that I then checked against quantitative data for the manufacturing sector as a whole, information from the case studies, and secondary literature on industries other than paper and steel. The models and verified predictions form the analytical substructure of my narrative.[19]

This narrative develops according to the following plan. After discussing the main competitive strategies pursued by firms in the late nineteenth century, I argue (in Chapter 2) that the entrepreneurial model does not fit many large-scale industries, including most that subsequently formed consolidations. Far from being dominated by extraordinary entrepreneurs or robber barons who managed to overwhelm their competitors, the more common experience, even in most branches of the steel industry, was rivalry among a relatively small number of evenly matched firms, no one of which was able to secure a permanent advantage. I then develop a model (Chapter 3) that represents the essential features of this more common type of industry and show how, under certain specified conditions, rapid industrial growth might lead to price warfare and ultimately to consolidation. In Chapter 4 I test this explanation for the great merger move-

[19] See Charles A. Lave and James G. March, *An Introduction to Models in the Social Sciences* (New York: Harper & Row, 1975), especially Chapters I-III.

ment, using quantitative data from the manufacturing census, secondary literature on consolidations, and data on the steel and paper industries. My conclusion is that the consolidation movement was by no means an inevitable component of the development of large-scale industry; oligopolistic market structures could also have emerged as a result of a more gradual process of growth and adjustment. In the case of the late nineteenth-century United States, however, a particular conjunction of circumstances – specifically the simultaneous rapid expansion of many capital-intensive industries in the early 1890s, followed by the deep depression of 1893 – gave rise to abnormally serious price wars and consequently to the great merger movement.

Chapters 5 and 6 explore the aftermath of the merger movement, the economic and political implications of this chance occurrence. In Chapter 5 I use a dominant-firm model to analyze whether or not consolidations were able to control the competitive environment. My conclusion is that in the short run many were, regardless of their relative efficiency. In the long run, however, the higher costs that most of the consolidations entailed prevented their continued dominance – except where they were able to erect barriers to entry. The ball was thus in the politicians' court. Chapter 6 evaluates the government's response to the great merger movement, in particular its ability to prevent barriers to new competition from being erected. I argue that government action at all levels was handicapped by the peculiar division of power and authority that characterizes our federal type of government. The result was a system of rules and precedents that outlawed some kinds of barriers to entry – those that explicitly imposed limits on the actions of other firms – but did not prevent the erection of other, more subtle barriers. Ironically, this system weighed more heavily on small firms than on large ones, on single-unit enterprises rather than consolidations, on competitive rather than oligopolistic industries. Yet it also encouraged large firms to improve their efficiency.

One final note on presentation. In the interest of reaching as diverse an audience as possible I have endeavored to explain all of the economic models I use in simple fashion and to include appropriate diagrams. These aids will be most useful to readers who have had a little training in economics (i.e., those who recognize terms such as "fixed cost" and "marginal revenue"). Readers who have not had this background may find the expositions difficult. They may wish to skim through these sections, but they should still be able to follow the basic argument. Economists will probably want to skip these elementary discussions altogether.

2. Product differentiation, mass production, and the urge to merge

Competitive strategies and collusion in the late nineteenth century

In early 1896, competition among domestic manufacturers of tin plate sent prices tumbling below the level at which plates could be imported into the country. That April the manufacturers met under the aegis of the Tin Plate Manufacturers' Association to fix prices just below the import level. All but two of the firms in the industry signed the resulting "gentlemen's agreement" (and even one of those promised to abide by it), but by May reports of violations had already proliferated. To make matters worse, in August the industry's largest producer, the American Tin Plate Company (of Indiana), resigned from the association, in effect nullifying the agreement. The other members of the association attempted in November to revive the pact without the participation of this company, but met with only temporary success: "the temptation to do a larger business at lower prices was too great."[1] In December they determined to alter their strategy. Because the American Tin Plate Company was still operating independently, "it was decided that the other Indiana mills should be recognized as free to make their own market in their own territory, with the understanding that the combination prices be maintained in the East and other sections."[2] By the end of January this effort, too, had collapsed. Finally, in March 1897, after much urging by the other manufacturers, the American Tin Plate Company consented to join a new Association of Tin Plate Makers of the United States, with its own Daniel G. Reid as chairman. Still nothing availed to stem the competition and the downward slide in prices. Between 1896 and 1897 the real price of common-grade tin plate

---

[1] D. E. Dunbar, *The Tin Plate Industry: A Comparative Study of Its Growth in the United States and in Wales* (Boston: Houghton Mifflin, 1915), pp. 76-8.
[2] *Iron Age*, December 31, 1896, p. 1310.

14

had fallen 10 percent; from 1897 to 1898 it dropped another 12 percent.[3]

"People of the same trade seldom meet together, even for merriment and diversion, but the conversation ends in a conspiracy against the public, or in some contrivance to raise prices."[4] Adam Smith's often quoted dictum has become an article of popular faith. But outcomes are at least as important as actions taken, and, as the foregoing example suggests, many of the conspiracies and contrivances that Smith warned against soon fell apart. The question that concerns us is, which ones? The purpose of collusion was typically to relieve downward pressure on prices by restricting output and to distribute the costs of this curtailment evenly across the industry. It was one means of protecting the firm from the dangers of competition. But the success of (and willingness to engage in) collusion depended to a large extent on what overall competitive strategy a firm pursued. In the United States during the late nineteenth century, most firms adopted one of two basic strategies. Either they manufactured small quantities of carefully differentiated, high-quality products, or they mass-produced a cheap homogeneous output. Where the first strategy was successfully pursued, collusion was for the most part unnecessary, for prices were relatively stable, and production adjusted easily to fluctuations in demand. Although manufacturers often banded together to act in their common interest, their purpose was rarely to fix prices or restrict production – Adam Smith's dictum notwithstanding. In those few cases in which price fixing was the aim, it was usually successful, but typically the result was little differ-

[3] Dunbar, *The Tin-Plate Industry*, pp. 76-8; *Iron Age*, April 23, 1896, p. 980; November 26, 1896, p. 1005; December 31, 1896, p. 1310; January 4, 1897, p. 12; March 4, 1897, p. 12; April 15, 1897, p. 22; *Metal Worker, Plumber and Steam Fitter*, May 9, 1896, pp. 36-7; August 29, 1896, p. 48; November 21, 1896, p. 44; January 30, 1897, p. 27; March 6, 1897, p. 38; April 10, 1897, p. 47; April 17, 1897, p. 42; *American Metal Market and Daily Iron and Steel Report*, November 21, 1896, p. 2; *American Manufacturer and Iron World*, March 5, 1897, p. 343; U.S. Congress, House, *Hearings before the Committee on Investigation of United States Steel Corporation* (Washington, D.C.: U.S. Government Printing Office, 1912), Vol. VII, p. 5562; George F. Warren and Frank A. Pearson, *Prices* (New York: Wiley, 1933), p. 13.
[4] Adam Smith, *An Inquiry into the Nature and Causes of the Wealth of Nations* (New York: Modern Library, 1937), p. 128.

ent from what the workings of the market would have brought about anyway.

In the case of industries in which the mass-production strategy prevailed, the response to fluctuations in demand was more problematic. Despite the stereotypes we have of nineteenth-century industries dominated by a single entrepreneur or robber baron, there were many mass-production industries in which no one firm managed to outdo its competitors – industries that were populated by relatively small numbers of evenly matched firms, each of which could affect the pricing and production decisions of its rivals. In this type of industry there were certain conditions (to be specified in Chapter 3) under which output failed to adjust to fluctuations in demand, so that a decline in demand might actually elicit an increase in production (the tin-plate industry in the 1890s is a good example). When this happened, manufacturers often resorted to pools, gentlemen's agreements, and other similar devices to bring production into line with demand. As we shall see, however, these attempts at collusion rarely succeeded.

The strategy of product differentiation

Companies chose the strategy of product differentiation for two basic reasons: to isolate and protect themselves from the actions of competitors, and to escape the worst effects of fluctuations in business conditions. A firm might accomplish both of these purposes simultaneously by specializing in a high-quality product (especially a luxury item) and working to build a good reputation for its brands.[5] By the first means, a firm could reduce the income elasticity of demand for its output – and hence the variability of both prices and revenues over the course of the business cycle. The second helped the firm establish its claim to be a high-quality producer. It also reduced the firm's price elasticity of demand and enabled it to erect barriers to entry in its part of the industry.

Firms that adopted this strategy in the paper industry, for example, devoted their resources to the manufacture of fine, "loft-dried" (as

---

[5] I am using the term "product differentiation" for both of these tactics, not simply in the conventional sense of distinguishing one's product from those of competitors.

opposed to "engine-sized") writing paper. Their counterparts in the whiskey industry concentrated on the preparation of aged bourbon and rye, rather than on mass production of cheaper "pure spirits" for immediate consumption. Similarly, in the starch industry, this type of firm produced a high-quality output, branded and packaged for use in the home, instead of the generic product sold in quantity to the textile and candy industries. Although the strategy of product differentiation was much easier to pursue in the case of consumer goods, firms applied it to intermediate products as well. The great majority of pig-iron producers specialized in one or more of the numerous grades of foundry and forge iron, marketing their products under such evocative brand names as Charlotte, Rebecca, Mount Vernon, and Riverside. Small independent petroleum refiners concentrated their energies on the production of special by-products such as lubricants, matching their products to the particular requirements of their customers' machinery.[6]

Implicit in the strategy of product differentiation was a particular philosophy of doing business: Earn profits on high margins rather than volume production; strive in times of reduced demand to maintain prices rather than output; avoid cutting prices for fear of cheapening the image of one's product. Where the strategy was most successful, as, for example, in the case of the ledger-paper industry, the degree of price stability achieved was truly remarkable. Thus, in 1903, paper dealers greeted an increase in prices by the manufacturers of linen ledger paper with astonishment; no one in the trade could remember the last time these firms had altered their quotations: "One man ventured the guess that the last change was a reduction of 5 per cent., made on February 1, 1891, by the Parsons Paper

---

[6] Constance McLaughlin Green, *Holyoke, Massachusetts: A Case History of the Industrial Revolution in America* (New Haven: Yale University Press, 1939), pp. 153-5; U.S. Industrial Commission, *Preliminary Report on Trusts and Industrial Combinations*, 56th Cong., 1st Sess., 1900, House Doc. 476, "Topical Digest of Evidence," p. 75; Arthur S. Dewing, *Corporate Promotions and Reorganizations* (Cambridge: Harvard University Press, 1914), pp. 51-2; American Iron and Steel Association (hereafter AISA), *Directory to the Iron and Steel Works of the United States*, 1882 to 1901; Harold F. Williamson and Arnold R. Daum, *The American Petroleum Industry: The Age of Illumination, 1859-1899* (Evanston: Northwestern University Press, 1959), pp. 274, 464-5, 684-7.

Company."[7] The increase in 1903 was the first price change in per-haps twelve years; yet in the interim the economy had suffered one of the most severe depressions in American history.

This reluctance to cut prices was in part a matter of inclination, but product differentiation made it economically viable. By specializ-ing in the manufacture of quality products – staking out a position at the upper end of their markets – manufacturers could minimize the effects of general downward shifts in demand. Hence, in the paper industry as a whole, it was the manufacturers of undifferentiated, staple products – newsprint, wrapping, and to a large extent manila paper – who suffered most from fluctuations in business conditions. By contrast, makers of fine writing paper (including linen ledgers) were relatively immune. Many writing-paper mills had "an estab-lished trade of their own, so large and steady that fluctuations in the general trade [did] not much affect them."[8] Reviewing the year of depression that followed the Panic of 1893, the New York corre-spondent for *Paper World* remarked that fine writings had held their own most nearly in price, and with the best demand, of any type of paper. One had to move down the scale of grades before the effects of the depression became apparent.[9]

This relationship between product differentiation and price stabil-ity existed in many other industries as well. It was always easier, for instance, to prevent price declines on the sale of packaged, trade-marked box starch than it was on the product sold in bulk for manufacturing purposes. Although severe competition in the 1880s sent the price of the latter plummeting, established firms with reput-able box-starch brands, such as Duryea and Kingsford in New York, were able to maintain both production and profits. During approxi-mately the same period, competition in cereals forced bulk oatmeal prices so low that it was said there was no profit left in the trade. Yet

[7] *Paper Trade Journal*, February 5, 1903, p. 163. Linen ledger paper was a high quality intermediate good with an inelastic demand curve. According to *Paper World*, the strength of brand loyalties made it extremely difficult for a new firm to enter this market. Crane Brothers, for example, had to run their machines on writing paper and other types that were relatively easy to sell while they slowly built up a market for their ledger paper. See December 1888, p. 1.
[8] *Ibid.*, September 1889, p. 12.
[9] *Ibid.*, June 1894, p. 218.

Henry Parsons Crowell, who marketed his oatmeal under the popular Quaker label, managed to sustain an advance.[10]

Similarly, in the tin-plate industry, small finishing works (known as dipperies) that had achieved good reputations for their brands, particularly of terne plate (special roofing plate coated with a mixture of tin and lead), were successful in maintaining stable prices. From January 1896 to July 1897 the average price of common-grade tin plate fell from $3.80 to $3.17 per box, a decline of 17 percent. Over the same period of time, the price of branded tin plates quoted in the *Metal Worker* fell only 4 percent on the New York market, while branded roofing plates fell a scant 1 percent. Some of the most prestigious firms – John Hamilton & Company, Meurer Brothers, and N.& G. Taylor – did not reduce quotations at all during this period.[11]

In general, the more successful a firm was in differentiating its product from potential substitutes and in staking out its claim to the upper end of the market, the more freedom from general price trends it was able to secure. This can be shown in the case of the pig-iron industry by comparing records of actual market transactions for two different grades of pig iron in Pittsburgh in the 1890s.[12] Pig-iron producers never had as much scope for product differentiation as manufacturers of writing paper and other consumer goods. Nonetheless, firms that specialized in one or more of the numerous grades of foundry or forge iron had more opportunity to distinguish their products than those that produced mainly Bessemer-grade pig. Whereas Bessemer producers sold the greater part of their output in bulk to large steel works whose raw-material requirements were fairly homogeneous, foundry and forge producers catered to the special needs of a multitude of small rolling mills, foundries, and machine shops.

[10] Dewing, *Corporate Promotions and Reorganizations*, pp. 51-3; Arthur F. Marquette, *Brands, Trademarks and Good Will: The Story of the Quaker Oats Company* (New York: McGraw-Hill, 1967), pp. 18-26.
[11] It is possible that these firms secretly shaded prices. Nonetheless, the fact that they refused to follow other firms in openly lowering quotations is significant. See quotations of tin-plate brands in *Metal Worker*, 1896-7; AISA, *Statistics of the American and Foreign Iron Trades: Annual Report of the Secretary*, 1897, p. 28.
[12] The AISA *Bulletin* reported market transactions on a weekly basis in the 1890s. It recorded the price and quantity of iron sold, the terms of the transaction (cash or credit), and often the date for which delivery was contracted.

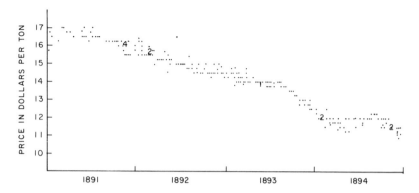

Figure 2.1. Transactions in no. 1 foundry pig iron, Pittsburgh market, by weeks, 1891–4. Transactions were published by the AISA *Bulletin*. Data are only for weeks in which the *Bulletin* was published, generally three out of every four weeks. Dots represent single transactions. Whenever more than one sale occurred at the same price during the same week, a single-digit number is used to indicate the number of transactions.

Figure 2.1 records the prices for which lots of no. 1 foundry pig iron sold during each week of the period 1891-4. Although the market as a whole displayed a general downward tendency, in most weeks there was a considerable dispersion of prices, amounting at times to more than 10 percent of the average price. Product differentiation allowed some firms to maintain prices long after their competitors had made cuts. For instance, although the average price of no. 1 foundry pig iron dropped from slightly more than $15.00 per ton in June 1892 to a little less than $14.00 a year later, some firms were able to sell their product for $15.00 as late as December 1892 and for $14.75 until March 1893, despite the fact that similar iron had sold for $14.50 as early as August, for $14.25 in October, and for $14.00 beginning in February.[13]

[13] Unfortunately, it is impossible to associate specific sales with specific firms. But trade-journal reports indicate that, if anything, the graph understates the strength of the more reputable brands, because established firms often sold out their product before the rest and hence did not participate in the ensuing declines: "Many of the leading companies are practically out of the market. Some of the smaller concerns, however, are less favorably situated, . . . so there is no alternative but to accept such prices as consumers are willing to pay." In addition, established firms sometimes continued to supply their regular customers without stipulating a price, confident

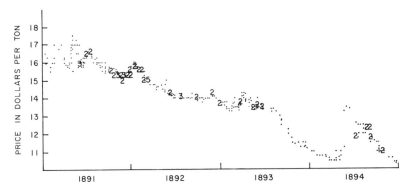

Figure 2.2. Transactions in Bessemer pig iron, Pittsburgh market, by weeks, 1891–4.

For those furnacemen who specialized in Bessemer pig iron – a grade that did not lend itself to product differentiation – there was much less leeway for independent price setting, although this fact may not be immediately apparent from Figure 2.2. The transactions of Bessemer pig iron recorded on the graph seem, at first glance, to be as widely dispersed as those of the foundry grade. Their average weekly standard deviation was less, however – $0.11 per ton for Bessemer iron as compared with $0.16 per ton for foundry no. 1. Moreover, the actual difference was greater than these numbers would suggest. Much of the variation in the price of Bessemer iron – unlike that in the foundry grade – was accounted for by differences in the timing of deliveries. Whenever prices began to rise, buyers rushed to contract for their present and future needs at as low a price as possible. Shortages often developed on metal for immediate delivery, sending the price at which prompt sales were made soaring above that for future contracts. In periods of rising prices, therefore, the average weekly standard deviation for Bessemer pig iron climbed to $0.15 per ton. Whenever prices began to decline, on the other hand, this source of variation disappeared, and the average weekly stan-

that when business conditions stabilized they would be able to negotiate a settlement satisfactory to both parties. The quotation is from *Iron Age,* March 20, 1890, pp. 470-3; see also March 11, 1880, pp. 18-19; March 25, 1880, pp. 18-19; March 29, 1894, pp. 620-2.

dard deviation fell to $0.07 per ton. In the absence of product differentiation, the manufacturers had little power to resist the general downward trend.[14]

Not only did firms that successfully pursued the strategy of product differentiation achieve greater pricing freedom – and greater price stability – than their less well established competitors, they also tended to run more constantly.[15] For instance, according to *Iron Age*, in the tin-plate industry during the depression of the nineties,

> Some few [of the dipperies] which make special plates, such as high grade roofing ternes, the reputation of which is established and for which there is a steady demand, have been enabled to keep fairly busy. But the majority of these firms . . . have not operated to anything like their full capacity. Some have run only at intervals and others have been closed down all or most of the time. The close margin at which the ordinary qualities of tin and terne plate have been selling [by large rolling mills] has made the dipping business unprofitable . . . except, as we have said, special plates which have made a name for themselves and which command high prices.[16]

Although most of the dipperies ran substantially below their full capacity during the depression (and nine of thirty-two actually failed), the reductions in demand that caused these curtailments and failures weighed less heavily on the firms with popular, high-quality brands. Thus, despite the fact that John Hamilton & Company, Meurer Brothers, and N. & G. Taylor refrained from lowering quotations in 1896 and 1897, their sales seem not to have suffered much. Notices in the *Metal Worker* reported continuing strong sales of "Hamilton's Best Redipped." Meurer Brothers expanded its tinning sets from six to eight because of the large demand for its old-style,

[14] Foundry iron was purchased in much smaller quantities than Bessemer iron and seems to have been bought as needed rather than in advance of requirements. The AISA *Bulletin* recorded no differences in delivery dates for foundry iron, whereas it distinguished between prompt sales and future sales in a number of transactions of Bessemer iron. The average weekly standard deviation in the price of no. 1 foundry pig iron was $0.18 per ton during upswings and $0.16 during downswings. In calculating the weekly standard deviations, I weighted prices by the quantity of metal sold. Weeks in which only one transaction was recorded were excluded from the analysis.

[15] I am arguing only that firms that successfully pursued the strategy of product differentiation achieved greater stability, not that they earned supernormal profits (though they might have). I recognize that specialization in a high quality product entailed extra costs.

[16] *Iron Age*, January 13, 1898, p. 10.

hand-dipped roofing plates. Similarly, Nathan Taylor, one of the partners in N. & G. Taylor, subsequently testified before the Industrial Commission:

Our business is prosperous and it always has been. We have not been affected in the past when business has been depressed in tin plates . . . We have always catered to the very best buying element, have always striven to make the very best tin plates, have always found buyers for them who have made no complaint of our prices.[17]

Similarly, in the pig-iron industry the burdens of curtailment were distributed unevenly during depressions. According to testimony before the House Ways and Means Committee in 1896, 82 of 104 furnaces east of the Alleghenies were idled by the depression, and many would not start up again until they were reorganized. Yet the Warwick Iron Company, a well-established producer in the same region, increased its production in every year of the depression except 1896. Likewise, during the downturn of the previous decade, production at the renowned Thomas Iron Company never fell more than 9 percent below its average for the prosperous years 1879-82.[18]

[17] U.S. Industrial Commission, *Preliminary Report on Trusts and Industrial Combinations*, "Testimony," p. 935; *Iron Age*, February 6, 1896, pp. 365-6; September 3, 1896, p. 451; scattered reports and price quotations in *Metal Worker*.

[18] In the case of the pig-iron industry, in which there was much more direct price competition than in roofing plates, efficiency was also a significant factor. It is difficult to know which was more responsible for steady operations – low variable costs, which permitted a firm to continue producing after price declines forced less efficient firms to shut down, or an income-inelastic demand curve, which resulted from specialization in a high-quality product. We know that the Thomas Iron Company was a low-cost producer (partly because it had access to inexpensive iron ore), but it was also conservative about cutting prices to meet competition or stimulate sales. For example, when the demand for pig iron dropped in 1883, *Iron Age* reported:

> After several weeks of unrewarded waiting for an improvement in the market, the Thomas Iron Company have reduced the price of their No. 1 foundry pig iron from $22 at tidewater to $21. No change was made in the price of other grades. It is hoped that this concession will induce a more active movement, especially as it is accompanied by the assertion that a number of furnaces will be blown out in the Eastern part of the country and will be kept idle until better times. There are a great many pig-iron manufacturers who cannot make iron profitably at current prices.

Iron Age, October 4, 1883, p. 14; May 25, 1893, p. 1183; U.S. Congress, House, *Tariff Hearings before the Committee on Ways and Means, 1896-1897*, 54th Cong., 2d Sess., 1897, Doc. 338, pp. 310-13; *Tariff Hearings before the Committee on Ways and Means, 1908-1909*, 60th Cong., 2d Sess., 1909, Doc. 1505, p. 1413.

The leading firms not only suffered less from depressions but also benefited directly from the curtailments and failures of weaker enterprises. In addition to relieving some of the downward pressure on prices, the reductions in output decreased the demand for raw materials and labor, lowering the costs of these factors of production. During the depression of the 1880s, for example, operating costs at the Thomas Iron Company dropped from a high of $17.73 per ton in the last half of 1881 to $13.06 four years later, with 86 percent of the decline attributable to the cost of iron ore and coal alone. Over the same period of time, the average price of no. 1 foundry pig iron in the Philadelphia market fell from $26.00 per ton to $18.25. A reputable, high quality producer, the Thomas Iron Company probably did not experience the full magnitude of the price decline; the firm's profits undoubtedly suffered, but it still seems to have had plenty of margin for survival.[19]

Not surprisingly, then, in industries such as tin plate and pig iron, where leading firms with differentiated products had a distinct advantage over their competitors and indeed often benefited from the distress of their weaker rivals, there was rarely much support for collusion. When the chairman of the Eastern Pig Iron Association (organized mainly to lobby for favorable tariff legislation) proposed the formation of a pool during the depression of the nineties, only one important furnaceman expressed himself in favor of the combination. Similarly, successful tin-plate dipperies displayed little disposition to participate in the gentlemen's agreements that the large rolling mills, quantity producers of common-grade tin plate, organized repeatedly in the mid-1890s. For them, the Tin Plate Manufacturers' Association had been useful primarily as a lobbying agent for protective tariffs. When the rolling mills consolidated to form the American Tin Plate Company in late 1898, the dipperies generally remained aloof from the organization.[20]

In industries such as tin plate and pig iron, firms that had successfully differentiated their products occupied a few choice positions in the upper strata of the market and had no incentive to collude with

[19] *Iron Age*, May 25, 1893, p. 1183; AISA, *Statistics of the Iron Trades*, 1899, p. 67.
[20] *Iron Age*, July 16, 1896, p. 123; February 16, 1899, p. 17; see also the citations listed in Note 1.

their less successful competitors. There were other cases, however, in which an entire industry consisted of specialty producers. When firms in such industries were also evenly matched, instances of collusion might occur, though the end result typically differed little from what market forces would have produced on their own. A case in point was the fine-writing-paper industry after the Civil War. Production was concentrated in the region around Holyoke, Massachusetts, and this proximity worked to reduce differentials in production and distribution costs and also marketing advantages (at that time a Holyoke location conferred national prestige). It also, as Adam Smith might have foreseen, brought manufacturers together to act in their common interest. When the demand for paper fell during the depression of the seventies, for example, the paper makers met and instituted a series of industry-wide shutdowns and curtailments. So successful seemed the initial experiment that it was frequently repeated – at the end of 1884, during the summer of 1885, in December 1889, in July 1890, and in July 1892.[21]

This series of industry-wide curtailments ended after the Panic of 1893, largely because the growing production of cheap, "enginesized" writing paper broke down the manufacturers' unanimity of interest. Rifts had already begun to develop by the late 1880s; with the added pressure of severe depression, the divisions became too great to overcome, and the collusive arrangements of the previous twenty years were abandoned. Subsequent events suggested, however, that continuation of these organized curtailments was largely unnecessary – at least as far as fine writing paper was concerned – for manufacturers easily reduced production on their own initiative. The Panic of 1893 was followed by widespread plant closings and curtailments, and though most mills in Holyoke were running again by the following February, they were only operating at an estimated three quarters of capacity. The rest of the year production remained below normal. Nearly every mill in the city shut down in July, and reports set August's production at one-half to three-quarters of capacity.

[21] Green, *Holyoke, Massachusetts*, pp. 137-8, 145-7. *Paper World*, February 1885, p. 14; June 1885, p. 12; August 1885, p. 9; December 1889, pp. 9, 18; January 1890, p. 22; July 1890, p. 14; August 1890, p. 16; June 1892, p. 16.

Two Augusts later, almost 50 percent of the mills in western Massachusetts were idle.[22]

These curtailments prevented a drastic erosion in prices, especially where the best brands of writing paper were concerned. As the *Paper Trade Journal* commented in its review of the market for the year 1897,

> Writing papers were in quiet but steady call, and during the dullest period there was a shutting down of machines which prevented demoralization, even if it did not enable prices to harden. There was at times a yielding in prices, but as a rule standard makes held their own very well.[23]

Although manufacturers complained about low prices, over the entire period 1883 to 1897 the price of high-grade writing paper fell only 20 percent, as compared with 33 percent for wholesale prices in general, 46 percent for engine-sized writing paper, and 67 percent for newsprint.[24]

Because the fine-writing firms were relatively evenly matched, the burdens of curtailment were more widely distributed than in the tin-plate and pig-iron industries. On the one hand, even as prestigious a firm as the Parsons Paper Company had to draw on the accumulated profits of past years in order to survive the crisis. On the other hand, failures were comparatively few. Only six of the sixty-eight writing paper manufacturers listed in the 1892 edition of *Lockwood's Directory of the Paper, Stationery and Allied Trades* disappeared from the ranks of paper producers by 1896, and only four more by 1900. None of these was a Holyoke firm.[25]

In other words, the effects of the depression of the nineties on fine-writing-paper manufacturers, acting individually, were much the same as if they had acted in concert. Output declined in accordance

---

[22] U.S. Congress, Senate, *Replies to Tariff Inquiries*, 53rd Cong., 2d Sess., 1894, Rept. 513, Pt. II, pp. 29, 34-5; Pt. III, pp. 28-30; *Paper World*, August 1893, p. 16; February 1894, p. 54; June 1894, p. 226; August 1894, pp. 49, 64; August 1896, p. 60; *Paper Trade Journal*, May 8, 1897, p. 369; May 15, 1897, p. 395; May 22, 1897, p. 408.

[23] *Ibid.*, January 8, 1898, p. 26.

[24] *Paper World*, September 1897, pp. 90-1; Warren and Pearson, *Prices*, p. 13.

[25] One of the firms that disappeared was located in nearby Westfield, however. *Lockwood's Directory of the Paper, Stationery and Allied Trades*, 1892 to 1900.

with the drop in demand; prices fell, but not excessively (especially on "standard makes"); and the burdens of curtailment were spread throughout the industry. The spontaneous, reflex response that produced these results suggests that it was the firms' predisposition to restrict output and support prices that had made collusion so successful in the past, not the reverse.

Most small-firm industries were more like the tin-plate and pig-iron industries than the writing-paper industry: A few established firms had a distinct advantage over their competitors, making collusion an unattractive proposition for them. In such industries, firms frequently joined together in associations; typically, however, their purpose was to defend the industry as a whole against some external threat (e.g., unfavorable tariff legislation) rather than to restrict output or support prices.[26] In those industries in which price-stabilizing agreements were attempted, they were most likely to be successful where a comparatively small number of firms produced a highly specialized product – once again, where they were least likely to be needed. Thus, William H. Becker has found that, in the hardware industry, successful price-fixing associations arose among manufacturers of differentiated products such as copper ware or stamped ware. Agreements were rarely successful among manufacturers who produced staple goods, that is, in industries in which the strategy of mass production prevailed.[27]

The strategy of mass production

Many, though by no means all, of the manufacturers of differentiated products were technologically conservative. They were reluctant to tamper with a successful formula, and their concern with quality often signified a commitment to the way things were done in the past. Yet even though this backwardness infected many of the nation's most successful enterprises in the mid-nineteenth century, it did

[26] See, for example, Louis Galambos's study of trade associations in the cotton-textile industry, *Competition and Cooperation: The Emergence of a National Trade Association* (Baltimore: Johns Hopkins Press, 1966), pp. 11-36.
[27] William H. Becker, "American Wholesale Hardware Trade Associations, 1870-1900," *Business History Review*, XLV (Summer 1971), pp. 182-5.

the economy as a whole little harm. The leading manufacturers of differentiated products generally occupied only a small portion of their industries, leaving plenty of other firms, plenty of experienced entrepreneurs, plenty of opportunity for innovation elsewhere. For example, when J. S. McElwain, manager of the Parsons Paper Company, failed to convince Parsons to invest in a new mechanized process for making writing paper, he founded a new firm himself.[28]

Common-grade producers had the most incentive to innovate, for it was they who bore the brunt of competition and of fluctuations in the market. Moreover, as the nineteenth century progressed, the opportunities for innovation in this sector grew as improvements in transportation and communications and rising per capita income expanded the market for manufactured goods. Increasingly, common-grade producers responded by adopting a completely new manufacturing strategy – earning profits on volume of output rather than on a high margin per unit. Firms that adopted this strategy of mass production had essentially the same goals as those that differentiated their products: to defend the firm against competitors and withstand fluctuations in business conditions. However, the means they used to achieve these goals differed significantly. By producing large quantities of homogeneous goods, they intended to exploit the efficiencies of volume production, reduce unit costs to the minimum, and protect themselves against price cutting by rivals. In times of depression they aimed to expand their share of the market at the expense of weaker, less efficient competitors, and in that manner maintain both production and profits.

The essential elements in the story of the emergence of this strategy were a large potential market and an innovation or discovery (or change in the tariff) that made it possible to exploit that market: the refrigerated car, which permitted the shipment of perishable goods long distances; the Bessemer process for large-scale conversion of pig iron to steel; continuous-process rolling mills that made cheap steel rods for wire production; wood-pulp based paper for mass-circulation newspapers; the Bonsack machine for manufacturing cigarettes; new products such as glucose, barbed wire, the bicycle; new raw-

---

[28] Green, *Holyoke, Massachusetts*, pp. 153-5.

material discoveries such as Pennsylvania petroleum and Western copper, lead, silver, and gold; new opportunities created by protective tariffs in industries such as linseed oil, tin plate, and iron and steel tubes.[29]

The general effect of these developments was to stimulate the growth of large, capital-intensive, often vertically integrated firms – a trend that is apparent even in the aggregate statistics. Between 1880 and 1900, the average amount of capital invested per manufacturing establishment increased 75 percent, from $11,000 to $19,200, while the capital-output ratio for the manufacturing sector as a whole rose 44 percent, from 0.52 to 0.75 year.[30] Vertical integration, unfortunately, is more difficult to measure than size or capital intensity, but Harold C. Livesay and Patrick G. Porter have estimated the extent to which the nation's 100 largest manufacturing companies were vertically integrated in 1899, 1909, and subsequent years. Already by 1899, 54 percent of the firms in the food products industry had integrated forward into marketing, as had 82 percent of the firms in

[29] Alfred D. Chandler, Jr., *The Visible Hand: The Managerial Revolution in American Business* (Cambridge: Harvard University Press, 1977), pp. 249, 290-2, 300-1; Stanley Baron, *Brewed in America: A History of Beer and Ale in the United States* (Boston: Little, Brown, 1962), pp. 257-61; Peter Temin, *Iron and Steel in Nineteenth-Century America: An Economic Inquiry* (Cambridge: M.I.T. Press, 1964), pp. 125-93; *Iron Age*, January 2, 1896, pp. 15-20; Stephen L. Goodale, *Chronology of Iron and Steel* (2nd ed.; Cleveland: Penton Publishing, 1931), pp. 197-8; Dewing, *Corporate Promotions and Reorganizations*, pp. 73-6, 249-56; Henry D. and Frances T. McCallum, *The Wire that Fenced the West* (Norman: University of Oklahoma Press, 1965); David C. Smith, "Wood Pulp and Newspapers, 1867-1900," *Business History Review*, XXXVIII (Autumn 1964), pp. 328-45; Williamson and Daum, *The Age of Illumination*, pp. 63-231; Orris C. Herfindahl, *Copper Costs and Prices: 1870-1957* (Baltimore: Johns Hopkins Press, 1959), pp. 73-6; James E. Fell, Jr., *Ores to Metals: The Rocky Mountain Smelting Industry* (Lincoln: University of Nebraska Press, 1979), pp. 1-75; Whitney Eastman, *The History of the Linseed Oil Industry in the United States* (Minneapolis: T. S. Denison & Co., 1968), pp. 27-30; Dunbar, *The Tin-Plate Industry*, pp. 14-17; U.S. Congress, House, *Investigation of United States Steel Corporation*, Vol. VII, pp. 5075-6.

[30] U.S. Census Office, *Twelfth Census: Manufacturers* (Washington, D.C.: U.S. Government Printing Office, 1902), Pt. I, p. 3. The Census figures probably overstate the rise in the capital-output ratio, owing to changes in the way borrowed capital was treated in the schedules. The appropriate units for the capital-output ratio are years, because the numerator, capital (a stock), is measured in dollars and the denominator, output (a flow), is measured in dollars per year. The ratio can be interpreted as the number of years it takes to earn revenues equivalent in value to the amount of capital invested. For this reason it is also known as the capital-turnover ratio.

petroleum, 100 percent in stone, clay, and glass producsts, and 100 percent in fabricated metals. Similarly, 100 percent of the firms in the tobacco industry had integrated backward into raw-material production by 1899, as had 50 percent of the firms in lumber and paper, 67 percent in petroleum, 100 percent in stone, clay, and glass products, and 79 percent in primary metals.[31]

As a result of these trends, the large mass-production enterprises that emerged in this period differed from the small differentiated firms described earlier in several important ways. To begin with, because they tended to employ more capital-intensive production processes and to be more vertically integrated, their fixed charges constituted a higher proportion of total costs. Total costs, by definition, equal the sum of variable costs (mainly raw materials and labor) plus fixed costs (mainly interest and depreciation charges on capital). All other things being equal, it follows that if capital is substituted for labor or raw materials, the proportion of fixed in total costs will rise. Similarly, vertical integration, because it results in internalization of costs that otherwise would be variable, also raises the proportion of fixed in total costs.[32]

In the paper industry, for example, the capital-output ratio for the

[31] Harold C. Livesay and Patrick G. Porter, "Vertical Integration in American Manufacturing, 1899-1948," *Journal of Economic History*, XXIX (September 1969), pp. 494-500.

[32] Forward integration simply raises overhead expenses without altering production costs. For the case of backward integration, let

R_1 = cost of materials purchased by an unintegrated firm to produce some given level of output
L_1 = remaining variable costs expended by unintegrated firm
F_1 = fixed costs of unintegrated firm
R_2 = cost of raw materials used by suppliers to produce R_1
L_2 = other variable costs of producing R_1
F_2 = fixed costs of producing R_1

For the given level of output, the proportion of fixed in total costs faced by the unintegrated firm is $F_1/(R_1 + L_1 + F_1)$. If we assume that vertical integration does not change the level of output or any of the costs (except for raw materials) associated with either stage of the production process, the proportion of fixed in total costs for an integrated firm will be $(F_1 + F_2)/(R_2 + L_2 + L_1 + F_1 + F_2)$. Because $R_2 + L_2$ must be less than R_1 (which includes payments to suppliers to cover fixed charges and profit), and because the addition of F_2 to both the numerator and denominator will increase the former proportionally more than the latter, the second ratio will be greater than the first. [We do not have to assume that the fixed costs of the integrated firm (call them F_3) equal $F_1 + F_2$. This result holds so long as F_3 is greater than or equal to F_1.]

industry as a whole rose from 0.71 year in 1870 to 1.32 years in 1900. This meant that if a firm had to set aside each year the equivalent of 10 per cent of its capital investment to meet interest and depreciation charges, the proportion of each dollar of sales needed to pay these expenses increased 86 percent between 1870 and 1900. Within the paper industry, of course, the capital-output ratio varied enormously, depending on the commodity produced. Newsprint was the most capital-intensive branch of the industry by 1900 (its capital-output ratio was about 1.8 years).[33] It was also the most vertically integrated, and the effect of vertical integration on fixed charges can be seen from the following figures. According to a report made by U.S. paper manufacturers in 1899, the capital cost of an integrated mill with a capacity of fifty tons of paper per day was $350,000 for the paper mill and $250,000 for the ground-wood mill. Addition of a sulphite-pulp facility necessitated an expenditure of another $5,000 per ton of daily product. Vertical integration thus nearly tripled capital investment without increasing the capacity for making paper, the final product. But this was only part of the story. Ground-wood production required a more extensive water-power development than that needed for paper alone, adding another $250,000 to total capital costs. Moreover, beginning in the 1890s, manufacturers moved to acquire and lumber their own woodlands, increasing their investments still further.[34]

Because the burden of fixed charges per unit of output was inversely proportional to the quantity of production, manufacturers with high fixed costs had an incentive, in the parlance of the times, to

[33] U.S. Census Office, *Twelfth Census: Manufacturers,* Pt. III, p. 1015. The newsprint figure is estimated from state-level data in U.S. Census Office, "Paper and Wood Pulp," *Census of Manufactures: 1905,* Bulletin 80, p. 10.

[34] David S. Cowles, president of the American Pulp and Paper Association and of several newsprint mills, testified in 1908 that a 100-ton newsprint mill required $1,125,000 worth of woodlands, based on a cost of $10 per acre. U.S. Congress, House, *Pulp and Paper Investigation Hearings,* 60th Cong., 2d Sess., 1909, Doc. 1502, Vol. II, pp. 893-4. The report was "Memorandum to the Joint High Commission *re* Duty on Paper and Pulp," reprinted in U.S. Industrial Commission, *Report on Trusts and Industrial Combinations,* 57th Cong., 1st Sess., 1901, House Doc. 182, p. 441. The manufacturers had every reason to exaggerate the sizes of their investments, but later estimates by less biased observers, though different in detail, point to the same conclusion: Vertical integration added substantially to capital costs. See, for example, Royal S. Kellogg, *Pulpwood and Wood Pulp in North America* (New York: McGraw-Hill, 1923), pp. 13, 17-25, 33-4.

run their plants "full." As one newsprint manufacturer, G. W. Knowlton, wrote in the early 1890s, "Prices are low and if a mill does not make big runs there is little in it in the way of margin." He elaborated in another letter: "It is the last ton or two that pays the profit. Five tons today 10 tons tomorrow and three tons next day will not do in these times and that is what hurts many manufacturers. If it had not been for break downs – repairs and lost time you and I would be rich men today."[35]

Vertical integration heightened the incentive to run full, in part because it raised the proportion of fixed in total costs, but also because it created the potential for what Alfred D. Chandler, Jr., has called "economies of speed."[36] For example, whenever pulp and paper mills were located in the same vicinity (a spatial arrangement that characterized all the largest newsprint mills and many smaller ones as well),[37] wood pulp could be pumped directly from the grinders into the paper mills while still in a liquid state. Where pulp and paper mills were directly linked in this manner, production at less than capacity meant either that the pulp mill had to reduce its output, resulting in a costly waste of water power, or that the excess pulp had to be dried into "laps" and stored. Before it could be further processed it had to be reliquified to the proper consistency, adding to the cost of the paper.[38]

The iron and steel industry provides an even clearer example of the workings of economies of speed. By the 1890s, large crude-steel manufacturers had so integrated successive stages of production that molten pig iron could be converted into steel and then into rails or

[35] G. W. Knowlton, letters for March 9, 1893, and July (undecipherable), 1893, Knowlton Bros., Watertown, N.Y., Papers, 1813-1964, Cornell University, Regional History Archives, Collection 2877, Reel 5.

[36] See *The Visible Hand*, pp. 281-3.

[37] For example, all but six of the thirty-two Eastern newsprint firms that produced all their own ground-wood pulp had pulp facilities in the vicinity of their paper mills. *Lockwood's Directory*, 1896-7.

[38] John Norris, business manager of the *New York Times*, estimated that pumping liquid pulp directly into the paper mill saved a manufacturer $1.00 per ton on newsprint selling for $40.00 to $50.00 per ton. U.S. Congress, House, *Pulp and Paper Investigation Hearings*, Vol. I, p. 472. See also U.S. Federal Trade Commission, *Newsprint Paper Industry*, 65th Cong., 1st Sess., 1917, Senate Doc. 49, pp. 26-30; Louis Tillotson Stevenson, *The Background and Economics of American Papermaking* (New York: Harper & Brothers, 1940), pp. 125, 149-53.

billets without reheating. Because blast furnaces could not be run intermittently or at less than capacity, economical operation of a steel works required the maintenance of a smooth, continuous flow of output from the blast furnaces to the Bessemer converters to the rolling mills. If for any reason production at the latter two plants was curtailed, blast furnaces had to be shut down – an expensive proposition[39] – or pig iron had to be cooled, stockpiled, and later reheated – adding, of course, to the cost of the product. As E. C. Felton, president of the Pennsylvania Steel Company, explained,

We take our pig iron in the molten state directly from the blast furnace, and it goes into the converting works, and so on through to the finished rail without ever losing its heat. If we slacken up and stop our converting mills, then that pig iron which would otherwise go through continuously in this operation must be piled up cold. Then when we start up again it must be remelted at very considerable expense.[40]

The capital-intensive nature of production and the existence of these economies of speed convinced manufacturers of steel, as they had convinced manufacturers of newsprint, "that best results in every way were gained by pushing their production to its limit . . . and spreading fixed charges over a greater tonnage."[41] The result was a radically new approach to business. In contrast to the small manufacturers, who adjusted their production to conform to fluctuations in market demand, large firms sought to operate their plants at full capacity, regardless of the state of business. A fundamentally different set of priorities had gained ascendancy. Replacing the old preoccupation with price maintenance and output restriction was a new imperative: "run full," even if it meant a reduction in prices. Accord-

[39] Work stoppages often caused extensive damage to furnace linings. William A. Ingram, a representative of the Eastern Pig Iron Association, testified in the late 1880s that "blowouts" usually involved repairs costing $5,000 to $10,000. In addition, it sometimes took several weeks to ease a furnace back into production. U.S. Congress, Senate, *Testimony Taken by the Subcommittee on the Tariff of the Senate Committee on Finance, 1887-1888*, 50th Cong., 1st Sess., 1888, Rept. 2332, pp. 1032-3.

[40] Felton estimated that continuous operations saved $0.80 to $0.90 per ton on rails selling for $28.00 per ton. Julian Kennedy, a prominent steel-industry engineer, estimated the savings to be $1.00 to $1.25 per ton. U.S. Congress, House, *Tariff Hearings, 1908-1909*, pp. 1574-6; U.S. Congress, House, *Investigation of United States Steel Corporation*, Vol. VII, pp. 5100-1.

[41] *Iron Age*, April 7, 1898, p. 17.

ing to the Illinois Steel Company's annual report for the year ending December 31, 1897: "For many years American manufacturers attempted to do business on the basis of large profits for comparatively small tonnage; but there has been a revolution in this condition of affairs, and it seems to have been demonstrated that for the future the policy of small profits on large tonnage furnishes the best assurance of success."[42] As Illinois's president, J. W. Gates, later explained, "My theory is that I would rather have an open market and be able to run full and not be hampered by any competitors saying: 'You are selling goods too low,' than to have a fictitious market, where I could only run 40 or 50 or 60 per cent."[43] Only slightly more extreme was Andrew Carnegie's exhortation to his staff: "To keep running, not to make profit is the point we should steer to."[44]

With volume of output their primary concern, large firms in the late nineteenth century tended to neglect most means of differentiating their products. In this way, too, they differed significantly from their smaller competitors. In part, the change was a function of the process of staple-goods manufacture itself, for in the nineteenth century most product differentiation depended on real differences in the composition or quality of commodities and, to some extent, on consumers' uncertainty about standards. For instance, although years of custom and practice had evolved a set of criteria to distinguish the different grades of pig iron by their carbon and silicon content and by the uses for which they were best suited (foundry no. 1 or no. 2, gray forge, car wheel, etc.), it was not yet common to use chemical analysis to identify the various grades. Instead, manufacturers fractured a sample of the iron and determined the metal's characteristics by examining the surface of the break. So imperfect was this technique that even the most experienced buyers found it useful to purchase their product by brand name, in order to assure as uniform a quality of iron as possible and avoid costly adjustments in their

[42] Reprinted in U.S. Supreme Court, *The United States of America, Appellant v. United States Steel Corporation, et al.: Brief for the United States* (Washington, D.C.: U.S. Government Printing Office, 1917), Vol. II, p. 87.
[43] U.S. Congress, House, *Investigation of United States Steel Corporation*, Vol. I, p. 43.
[44] U.S. Supreme Court, *The United States v. United States Steel Corporation, et al.: Transcript of Record: Government Exhibits*, Vol. III, pp. 1035-6.

equipment.[45] In other industries, where quality was more easily recognized, brands often conveyed information about differences in factory procedures, particularly in the amount of care taken during the manufacturing process. Thus, it was well known that the L. L. Brown Paper Company of Adams, Massachusetts, made its famous ledger paper exclusively from imported linen rags and from shirt cuttings shipped directly from garment factories: "These are sorted carefully and cut by hand, no machine cutting being adequate for the paper that it is desired to make."[46] Similarly, at Byron Weston's fine paper mill in Dalton, Massachusetts,

The washing and beating occupy double the usual length of time that is given to the process, so that fibers may be separated from each other without cutting; the result is a long fibre, uninjured by chemicals, and possessing the utmost strength and the purest whiteness. The machine is run very slowly, that the paper may be thoroughly closed. So painstaking is the process of manufacture here that, while the fourteen 500-pound engines and the two machines have a producing power of four tons a day under ordinary requirements, the actual product is but two tons. The loss in quantity is more than made up in extraordinary excellence of quality.[47]

In contrast to Byron Weston or L. L. Brown, large mass-production firms concentrated on what Nathan Taylor (the renowned tin-plate manufacturer) called "the calico end" of the business, "turning out product" by specializing in "the kinds that entail the least

---

[45] Even with the advent of chemical analysis, brands retained much of their importance: "In foundry iron there are various fine points, determined by the exact relations between silicon, phosphorus, and manganese, which the consumer, if he understands them, will take care of by making purchases from two or three furnaces with the product of which he is familiar. With small consumers, not so well acquainted with details, the experienced pig-iron salesman will frequently make selection of the iron he delivers, to suit it to particular requirements, without divulging his reasons, thereby aiming to hold a customer for his particular brands." B. E. V. Luty, "Iron Ore and Pig Iron," *The Marketing of Metals and Minerals: A Series of Articles by Specialists,* eds. Josiah Edward Spurr and Felix Edgar Wormser (New York: McGraw-Hill, 1925), pp. 82-7; W. K. V. Gale, *The Iron and Steel Industry: A Dictionary of Terms* (London: David and Charles, 1971), pp. 88-9, 98, 131, 142, 180, 228.
[46] *Paper World,* October 1885, pp. 1-4. The article continued: "There is no better test of the approval of goods than the constancy with which customers return year after year; the L. L. Brown Paper Company still carries on its books the names of ledger manufacturers who bought the company's paper thirty-five years ago."
[47] *Ibid.,* January 1886, pp. 1-5.

trouble."[48] This decision eliminated one important source of product differentiation. At the same time, mass-production techniques removed much of the variability in manufacturing conditions that previously had been responsible for lack of uniformity in finished products. For example, by the 1870s, improved methods of refining had eliminated most of the variation in processed sugar, leaving two basic grades – centrifugal and granulated – each with its own easily recognizable characteristics. Although a few brands of "cut loaf sugar" retained their popularity, their content was the same as other granulated sugars on the market, and they sold for practically the same price.[49]

In the twentieth century, of course, many giant firms became adept at differentiating common-grade products, but this was for the most part a later development in corporate strategy.[50] In the nineteenth century, by contrast, some mass-production enterprises went so far as consciously to reject product differentiation, which they perceived as contrary to their goal of increasing output, as a device that partitioned the market and erected barriers to the expansion of their product. For instance, in the cereals industry, Ferdinand Schumacher, the "oatmeal king," devoted a lifetime of effort to broadening the domestic market for oatmeal, which entailed breaking down the American prejudice that oats were fit only for horsefeed. Advertising individual brands was, in his opinion, a waste of resources and a distraction from this larger task. Even after oatmeal producers consolidated their enterprises into the American Cereal Company (now Quaker Oats), he resisted expenditures for product differentiation.[51]

Similarly, in the tin-plate industry, large rolling mills were less likely than dipperies to differentiate their products. Of the manufacturers' special brands for which the *Metal Worker* quoted prices in 1896 and 1897, most (84 of 115) were traceable to dipperies. The

[48] U.S. Industrial Commission, *Preliminary Report on Trusts and Industrial Combinations*, "Testimony," p. 940.

[49] Alfred S. Eichner, *The Emergence of Oligopoly: Sugar Refining as a Case Study* (Baltimore: Johns Hopkins Press, 1969), p. 46.

[50] See Chapter 6. For some early exceptions see Chandler, *The Visible Hand*, pp. 290-9.

[51] Marquette, *Brands, Trademarks and Good Will*, pp. 10-25, 45-9.

rest belonged to small rolling mills, with three exceptions: the ninth largest firm in the industry (which was the oldest tin-plate manufacturer in existence); the number five firm (whose only brand was synonymous with the name of the company); and the number three firm (which stopped quoting prices on most of its brands in early 1897). Not only were rolling mills less likely to differentiate their products, but the officers of the industry's largest enterprise concluded that consumers were being confused and intimidated by the proliferating variety of brands, sizes, and types of tin plate. In 1897 their drive to standardize the different grades and qualities of material was so successful that the trade journals stopped quoting prices by brands.[52]

Industries without Andrew Carnegies

Firms that adopted the mass-production strategy differed from the small differentiated firms in another important respect: They faced the critical problem of oligopolistic pricing. Because they tended to be large relative to the market, they could affect the selling prices of their goods. But lack of product differentiation meant there was little leeway for independent price setting. The individual decisions of all the major firms in the industry determined the prices at which goods would be sold. Each firm's price and output decisions affected those of its rivals, and vice versa. If one cut prices, the rest had to follow, or else risk losing their share of the market.

Occasionally a manufacturer succeeded in bypassing the entire problem of oligopolistic pricing by outdistancing his rivals and exploiting or erecting barriers to new competition. He might gain an advantage, for example, by investing in plant and equipment or in vertical integration the enormous sums necessary to capture economies of scale and economies of speed, by acquiring control of critical patents and resources, or by effectively manipulating his company's

[52] I ranked the firms in order of their capacity as listed in the AISA *Directory* for 1896. See quarterly list of tin-plate brands in *Metal Worker*, 1896-7, and price quotations in the same issues. See also the repeated discussions of standardization of tin-plate products in the *Metal Worker* in late 1896 and early 1897.

market power. Andrew Carnegie was a prime example of this type of manufacturer. Carnegie operated in a branch of the steel industry in which both patents and economies of scale had already restricted entry. But he further reduced the number of competitors by relentlessly cutting costs, using the advanced methods of accounting developed by the railroads. Whenever his cost statistics signaled the possibility of improvement, he willingly scrapped expensive equipment for more productive machinery. In order to save on raw-material costs, he led the industry in vertical integration, integrating backward first into coal extraction and then into transportation and iron ore. By such means he built the most efficient crude-steel works in the United States, and perhaps the world, capable of underselling his competitors in most domestic markets. Even so, Carnegie was not above using market power to protect his interests. When investors built the Duquesne Steel Works in Carnegie's own territory, he used his influence to exclude the firm from the rail pool. He also warned railroads not to buy Duquesne's rails, because, he claimed, its manufacturing process was defective. As a consequence of this and other problems, Duquesne experienced financial difficulty, and Carnegie bought up its assets.[53]

Much American business history has been devoted to the exploits of men like Carnegie, whether they have been considered robber barons or innovative entrepreneurs. But the dominance of men like Carnegie was the exception rather than the rule. In many industries, even many mass-production industries, no one entrepreneur emerged to outdistance his rivals by means fair or foul. Rather, the typical mass-production industry was dominated by a whole coterie of large firms, most of which had entered the market at approximately the same time, none of which had managed to secure a competitive advantage over the others.

This was true even in steel, where Andrew Carnegie ruled only one

[53] For an excellent discussion of Carnegie's achievements, see Harold C. Livesay, *Andrew Carnegie and the Rise of Big Business* (Boston: Little, Brown, 1975), pp. 77-166. Although all writers agree that Carnegie Steel was the most efficient firm in the industry, some deny that credit should go to Carnegie alone. See James Howard Bridge, *The Inside History of the Carnegie Steel Company: A Romance of Millions* (New York: Aldine, 1903). On the industry in general, see Temin, *Iron and Steel in Nineteenth-Century America*, pp. 133-83.

sector. The tin-plate branch of the industry serves as an excellent example. After passage of the McKinley tariff in 1890 had made tin-plate production profitable in the United States, domestic output boomed. Because of the small amount of capital required for their construction, most of the industry's earliest entrants were small finishing works, or dipperies. Built to coat imported black plate (a highly finished steel sheet), they located in port cities such as New York and Philadelphia. To the west, however, where higher transportation costs added to the protection of the duty, construction soon commenced on larger, vertically integrated works – plants that rolled as well as coated black plate. By 1894 there were already fifteen rolling mills in production; two years later the number had increased to thirty-two.[54]

Unlike most dipperies, which specialized in the production of expensive terne (or roofing) plate, the rolling mills concentrated on the manufacture of common-grade tin plate for the canning industry.[55] Each firm's product was a close substitute for that of its competitors. Moreover, none of the more than thirty rolling mills in production by the mid-1890s appears to have had a competitive edge over the rest. In the first place, there were no economies of scale over a wide range of production. The total number of rolling stands varied widely from one firm to the next, but as the well-known steel engineer Julian Kennedy pointed out, a man with six could make tin plate as cheaply as a man with sixty.[56] Second, none of the important firms had integrated backward into steel production to save on the cost of billets (most likely because their steel requirements were not great enough to justify an investment sufficient to capture scale

[54] AISA, *Directory*, 1892-8; Dunbar, *The Tin-Plate Industry*, pp. 13-18, 21-2; Thomas William Hundermark, "The Changes in Distribution of Tin Plate Works in Pennsylvania during the Various Stages of Development of the Industry" (unpublished master's thesis, University of Pittsburgh, 1948), pp. 15-16.

[55] Of the thirty-two dipperies that were in existence at some time during the period 1892-8 and whose mix of output is known, fifteen produced nothing but terne plate, and ten made more terne than tin plate. Of the thirty-four rolling mills for which the same information is available, four produced only tin plate, and twenty-one manufactured more tin than terne plate. AISA, *Directory*, 1892-8.

[56] U.S. Congress, House, *Investigation of United States Steel Corporation*, Vol. VII, p. 5128.

economies).[57] At the same time, those manufacturers who believed their connections with neighboring steel mills gave them a cost advantage quickly discovered that their competitors could obtain similar concessions. As *Iron Age* reported in 1896,

> Those who have led the way in reductions have given to their customers supposed advantages in cheap billets or tin plate bars. In this they found themselves mistaken, since other manufacturers proved themselves equal to the emergency. They have gone into the market at even lower rates and have taken large contracts, having evidently found powerful backing.[58]

Because the basic technology of tin-plate manufacture had been developed earlier in Wales, there were no crucial patents to provide one American firm with an advantage over the rest. Those improvements in technique that did occur in the United States (increases in the size of hot rolls, reductions in the number of rolls and in the number of separate heatings, improvements in the design of annealing furnaces, elimination of handwork in finishing) appear to have diffused rapidly throughout the industry in the early 1890s.[59] Moreover, whatever benefits might otherwise be derived from innovation were greatly reduced as a result of the strength of the workers' union, the Amalgamated Association of Iron, Steel, and Tin Workers. The Amalgamated Association used its control over skilled labor, vital in this branch of the steel industry, to enforce strict limitations on tonnage and a uniform wage scale throughout the industry.[60]

---

[57] When a short-lived billet pool inflated the price of crude steel in 1896, several tin-plate manufacturers threatened to construct their own steel plants, but the collapse of the pool relieved them of the necessity. The largest firm in the industry, the American Tin Plate Company (of Indiana), did in fact join with a wire mill to lease the idle Premier Steel Works, but the project was shortly abandoned. Aetna-Standard acquired a steel plant when it consolidated with the Laughlin & Junction Steel Company in 1897, but this firm mainly produced sheets. Several other tin-plate rolling mills in the vicinity of Wheeling, West Virginia, were connected by ownership ties with neighboring steel works. AISA, *Directory,* 1896, 1898; *Iron Age,* November 19, 1896, p. 968; quarterly reports on the tin-plate industry in *Metal Worker,* 1896-8; Henry Dickerson Scott, *Iron and Steel in Wheeling* (Toledo: Caslon, 1929), pp. 89-129; Earl Chapin May, *Principio to Wheeling, 1715-1945: A Pageant of Iron and Steel* (New York: Harper & Brothers, 1945), pp. 144-207.

[58] *Iron Age,* October 22, 1896, p. 779.

[59] There were some patents on automatic tinning and pickling machinery, but either these were held by independent equipment manufacturers or close substitutes for patented machines were available. Dunbar, *The Tin-Plate Industry,* pp. 30-49.

[60] *Iron Age,* March 31, 1898, pp. 16-17; Dunbar, *The Tin-Plate Industry,* pp. 51-65.

Finally, the fact that serious price competition failed to force significant shutdowns or curtailments provides further evidence of the close rivalry within the industry. Despite the price war that began during the downturn of 1896 and lasted until December 1898, when manufacturers formed the American Tin Plate consolidation, only four small plants were idle for any length of time in 1896; in 1897, only three; and in 1898, just one. Throughout this period of price warfare, only one firm (in a particularly poor location) actually failed.[61] Nor did any firm seem to benefit from the competition. After the manufacturers met in 1896 and attempted to fix prices, the largest firm in the industry, the American Tin Plate Company (not to be confused with the later consolidation of the same name) resigned from the Tin Plate Manufacturers' Association, determined to compete vigorously on its own. Apparently, however, the firm was unable to secure an advantage. Within approximately half a year, American was back in the fold. Its officers led in the formation of the new Association of Tin Plate Makers of the United States, and when this association also failed to stem the competition, they arranged for Judge William H. Moore's help in promoting a consolidation.[62]

In the tin-plate industry, neither American nor any other firm was able to obtain a competitive advantage. The situation was much the same in the newsprint branch of the paper industry. Again, most of the industry's capacity had been constructed in a short space of time. The substitution of wood pulp for rags had reduced the cost of newsprint by the 1880s and greatly stimulated consumption, attracting new investment to the industry. This influx grew especially heavy during the boom of the late 1880s and early 1890s, when most of the important mills of the next decade were built. It was in this period, for example, that construction began on the plants of three of the eight largest firms in the industry, and at least four of the remaining five firms made substantial additions to their works. A number of smaller, though still important, enterprises also entered the industry

[61] In 1896, the Baltimore Iron, Steel, and Tinplate Company, the only enterprise in Baltimore, failed. The plant was subsequently returned to production. Quarterly reports in *Metal Worker*, 1896-8; *Iron Age*, October 22, 1896, p. 779; November 19, 1896, p. 968; January 13, 1898, p. 10.
[62] See citations in Note 1; U.S. Industrial Commission, *Preliminary Report on Trusts and Industrial Combinations*, "Testimony," p. 866.

in this period. According to the *Boston Advertiser,* in the summer of 1891 there were forty-two paper mills (chiefly newsprint and book paper) under construction, and *Paper World* reported that in 1891 alone production of newsprint and book paper increased 20 percent.[63]

As in the case of the tin-plate industry, most of the larger newsprint firms seem to have been evenly matched. In the first place, there were no economies of scale over a wide range of production, as can be seen by applying George Stigler's survivor test. This procedure assumes that competition among different sizes of firms will sift out the enterprises of less efficient scale over time. By classifying firms in an industry according to their size and calculating the share of industry output produced by each size class of firms at different points in time, the extent of economies of scale can be assessed. If the market share of a given category of firms falls, that size is relatively inefficient. On the other hand, those classes with firms large enough to benefit from economies of scale will increase their shares of the market over time.[64]

Table 2.1 records the size distribution of eastern newsprint mills in 1892 and 1900. Although the intervening years were especially difficult ones, characterized by the most intense competition the industry had ever experienced, the main effect seems to have been an expansion of mills with at least 2 percent of total capacity at the expense of their smaller competitors. This pattern suggests that mills of this size (35 tons of paper per day, and there were as many as thirteen firms with mills of this capacity or greater in 1896) were large enough to capture whatever economies of scale characterized the industry. Moreover, the minimum efficient size for a newsprint plant was probably actually more like 30 tons, because mills of this scale continued to be built in large numbers throughout the next decade. If we lower

---

[63] See *Paper World,* August 1891, p. 12; January 1892, pp. 10-11; and the series of articles on the growth of the paper industry in Maine (February 1892, pp. 7-10; March 1892, pp. 5-6; April 1892, pp. 5-7; May, 1892, pp. 1-8); U.S. Congress, House, *Pulp and Paper Investigation Hearings,* Vol. II, p. 1213; Smith, "Wood Pulp and Newspapers."

[64] George J. Stigler, "The Economies of Scale," *The Organization of Industry* (Homewood, Ill.: Richard D. Irwin, 1968), pp. 71-94. For criticisms of the test, see F. M. Scherer, *Industrial Market Structure and Economic Performance* (2nd ed; Chicago: Rand McNally, 1980), pp. 92-3.

Table 2.1. *Size classification of Eastern newsprint mills,*[a] *1892 and 1900*

	1892		1900	
Size class of mills (% of total capacity)	Percentage of capacity in size class	No. of mills in size class	Percentage of capacity in size class	No. of mills in size class
0–1	21.1	37	9.0	19
1–2	29.2	19	14.8	11
2–3	24.5	10	26.6	11
3–4	9.9	3	10.7	3
4–5	9.1	2	9.1	2
5–6	0.0	0	22.7	4
6+	6.2	1	7.0	1

[a]When a firm had two or more plants in different locations, the mills are listed separately.
Source: Lockwood's Directory, 1892–3 and 1900–1.

the cutoff to this figure, we expand the list of efficient-size mills to seventeen.[65]

By the 1890s there were no longer any patents of importance that could give a newsprint manufacturer an advantage over his competitors.[66] The central item of capital equipment required for paper-making, the Fourdrinier paper machine, had been invented early in the nineteenth century. By the 1870s the machine had achieved a standard design that was to persist with few changes for decades. Technological improvements from that time on involved, for the most part, increases in the Fourdrinier's width and speed, and

[65] I restricted the table to Eastern newsprint firms because there was little interregional competition and because all the larger newsprint firms were located in the East. If anything, Table 2.1 probably exaggerates the gains made by the largest size classes of firms. The large firms escaped the worst effects of severe price competition by forming the International Paper Company in early 1898. *Lockwood's Directory,* 1892-3 to 1910.
[66] U.S. Industrial Commission, *Report on Trusts and Industrial Combinations,* p. 423. Some patents on the production of sulphite pulp remained, but these were not controlled by any of the newsprint manufacturers. Newsprint mills used comparatively little sulphite pulp, and many manufacturers preferred to buy this material on the market rather than produce it themselves.

these seem to have diffused rapidly throughout the industry.[67] In 1884 there were only three Fourdriniers in the United States 100 inches wide or better; by the mid-1890s widths greater than 100 inches were common. All but three of the seventeen firms with mills capable of producing 30 tons of paper per day had at least one Fourdrinier 100 inches or more wide, eleven firms had at least two machines of this width (all that was necessary to produce 30 tons of paper per day), four firms had at least three machines, and three firms had four or more.[68] All of the eleven firms with two or more Fourdriniers of modern width were located near raw-material resources, in the woodlands of northern New England or upstate New York, and nine of these had the capacity to produce all their own ground-wood pulp.[69]

The newsprint industry, in sum, was dominated by at least nine large firms that produced a homogeneous product and were equivalently equipped to compete for sales. So evenly matched were these firms that the long period of downward-spiraling price competition that lasted from the Panic of 1893 to the formation of the International Paper Company in January 1898 failed to divide the industry into winners and losers. Only two of the mills with at least 30-ton capacities actually failed (one could make exactly 30 tons, the other 33), and one of these was not vertically integrated.[70] Profits for the

---

[67] R. H. Clapperton, *The Paper-making Machine: Its Invention, Evolution and Development* (Oxford: Pergamon, 1967), p. 236; U.S. Congress, House, *Pulp and Paper Investigation Hearings*, Vol. I, p. 186.

[68] By 1896, widths were beginning to increase beyond 120 inches. Six firms had machines at least this wide. Clapperton, *The Paper-making Machine*, pp. 247, 252; *Lockwood's Directory*, 1896-7.

[69] Five also made sulphite pulp. Some qualifications: One firm, the Glen Falls Paper Mill Company, had a paper capacity of 250 tons per day and a ground-wood capacity of only 165 tons. The firm had seven Fourdriniers in excess of 100 inches wide and seven narrower machines. I suspect that some of the narrow machines were held in reserve and that this explains the discrepancy between the firm's pulp and paper capacity. The same was probably the case for the Jay Paper Company, which had a paper capacity of 30 tons per day and a ground-wood capacity of 25 tons; it listed three modern Fourdriniers and one old one. *Lockwood's Directory* does not record ground-wood facilities for the Niagara Falls Company, but I know from other records that the company had them. See U.S. Congress, House, *Pulp and Paper Investigation Hearings*, Vol. II, p. 1213.

[70] *Paper World*, February 1897, p. 48; January, 1898, p. 6; *Paper Trade Journal*, February 13, 1897, p. 124. Both of the firms that failed later returned to production.

rest fell sharply, but none appeared able to win the competitive struggle for survival of the fittest. Rather, the price warfare inflicted serious damage on them all.[71]

It was generally this type of mass-production industry, in which no one firm had a clear-cut advantage over the rest, that suffered the most severe price competition during the depression of the nineties. The next chapter will attempt to explain why. In striking contrast to the experience of small firms that differentiated their products, firms in industries such as tin plate and newsprint failed to adjust their production to declines in demand. Indeed, despite sharply falling prices, production often increased dramatically as firms struggled to run their plants at full capacity. Normal collusive arrangements proved utterly incapable of stemming this virulent competition. So, as we shall see, did the increasingly sophisticated and formal pools that the manufacturers devised. By the end of the decade, only consolidation seemed to offer a chance for relief.

[71] See Chapter 4.

3. High fixed costs and rapid expansion
A model of price warfare and two examples

By the 1890s, then, there had developed in industries such as tin plate and newsprint a type of industrial structure significantly different from what had prevailed earlier in the century. Replacing the small firms, with their concern for product differentiation and price stability, were large, mass-production enterprises whose heavy capital investments gave rise to new forms of competitive behavior – an emphasis on "running full" and a neglect of product differentiation. Conventional notions notwithstanding, these mass-production industries were typically dominated neither by innovative entrepreneurs nor by ruthless robber barons. More often than not they were the preserve of a dozen or more large firms, all of which were equivalently equipped to compete for sales, none of which was able to secure an exclusive advantage for itself.

It is important to understand the relationship between this new type of industrial structure and the severe price competition of the 1890s. The purpose of this chapter is to develop a model that captures the essential characteristics of firms in these mass-production industries and then to trace the model's implications for competitive behavior.

A preliminary model

Imagine an industry populated by a small number of firms, say ten.[1] In this hypothetical industry each firm possesses one and only one plant; all plants are identical in size and efficiency, and all produce the same homogeneous product. There are no barriers to prevent new firms from entering this industry, but otherwise no assumptions are made to ensure perfect competition. On the contrary, it is as-

---

[1] The following discussion is based on Don Patinkin's analysis in "Multiple-Plant Firms, Cartels, and Imperfect Competition," *Quarterly Journal of Economics*, LXI (February 1947), pp. 173-205.

sumed that firms are large relative to the market, that they are inter-
dependent and aware of this fact, and that each firm's price and
output decisions directly affect those of its rivals. In other words,
imagine an industry with characteristics similar to (though more extreme in form) those of the tin-plate and newsprint industries in the
1890s.[2]

These characteristics are embodied in Figures 3.1 and 3.2, which
depict cost curves for a single firm and for the industry as a whole.
Suppose initially that the total industry demand curve is D_0 in Figure
3.2 and that all firms possess equal shares of the market. Facing
individual demand curve d_0 in Figure 3.1, each firm operates at its
least-cost level of production, q_0. Total industry output is Q_0 ($Q_0 =$
$q_0 \times 10$), price is P_0, and each firm earns a per-unit profit of ab. This
is not a stable situation, however, for with no barriers to entry, the
existence of positive profits attracts additional firms to the industry.
The total industry demand curve remains the same, but (retaining for
the time being the assumption of equal market shares and identical
one-plant firms) each firm's share of the market is reduced. Each firm
now faces demand curve d_1. The price of its output falls to P_1, per-
unit profit drops to cd, and the firm curtails its production to q_1. In
the industry as a whole, however, output increases to Q_1 ($q_1 \times n$,
where n is the current number of firms) as the addition of new firms
shifts the industry's marginal-cost curve from MC_0 to MC_1 and hence
moves the equilibrium output to the right.

---

[2] All these assumptions except the one concerning single-plant firms follow directly
from the description of the tin-plate and newsprint industries provided in Chapter 2.
Large firms in these two oligopolistically structured industries did not differentiate
their products, they were for the most part equivalently equipped to compete for
business, and there were no barriers to prevent the entry of new competition. The
assumption of single-plant firms is also reasonable. For example, in 1896 all but one
of the thirty-three tin-plate rolling mills in existence were single-plant enterprises.
Similar figures for the newsprint industry are difficult to obtain, because some firms
housed their paper machines in separate "mills" at the same location, whereas
others considered all machines at the same location, however housed, as constituting
one mill. Nonetheless, we know that only eight of the ninety-eight firms that produced at least some newsprint in 1896 had mills in different geographic locations,
whereas only one of the seventeen firms with efficient-sized mills (see Chapter 2) had
plants in separate places. American Iron and Steel Association (hereafter AISA),
Directory to the Iron and Steel Works of the United States, 1896; *Lockwood's
Directory of the Paper, Stationery and Allied Trades*, 1896-7.

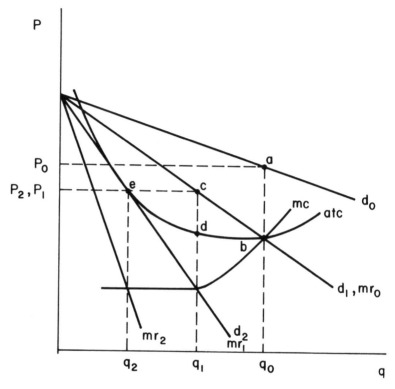

Figure 3.1. Cost and revenue curves for the firm.

At this point there are still profits to be made in the industry. So long as these profits persist, new competitors will continually appear, shifting the industry's marginal-cost curve to the right and reducing each firm's share of the market, its equilibrium output, and its per-unit profit. But notice that industry output cannot increase beyond Q_1. As new firms continue to enter the industry, therefore, they receive diminishing shares of a no-longer-growing pie, until finally per-unit profits fall to zero and new investment ceases.

In this description of the process by which long-run equilibrium is attained, price warfare is precluded by the assumption that firms accept an equal division of the market and that they accommodate new entrants by immediately redividing sales. Given the assumption

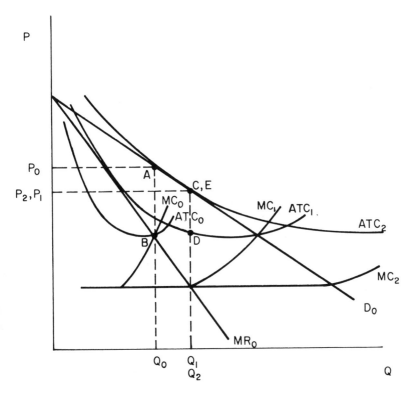

Figure 3.2. Cost and revenue curves for the industry.

of evenly matched firms, this sharing would constitute rational economic behavior. If one firm were to cut prices below the equal-mar-
ket-division level with the aim of increasing its proportion of sales,
all the others could easily meet its price. Assuming that the price cut
was promptly discovered (a reasonable assumption, as we shall see),
market shares would remain unchanged, but prices would be
lowered. Everyone would be worse off than before, including the
firm that initiated the cuts. Rational calculation, in sum, would dic-
tate that these firms accept the demand curves drawn in Figure 3.1.
Yet history tells us that there were many instances in which firms in
exactly this situation cut prices in an attempt to increase their share
of the market. The question that needs to be answered is why.

The fixed-cost explanation

The answer, as a venerable line of scholars has suggested,[3] requires two changes in the model. First, one must relax the assumption that the demand curve for the industry's product is constant (not unreasonable, given the dramatic shifts in business conditions that occurred in the nineteenth century). Second, another variable must be taken into account: the industry's cost structure, the proportion of fixed to total costs that firms had to meet. In the late nineteenth century, so the argument goes, the increased capital intensity of American manufacturing raised the proportion of fixed in total charges and, as a consequence, increased the likelihood that firms would respond to severe declines in demand by cutting prices to improve their share of the market.

The argument can be followed with the aid of Figure 3.3, which shows the costs and revenues associated with various levels of production and demand for a firm with high fixed costs.[4] To begin with, assume that the firm's (constant-share-of-the-market) demand curve is d_0 and that the firm is producing at its profit-maximizing level of output, where marginal cost and revenue are equal. At that position it produces output q_0, receives price P_0 for its product, and earns a per-unit profit equal to ab. Now suppose that the economy sinks into depression, and the demand for the firm's product declines to d_1. If the firm responds in the conventional fashion by equating its marginal costs with the lower marginal revenue curve, it will reduce production to the new profit-maximizing level, q_1, receive price P_1 for its

---

[3] The theory that follows appeared very early in the literature on large-scale corporations and occasioned much debate. See, for example, Spurgeon Bell, "Fixed Costs and Market Price," *Quarterly Journal of Economics*, XXXII (May 1918), pp. 507-24, and Eliot Jones's opposing view, "Is Competition in Industry Ruinous?" *ibid.*, XXXIV (May, 1920), pp. 473-519. For more recent discussions of the fixed-cost theory, as I shall call it, see F. M. Scherer, *Industrial Market Structure and Economic Performance* (2nd ed; Chicago: Rand McNally, 1980), pp. 205-12, and Alfred S. Eichner, *The Emergence of Oligopoly: Sugar Refining as a Case Study* (Baltimore: Johns Hopkins Press, 1969), pp. 93-119. For a sophisticated version, see George Bittlingmayer, "Decreasing Average Cost and Competition: A New Look at the Addyston Pipe Case," *Journal of Law and Economics*, XXV (October 1982), pp. 201-79; and "Price Fixing and the Addyston Pipe Case," *Research in Law and Economics*, V (1983), pp. 57-128.

[4] This drawing is based on Scherer, *Industrial Market Structure and Economic Performance*, pp. 206-7.

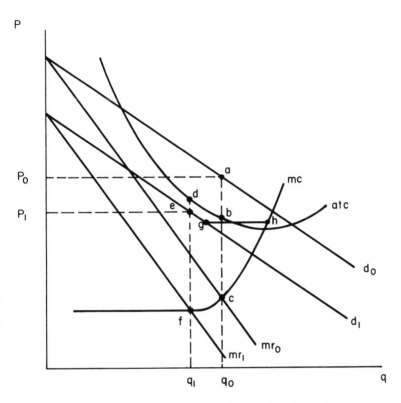

Figure 3.3. Cost and revenue curves for a firm with high fixed costs.

goods, and find itself losing an amount equal to *de* on each unit of output it makes. This is because its fixed charges are so large that average total costs rise steeply whenever production is curtailed. At its new profit-maximizing position, then, the firm will discover that, after paying for raw materials and labor, it is unable to meet all the charges on its fixed investments. As pressures mount to meet interest (and, as well, dividend) payments, or to replace obsolete and worn-out equipment, the incentive to adopt another pricing strategy will grow. Realizing that by increasing output it can reduce unit costs, the firm will be tempted to cut prices in order to increase its share of the market. By moving off its original (constant-share-of-the-market) demand curve along some line such as *gh*, it can reduce or possibly even eliminate its losses.[5]

The problem was, of course, that in an industry in which firms were evenly matched, the result was often a downward-spiraling price war. One firm's price cuts were quickly matched by the rest, resulting in a lower level of prices, but no net shift in market shares. Yet the lower price level increased losses and hence the temptation to cut prices. Nor could market forces provide relief (at least not in the near future). The high proportion of fixed in total costs meant that there was a wide range of prices within which firms would continue to produce at a loss. At the same time, because firms were evenly matched, none could cut prices low enough to force any of the others out of business; what one could withstand, the rest could tolerate as well. As a result, prices might hover indefinitely at a level too low to enable firms to break even, but too high to compel them to shut down.[6]

Criticism of the fixed-cost explanation

This fixed-cost explanation seems plausible, especially in light of what we know about the large firms' determination to run full, regardless of the state of business. Nonetheless, the foregoing scenario also points to a major deficiency in the fixed-cost theory: It cannot explain why a firm would initiate a price cut, knowing that as a consequence of its actions it would end up worse off than before. Indeed, for this very reason, some theorists have cited high fixed costs as an explanation for the lack of (rather than the existence of) price competition. Arthur R. Burns, for example, argued that one of the conditions in the steel industry "peculiarly calculated to induce attempts to avoid price competition" was that "overhead costs

---

[5] Of course, firms always had an incentive to cut prices in order to increase their share of the market. But the argument assumes that they would not be willing to risk retaliation until they found themselves actually losing money.

[6] Firms will continue to operate at a loss so long as prices cover variable costs – that is, labor, materials, and other items of expense whose magnitude varies with the level of output. Because fixed charges do not fluctuate with output and have to be met whether the firm operates or not, as long as revenues exceed variable costs the firm is better off running at a loss than shutting down.

represent[ed] a very high proportion of total costs." He suggested that firms in industries with high fixed costs recognized their suscepti- bility to ruinous price wars and went to great lengths to avoid any hint of price competition.[7] Before we can make use of the fixed-cost explanation, then, some qualifier must be added to enable us to distinguish those situations in which a high proportion of fixed in total costs led to price warfare and those in which it produced stable oligopolistic arrangements.

There is a second problem with the fixed-cost theory. It is uncom- fortably vague. Fixed costs had to be a high proportion of total costs, but how high did they have to be before they had the hypothesized effect on a firm's behavior? Because, as it turns out, a solution to the first problem follows from an answer to the second, the place to begin is with a discussion of fixed costs.

How large a proportion of total costs did fixed charges have to be? This is an important question, but one that is difficult to answer – first, because all the necessary data do not exist, and, second, because the answer depends on the particular accounting practices followed by individual firms. For the period under consideration, this latter point is especially critical. Most nineteenth-century firms, when they calculated their costs, simply did not account for depreciation, a major element in fixed charges. Manufacturers recognized that their equipment suffered from wear and tear and technological obsoles- cence, but instead of calculating depreciation as a cost, they financed replacements and improvements as needed out of revenues.

This difference in procedure was not simply an alternative route to the same end. As Richard P. Brief has shown, the cumulative effect of "replacement accounting" was to underestimate the consumption of capital.[8] More important for our purposes, however, the method had very different behavioral implications from depreciation accounting. Nineteenth-century (and even most early-twentieth-century) manu- facturers considered any reserve for replacements and improvements a subcategory of profits rather than expenses, and certainly not a

[7] Arthur Robert Burns, *The Decline of Competition: A Study of the Evolution of American Industry* (New York: McGraw-Hill, 1936), p. 78.
[8] Richard P. Brief, "Nineteenth Century Accounting Error," *Journal of Accounting Research*, III (Spring 1965), pp. 12-31.

pressing element of fixed charges. In the words of one contemporary observer, manufacturers viewed "the charge for depreciation as being an act of grace rather than of necessity."[9] If a firm's revenues were sufficient to cover interest payments and taxes, but not the depreciation of its capital, it might not even realize that it was operating at a loss. As officers of the International Paper Company admitted in 1908, "There is no question in our minds that it was a mistake not to have charged off depreciation. Had such charge been made, paper would never have sold at the prices for which we have sold it."[10] The concept of fixed costs under which nineteenth-century firms operated was thus limited as compared with modern business procedures. With depreciation excluded from the calculation by reason of the accounting practices of the time, other fixed charges had to be correspondingly larger in order for the proportion of fixed in total costs to be "high."

In a handful of cases, these "other" fixed charges clearly did constitute a large proportion of total costs. In the salt industry, for instance, the major expense a firm had to meet was the capital cost of acquiring land, drilling and preparing a well, and constructing a plant for evaporation and purification of brine. Operating expenses, consisting mainly of the cost of fuel for the pumps, were comparatively minor. In fact, where the well adjoined a lumber mill, as was often the case in Michigan's Saginaw Valley (one of the nation's chief salt-producing regions), operating costs might even be negative. Refuse from the saw mill served as fuel for the pumps, and it was estimated that it would cost a company more to haul the refuse away than to burn it as fuel, even with no return on the salt. It is not surprising, therefore, that salt manufacturers responded to declines in demand in the late nineteenth century by battling to undercut each other's prices, just as the fixed-cost theory would predict.[11]

[9] *Ibid.*, p. 26. See also Brief, "The Origin and Evolution of Nineteenth-Century Asset Accounting," *Business History Review*, XL (Spring 1966), pp. 1-23; Alfred D. Chandler, Jr., *The Visible Hand: The Managerial Revolution in American Business* (Cambridge: Harvard University Press, 1977), pp. 71, 111-15, 268, 278-9, 386, 397, 421, 431, 445-8.

[10] U.S. Congress, House, *Pulp and Paper Investigation Hearings*, 60th Cong., 2d Sess., 1909, Doc. 1502, Vol. II, p. 1079.

[11] J. W. Jenks, "The Michigan Salt Association," *Trusts, Pools and Corporations*, ed. William Z. Ripley (rev. ed.; New York: Ginn & Co., 1916), pp. 7-9; Arthur S. Dewing, *Corporate Promotions and Reorganizations* (Cambridge: Harvard University Press, 1914), p. 204.

In less clear-cut cases, however, the question of the magnitude of fixed charges is complicated by the different methods firms used to raise capital, because the method affected the degree of urgency with which they had to meet their liabilities. To the extent that businesses financed their investments by plowing back earnings without correspondingly increasing their capital stock, they could virtually ignore the problem of fixed charges. To the extent that they financed their investments through the sale of stock, their commitments were somewhat more pressing. Still, firms could and often did pass dividends without precipitating a stockholders' revolt, and in the case of the closed corporations that predominated in this period, investors were generally indulgent (particularly if profits in the industry had a history of cyclical fluctuations). Therefore, it is mainly in the case of firms that raised large amounts of capital by borrowing that the press of fixed charges can be expected to have exercised a significant effect on pricing behavior during depressions; the need to make regular interest payments on penalty of bankruptcy served as a powerful incentive to expand production whenever prices fell below costs.[12]

Again, in a handful of industries the latter method of financing was clearly important. In the newsprint industry, for instance, at least some firms raised a large proportion of their capital by borrowing. Although there is no information on the debt structure of newsprint firms in the 1890s, data on a few companies are available for the first decade of the twentieth century. Even at that time, when industrials had readier access to the nation's stock markets,[13] newsprint mills borrowed heavily in order to finance their investments. The Great Northern Paper Company issued $5,000,000 in stock and borrowed an additional $3,000,000 by selling bonds; the St. Regis Company issued $1,600,000 in stock and $1,130,000 in bonds; Remington-Martin, $350,000 in stock and $500,000 in bonds; Flambeau Paper Company, $200,000 in stock and $150,000 in bonds. Although the Northwest Paper Company reported to a congressional committee

---

[12] It might be added as a corollary that the same analysis would apply to less capital-intensive firms that for various reasons (including the need to carry large raw material stocks) had massive short-term debts.

[13] See Thomas R. Navin and Marian V. Sears, "The Rise of a Market for Industrial Securities, 1887-1902," *Business History Review*, XXIX (June 1955), pp. 105-38.

that it had $300,000 in stock and no bonded debt, Director Clarence I. McNair acknowledged that the firm had financed an additional investment of $800,000 to $900,000 by borrowing.[14]

That the need to make regular interest payments on their debts weighed heavily on paper manufacturers even in times of prosperity can be seen from G. W. Knowlton's 1893 resolution to "start no more big paper mills or if I do there must be money enough put up to do the business without borrowing."[15] In times of depression the payments could be extremely onerous, forcing papermakers to struggle to run their plants at full capacity, and in that way minimize their losses. Arthur C. Hastings of the Cliff Paper Company later testified before the House Pulp and Paper Investigation Committee:

Mr. Stafford: Then the manufacturers at that time [the 1890s] did not shut down their mills, but continued to manufacture.
Mr. Hastings: Very few of them that I know closed down. We did not. We ran pretty steadily.
Mr. Sims: You did not even curtail your time?
Mr. Hastings: No, sir; because we could dispose of our product.
Mr. Sims: At a loss?
Mr. Hastings: At a loss. It was merely a question whether you ran along and took care of your fixed charges and made a small loss on your tonnage.[16]

In the newsprint industry, manufacturers raised a large proportion of their capital by borrowing, and the necessity of meeting interest payments on this debt seems to have affected their behavior during depressions, just as the fixed-cost theory predicts. In the case of the steel industry, however (ironically, the industry most often cited by proponents of the theory), methods of raising capital were generally less burdensome. Steel companies often financed expansion out of earnings, rather than by selling stock or borrowing, and as a result

[14] The one exception to this pattern I could find was the Cliff Paper Company, which had a capital stock of $100,000 and financed its additional investment of $300,000 out of profits. U.S. Congress, House, *Pulp and Paper Investigation Hearings*, Vol. II, pp. 968, 1422, Vol. III, pp. 1635, 1644, 1648-50, 1796, Vol. V, pp. 3099-100.

[15] Letter from G. W. Knowlton, March 7, 1893, Knowlton Bros., Watertown, N.Y., Papers, 1813-1964, Cornell University Regional History Archives, Collection 2877, Reel 5.

[16] U.S. Congress, House, *Pulp and Paper Investigation Hearings*, Vol. III, pp. 1616-17.

many of them had assets far in excess of the par value of their stock. The huge Carnegie Steel Company, Ltd., had a total stock issue of only $25 million, until a dispute between Carnegie and Henry Clay Frick forced a reorganization of the firm in 1900. Stock and bonds were then reissued to correspond to the firm's more realistic valuation of $250 million.[17] According to Vice President Welsh of the Cambria Iron Company, by 1898 Cambria's works had "really outgrown the capital, owing to the very conservative course always pursued by the managers of not dividing all the profits, but using them for the construction of new plants." The firm was reorganized as the Cambria Steel Company in 1898, and its stock was expanded from approximately $8 million to $16 million.[18] Similar reorganizations indicate that other companies had assets whose value substantially exceeded their stock in the 1890s. The Bethlehem Iron Company doubled its stock issue (from $7.5 million to $15 million) when it reorganized as the Bethlehem Steel Company in 1899, and Lackawanna Iron and Steel's stock was increased from a meager $3.75 million to $25 million three years later.[19]

Although several enterprises carried a heavy burden of debt (Illinois Steel and Pennsylvania Steel are the primary examples),[20] the evidence suggests that steel firms were more reluctant than newsprint

---

[17] The Carnegie Company of New Jersey was capitalized at $320 million, but this included the H. C. Frick Coke Company, which was worth about $70 million. U.S. Commissioner of Corporations, *Report on the Steel Industry, Part I: Organization, Investment, Profits, and Position of the United States Steel Corporation* (Washington, D.C.: U.S. Government Printing Office, 1911), pp. 63-4, 160-2; James Howard Bridge, *The Inside History of the Carnegie Steel Company: A Romance of Millions* (New York: Aldine, 1903), p. 301.

[18] Although this increase was motivated by a need for funds, the circumstances of the issue indicate that stockholders' equity in the corporation previously exceeded the total value of the firm's stock. Shareholders were encouraged to subscribe to the new issue by the directors' assurances that they would be called on to pay only a fraction of the stock's par value – and that only as needed by the firm. Cambria's stock was increased to $50 million in the next decade. *Commercial and Financial Chronicle*, August 27, 1898, p. 427; September 24, 1898, p. 633; U.S. Commissioner of Corporations, *Report on the Steel Industry*, Part I, p. 95.

[19] *Ibid.*, p. 96; *Commercial and Financial Chronicle*, August 27, 1898, p. 427; *Moody's Manual of Industrial and Miscellaneous Securities*, I (1900), pp. 397-8.

[20] In 1896, Illinois Steel had outstanding about $18,650,000 worth of stock and $13,200,000 of bonds; Pennsylvania had approximately $7,500,000 in stock and $7,000,000 in bonds. *Iron Age*, April 23, 1896, p. 974; *Commercial and Financial Chronicle*, February 15, 1896, pp. 316-17; April 25, 1896, p. 776.

firms to finance their expansions by borrowing. For example, the Cambria Iron Company increased its capitalization in 1895 from $5 million to $7.875 million in order to finance improvements, increase its working capital, and free itself of floating debt (at that time it had no bonded debt). Although two years later it issued $2 million in bonds to purchase additional property, make improvements, and pay off loans, by 1900 there were only $254,300 of these bonds outstanding. The rest either had been repurchased or had never been marketed. In a similar move, the Lackawanna Iron and Steel Company paid off its entire funded debt of $1.2 million in 1899.[21] Carnegie Steel had mortgages totaling only $2.7 million on all its properties. The seven firms that merged into the National Steel Company (capital stock $59 million) had a combined bonded and mortgaged indebtedness of only $2.56 million, whereas those that formed the giant American Steel and Wire Company of New Jersey (capital stock $90 million) together owed a mere $750,000.[22] Finally, only two of the seven Bessemer steel producers surveyed by the commissioner of labor in 1890 included interest payments in their assessments of fixed costs. For one of the firms, these amounted to a charge of $0.35 per ton of output; for the other, less than $0.05 per ton. The rest reported that they made "no expenditure for interest."[23]

When applied to the late-nineteenth-century economy, then, the fixed-cost hypothesis suffers from several important liabilities. In the first place, nineteenth-century firms did not account for depreciation, a major element in fixed charges, when they totaled up their costs. As a consequence, other fixed charges had to be proportionally larger before they affected a firm's behavior. Second, firms in some capital-intensive industries (such as steel) financed the major part of their growth by plowing back earnings or issuing stock. As a result, their financial obligations were not as pressing as they would have been

[21] *Ibid.*, June 15, 1895, p. 1057; April 17, 1897, p. 753; March 4, 1899, p. 428; *Moody's Manual*, I (1900), p. 399.

[22] Bridge, *Inside History*, p. 313; *Commercial and Financial Chronicle*, January 14, 1899, p. 83; March 4, 1899, p. 429; April 8, 1899, pp. 672-3; July 8, 1899, p. 77; *Moody's Manual*, I (1900), pp. 430-1; *Iron Age*, February 16, 1899, p. 7.

[23] U.S. Commissioner of Labor, *Sixth Annual Report, 1890: Cost of Production: Iron, Steel, Coal, Etc.* (Washington, D.C.: U.S. Government Printing Office, 1891), p. 158.

had loans been their major source of funds. In times of depression, for instance, dividend payments could easily be postponed.

In addition to the liabilities already discussed, the fixed-cost hypothesis suffers from still another problem. The magnitude of fixed charges, even in the most capital-intensive industries, varied with the age of the firm and its plant and equipment. Whereas a firm with new capital had to shoulder the full cost of financing its investments, a firm with old capital might conceivably have paid off most or all of the obligations incurred when it built its plant and installed its equipment. Hence, even though the capital-labor ratios of the two firms might technically be the same, fixed charges weighed more heavily on the firm with the new capital than on the firm with the old.

A modification of the fixed-cost theory

This last point suggests a means of circumventing the liabilities of the fixed-cost theory – by formally combining this theory with our original model. One would expect the type of behavior predicted by the fixed-cost hypothesis to have occurred with greatest frequency in industries (such as tin plate and newsprint) in which the great majority of firms were new. In such industries the existence of a large potential market, and an innovation, discovery, or change in the tariff that made it possible to exploit that market, created an opportunity for profit such as that represented by demand curve d_0 in Figure 3.1. With no barriers to entry, the promise of profits attracted new firms to the industry, beginning the process of adjustment to long-run equilibrium described earlier. This process was unlikely, however, to be as smooth and continuous as I previously implied. In the case of capital-intensive industries, in particular, the long gestation period that elapsed before the product of new enterprises reached the market meant that price changes lagged seriously behind the decision to enter and sent misleading signals to potential investors. In the interval before new firms started production, the old prices continued to attract additional entrants, with the consequence that firms might ultimately find themselves facing individual demand curves below the long-run equilibrium, d_2.[24]

[24] For an analysis of the timing of entry in industries with long gestation periods, see Douglass C. North, *The Economic Growth of the United States, 1790-1860* (Englewood Cliffs, N.J.: Prentice-Hall, 1961), pp. 1-4.

Whether or not the result was actually overexpansion, firms had to adjust their pricing and output plans in response to the sudden increase in capacity. Some amount of price competition and instability was inevitable, even under conditions of prosperity. But now suppose that a sharp economic downturn interrupted the industry's adjustment process, that demand for the industry's product dropped, and that prices slid below costs – a result made more likely in rough proportion to the magnitude of new investment in the industry. Because the firms were new, their fixed charges were likely to be at or near their peak levels in terms of both size and urgency: Sufficient time had not yet elapsed to pay off debts; moreover, managers of new firms were reluctant to miss payments for fear of discouraging further investment in their enterprises. Newsprint manufacturer G. W. Knowlton expressed some of the anxieties owners of new mills experienced:

I had no picnic with our Ontario Paper Mill. We put in $150,000 and soon found ourselves with a debt of $260,000 and I was the man under the [gun] and I confess that it not only disturbed my waking hours but many hours when I should have been asleep. We paid $100,000 of this debt and last year paid 16 percent in dividends so we are more comfortable. . . .

My stockholders are lawyers and bankers and not used to the annoyances of paper mills and they not only worried themselves but worried us, but now they all feel better and if all goes well they may get to a point where they will think this [deal] is a good one after all, and then I suppose they may say pleasant things to me, but they did not say these when I was working under a debt of $260,000, but you know "nothing succeeds like success."[25]

As a result of such pressures, new firms felt particularly threatened whenever revenues fell below total costs, and they had a strong incentive to cut prices in an attempt to increase sales, decrease losses, and pay off as much as possible of their fixed charges. Moreover, many new firms were underfinanced. Short of working capital, they desperately needed sales to stay in business, and this need itself became an important stimulus for cutting prices. Thus, new rolling mills were major instigators of the price competition in tin plates in the mid-1890s:

[25] Letters from G. W. Knowlton, March 6, 1893, and March 7, 1893, Knowlton Bros., Papers, Reel 5.

It is the selling of their product at ruinously low prices, either through ignorance of cost or from excessive anxiety to secure business at almost any sacrifice, which has been the bane of several of the new American tin plate manufacturing concerns. Moreover, in some cases where the bulk of capital has been expended in building, equipping and starting up the works, the imperative need of funds to meet running expenses has induced pressure to realize stocks in hand, even at a loss.[26]

Not only did new firms have an incentive to cut prices, they also had good reason to believe that they could get away with it. Here I return to the first objection to the fixed-cost hypothesis: Why, if all the firms in an industry were evenly matched, would one manufacturer believe he could succeed in increasing his share of the market by cutting prices? In an already established industry, an industry not undergoing rapid growth, it is doubtful that he would. Regular marketing patterns would already have taken hold, and consumers would have grown accustomed to dealing with one or two firms that met their needs satisfactorily. If approached by another manufacturer who offered them a lower price, they would give their regular suppliers an opportunity to meet the bid before closing with the interloper. In such established industries, therefore, price cutting with the aim of increasing one's market share had little chance of success and involved considerable risk of lowering the general price level without altering the distribution of output.[27]

In an industry experiencing rapid growth, however, circumstances were often very different. New firms were continually entering the market, and prices were already in a state of flux. The equilibrium market shares of the firms had not yet been determined; neither had the competitive resources of the rivals been tested. Manufacturers who possessed new plants equipped with the most up-to-date machinery had faith that they could undersell at least some of their competitors and increase their shares of the market at their rivals' expense. Established marketing habits and consumer loyalties had not had time to take root, and there seemed to be the possibility that a

[26] *Metal Worker, Plumber and Steam Fitter*, February 8, 1896, p. 44.
[27] See, for example, John Norris's description of the effect of price cutting on the newsprint industry in the early twentieth century, when the industry was more established. John Norris was business manager of the *New York Times*. U.S. Congress, House, *Pulp and Paper Investigation Hearings*, Vol. I, p. 144.

manufacturer could make a "coup,"[28] capture enough orders to run his plant full before his competitors found out and were able to retaliate.

The problem was that competitors often did find out and often did retaliate. And because firms in these industries were evenly matched, the price wars that ensued were generally severe and long-lasting – so severe and long-lasting, in fact, that manufacturers felt compelled to take action to limit competition. In the competitive struggles that followed the Panic of 1893, manufacturers first resorted to the trade associations and gentlemen's agreements that had seemed to work so well for some small-firm industries in the past. When these failed, they experimented with more highly structured organizations, such as selling agencies and pools. Finally, when these, too, proved unable to stem the decline in prices, they turned to consolidation for relief.

Two contrasting examples

This modification of the fixed-cost explanation suggests that price wars (and consolidations) were likely to occur in capital-intensive industries that first underwent rapid expansion and then suffered a major downturn in demand. It was in such industries that fixed costs were likely to be highest and the chances of increasing one's share of the market greatest. Conversely, industries that had not recently undergone expansion were generally much less susceptible to price warfare during depressions, regardless of the capital intensity of their production processes.

These predictions are borne out by comparison of the different experiences during the depression of the nineties of firms in two branches of the steel industry: wire nails, which had recently undergone rapid expansion, and standard rails, which had not. In the former industry, the depression of the nineties provoked vigorous price cutting that pools and other price-fixing associations were helpless to stop. In the latter, competition was more restrained and collusion correspondingly more successful.

In the wire branch of the steel industry, the innovation of continu-

---

[28] The term was used by *Iron Age*; see October 22, 1896, p. 779.

ous rod rolling in the early 1880s had raised the scale and capital intensity of rod production and also, by lowering the cost of the finished product, opened up a multitude of new uses for steel wire. One of these was wire nails. According to Michael Baackes, an industry pioneer, the great majority of nails consumed in the United States until the late 1880s were of the cut variety; that is, they were made by slicing iron and steel plates into thin strips. Between 1886 and 1892 the cut-nail and wire-nail interests waged a furious battle to convince consumers of the superiority of their products. Wire nails eventually won (although the cut nail had greater holding power, the wire nail was less likely to split wood), and production boomed. Output soared from about 1,250,000 kegs in 1887 to 4,720,000 by 1892. Within five more years it nearly doubled again. In the meantime, production of cut nails dropped from 6,909,000 kegs in 1887 to 4,500,000 kegs in 1892 to 2,100,000 in 1897 (Table 3.1).[29]

As in the case of tin plate, most of the earliest entrants into the industry were finishing plants. Of the forty-nine wire-nail works in existence in 1888, for example, only two were integrated to the rolling-mill stage, and only four others had facilities for drawing rods into wire. As the wire nail established its superiority, however, the number of firms with rolling mills and drawing works increased, both absolutely and relatively. By 1894 there were forty firms in operation (ten rolling mills, eighteen drawing works, and twelve finishing plants), and the rolling mills alone accounted for nearly 70 percent of total capacity (Table 3.2).[30]

In the midst of this expansion, the Panic of 1893 occurred. The demand for nails dropped, and real prices fell 6 percent between April and October, despite the credit stringency that forced most of

[29] *Iron Age*, January 2, 1896, pp. 15-20, 105-6; Charles E. Edgerton, "The Wire-Nail Association of 1895-1896," *Trusts, Pools and Corporations*, ed. William Z. Ripley (rev. ed.; New York: Ginn & Co., 1916), p. 46; Stephen L. Goodale, *Chronology of Iron and Steel* (2nd ed.; Cleveland: Penton Publishing, 1931), pp. 197-8, 213; AISA, *Directory*, 1888, 1892, 1894; William T. Hogan, *Economic History of the Iron and Steel Industry in the United States* (Lexington, Mass.: Lexington-D. C. Heath, 1971), pp. 186-8; Peter Temin, *Iron and Steel in Nineteenth-Century America: An Economic Inquiry* (Cambridge: M.I.T. Press, 1964), p. 227; AISA, *Statistics of the American and Foreign Iron Trades: Annual Report of the Secretary*, 1914, p. 63.

[30] The ten firms had eleven mills, six of which were completely new. The rest had previously made at least some quantity of rods for other uses.

Table 3.1. *Production of wire and cut nails*

Year	Wire nails[a]	Cut nails[a]
1886	0.600[b]	8.161
1887	1.250[b]	6.909
1888	1.500[b]	6.494
1889	2.435	5.811
1890	3.136	5.641
1891	4.114	5.002
1892	4.720	4.508
1893	5.096	3.049
1894	5.682	2.425
1895	5.841	2.130
1896	4.720	1.616
1897	8.977	2.107
1898	7.418	1.572
1899	7.618	1.904

[a]Millions of 100-lb kegs per year.
[b]Estimated.
Source: U.S. Congress, House, *Tariff Hearings before the Committee on Ways and Means, 1896–1897*, 54th Cong., 2d Sess., 1897, Doc. 338, p. 2127; American Iron and Steel Association, *Statistics of the American and Foreign Iron Trades: Annual Report of the Secretary*, 1896, p. 45; 1898, p. 51; 1900, p. 29.

the mills to shut down (Figure 3.4)[31] The seventh largest firm in the industry, the Baackes Wire Nail Company, failed altogether; Andrew Carnegie withdrew from production his Beaver Falls mill, the fifth largest in the industry; and the H. P. Nail Company, the number three firm, informed the Senate Finance Committee that selling prices "decreased to an actual loss for 1893," a report that was confirmed

---

[31] *Iron Age,* January 4, 1894, p. 30; George F. Warren and Frank A. Pearson, *Prices* (New York: Wiley, 1933), p. 13. A note on prices: Wire nails of different sizes sold according to a schedule of extras charged above a base price. Market quotations listed this base price, but because manufacturers changed the schedule of extras from time to time, these quotations do not provide an accurate indication of the trend in prices. A better index is the price of size 8-d nails, because the extras on a well-assorted purchase of nails typically averaged out to the extra on 8-d nails. In fact, for many years this was a pricing rule in the industry. Edgerton, "The Wire-Nail Association," pp. 47-9, 58-9.

Table 3.2. *Changes in the numbers and capacities[a] of wire-nail firms*

	1892–4	1894–6	1896–8
Number of new rolling mills	3[b]	1[c]	3[d]
Net additions to industry capacity from new rolling mills	0.415	0.120	0.790
Number of rolling mills that disappeared	0	0[e]	1
Capacity of rolling mills that disappeared	0.000	0.000	0.030
Net changes in capacity of rolling mills in existence in first and last years	1.150	1.453	1.940
Total number of rolling-mill firms in last year	10	9	11[f]
Total number of drawing firms in last year	18	21	23[f]
Total number of nail-finishing firms in last year	12	13	29
Total capacity of rolling-mill firms in last year	6.807	8.380	11.080[f]
Total capacity of drawing firms in last year[g]	2.797	3.678	4.315[f]
Total capacity of finishing firms in last year[h]	0.323	0.522	1.260
Total industry capacity in last year	9.927	12.580	16.655

[a]Millions of 100-lb kegs of nails per year.
[b]Includes one completely new firm, one firm that integrated backward into rod production, and one barbed-wire producer that entered the nail industry as part of Consolidated Steel & Wire.
[c]One rod producer entered the nail industry.
[d]Includes two completely new firms (one of which was absorbed by American Steel & Wire of Illinois) and one rod producer that entered the nail industry in this period.
[e]Two mills closed in 1894, but by 1896 they had been acquired by Consolidated Steel & Wire.
[f]Before formation of American Steel & Wire of Illinois.
[g]There was no information on the capacities of three drawing works in 1894, two in 1896, and two in 1898. The capacities of several other firms had to be estimated.
[h]There was no information on the capacities of four finishing works in 1894, two in 1896, and three in 1898. The capacities of several other firms had to be estimated.
Source: AISA, *Directory to the Iron and Steel Works of the United States*, 1892 to 1898.

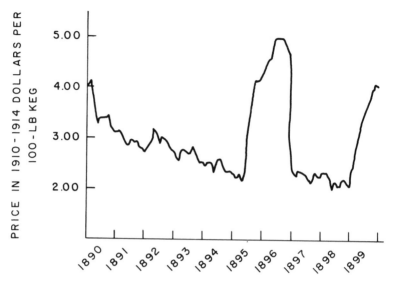

Figure 3.4. Real price of 8-d wire nails, by months, 1890–9. The sharp rise and decline in the price of wire nails in 1895–6 resulted from formation and collapse of a pool. The 1899 increase was due to the organization of the American Steel and Wire Company of New Jersey. Data from AISA, *Statistics of the Iron Trades*, 1896, p. 89; 1897, p. 28; 1898, p. 28; 1900, p. 17; Warren and Pearson, *Prices*, pp. 11–13.

by the following stockholders' resolution: "Notwithstanding the losses sustained in operating the works during the year 1893, we take advantage of this occasion to express our confidence in the officers of the Company."[32]

The drop in demand was so severe that *Iron Age* reported that "if all the wire mills in the country were operated to full capacity for four months, the consumption of the whole country for an entire year could be met,"[33] Yet running full was exactly what some of the

---

[32] The Baackes Wire Nail Company was a new firm and had a large bonded indebtedness. Carnegie's mill was fairly old and probably outmoded. *Iron Age,* January 4, 1894, p. 30; AISA, *Directory,* 1894; U.S. Congress, Senate, *Replies to Tariff Inquiries,* 53d Cong., 2d Sess., 1894, Rept. 423, pp. 14-15; Report of annual meeting of H. P. Nail Co., Baker Library, Harvard University Business School, American Steel and Wire Collection, Mss. 596, H. P. Nail Co., Vol. I, p. 33.
[33] *Iron Age,* January 4, 1894, p. 30.

largest manufacturers attempted to do when falling demand threatened them with losses. As soon as credit conditions improved toward the end of 1893, firms began to cut prices in order to keep their expensive, continuous-type rolling mills in operation, and at least some of them were able in this manner to secure a good run of orders. For instance, the New Castle Wire Nail Company drove its factory to the "utmost capacity" in early 1894, both Oliver & Roberts and the Pittsburgh Wire Company set new production records in April, and the American Wire Nail Company was running full in November.[34]

Despite the closing of the Baackes and Carnegie mills and a number of smaller concerns,[35] production continued to increase as firms struggled to run their plants at full capacity. Output rose from 5.1 million kegs in 1893 to 5.7 million in 1894 (Table 3.1), and even

---

[34] *Iron Age*, February 15, 1894, p. 308, April 5, 1894, p. 669, April 12, 1894, p. 713, November 15, 1894, pp. 852-3; AISA, *Directory*, 1894 and 1896. In 1894 the largest eight firms (in order of nail capacity) were Consolidated Steel & Wire, New Castle Nail, H. P. Nail, Salem Wire Nail, Beaver Falls, Oliver & Roberts, Baackes Wire Nail, and American Wire Nail. In 1896 the top eight firms were Consolidated Steel & Wire, Salem Wire Nail, H. P. Nail, New Castle Nail, Oliver Wire (formerly Oliver & Roberts), American Wire Nail, Grand Crossing Tack, and the Pittsburgh Wire Company.

These firms do not seem to have been as evenly matched as those in the tin-plate and newsprint industries. On the one hand, Consolidated Steel & Wire controlled (after its acquisition of the Baackes Company and Carnegie's Beaver Falls mill) nearly a third of total nail capacity. It was connected by ties of ownership with Illinois Steel, a major producer of billets and rods, and derived additional financial strength from a formidable market position in barbed wire. At the other extreme, a producer as important as the Salem Wire Nail Company had no rod-making capacity whatsoever.

Nonetheless, all of the top eight firms, with the possible exception of Grand Crossing Tack, were major competitors until 1898, when the American Steel and Wire consolidation was formed. After 1893, despite bouts of severe price competition, there were no more failures of importance in the industry, and all of the firms appear to have suffered from the declining prices. Whatever advantage any one firm had seems to have been offset by some disadvantage, and vice versa (in Consolidated's case the disadvantage was probably high overhead costs).

[35] The Baackes and Carnegie mills had a combined capacity of 1,450,000 kegs of nails per year, or 15 percent of industry capacity. They shut down in late 1893, at which time, according to *Iron Age*, their withdrawal appeared to have no effect in steadying the market. Apparently they were not operated again until they were acquired by Consolidated Steel & Wire in 1895. In addition to these two failures, nineteen smaller firms either disappeared altogether from the list of wire-nail producers between 1892 and 1894 or were reported to be idle in 1894. *Iron Age*, January 4, 1894, p. 30; AISA, *Directory*, 1892 to 1896.

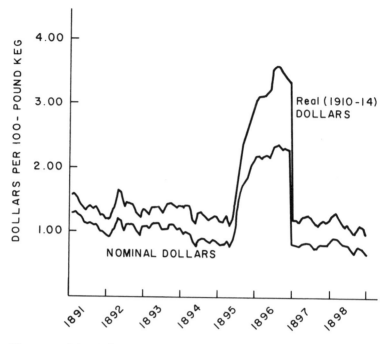

Figure 3.5. Margin between price of wire nails and cost of raw materials, by months, 1891–8. Data from the following sources: Prices: size 8-d nails delivered at Chicago, AISA, *Statistics of the Iron Trades,* 1896, p. 89; 1897, p. 28; 1898, p. 28. Cost (see text). Deflator: Warren and Pearson, *Prices,* p. 13.

though much of this gain came at the expense of cut nail producers, by the end of 1894 real prices had fallen another 11 percent. Raw-material costs also fell, but not enough to offset fully the decline in revenues. As can be seen from Figure 3.5, the margin between the market price of wire nails and that of the billets used to produce them dropped from a level of approximately $1.10 per keg in early 1893 to $0.80 per keg the first few months of 1895, a fall in real terms of 12 percent.[36]

---

[36] I am assuming that there was no technological change and that it took approximately 2,500 pounds of steel to produce 1 gross ton (2,240 pounds) of nails. This estimate is based on data collected in U.S. Congress, Senate, *Testimony Taken by the Subcommittee on the Tariff of the Senate Committee on Finance,* 1887-1888,

As wire-nail prices continued to fall, the manufacturers met repeatedly to urge one another not to cut prices, but their attempts met with little success. Finally, in the spring of 1895 they united to form the Wire-Nail Association, a powerful and well-organized pool engineered by John H. Parks, an outsider who specialized in industrial combination.[37] Parks's method was to jack prices up quickly – far above the equilibrium level – to give firms an incentive to accept the discipline of the pool. The idea was that manufacturers would recognize that only by working together through the agency of the pool could they sustain such a high level of prices. But because high prices also reduced consumption and stimulated entry, maintenance of this discipline would ultimately prove very costly.

Initially, however, the association was a great success. In the spring of 1895 the economy was beginning a temporary revival, and this, in conjunction with the mere rumor that a pool had been effected, sent customers and jobbers scurrying to buy nails, forcing prices up.[38] Whereas nails had been selling for some time at a base price of 75-85 cents per keg, prices advanced to $1.15-$1.20 per keg, and the association had no trouble in attaining its June goal of $1.20. In fact, manufacturers generally sold their allotments for the month as early as June 12. July was an even better month, and some manufacturers disposed of their entire outputs at pool prices before July 4. By August the association was demanding, and getting, $2.05 per keg. Though prices would go still higher, that was to be the peak of the pool's influence. By mid-fall the demand for nails had begun to shrink, and competition from independent firms began to increase.[39]

50th Cong., 1st Sess., 1888, Rept. 2332, Pt. II, pp. 110-15, 135-6, 145-6; U.S. Commissioner of Labor, *Sixth Annual Report*, pp. 183-93; U.S. Commissioner of Corporations, *Report on the Steel Industry, Part III, Cost of Production* (Washington, D.C.: U.S. Government Printing Office, 1913), p. 262. Steel prices are from U.S. Congress, House, *Hearings before the Committee on Investigation of United States Steel Corporation*, (Washington, D.C.: U.S. Government Printing Office, 1912), Vol. VII, p. 5555.

[37] See Edgerton, "The Wire-Nail Association," pp. 46-72; *Iron Age*, December 3, 1896, pp. 1106-7.

[38] I am suggesting that although the pool pushed prices above what, in a static analysis, would have been the firms' profit-maximizing level, this strategy seemed initially to work because it stimulated a buying movement.

[39] Edgerton, "The Wire-Nail Association," pp. 49-53; U.S. Industrial Commission, *Report on Trusts and Industrial Combinations*, 57th Cong., 1st Sess., 1901, House Doc. 182, pp. xcvii-xcviii; *Iron Age*, January 2, 1896, pp. 78, 81-2, December 3, 1896, pp. 1106-7.

Nonetheless, the association managed to hold itself together for another year. Advance announcements of price increases galvanized the dying market into activity, and guarantees against price declines encouraged wary jobbers to continue purchasing. For a time the association staved off the worst effects of the growing competition by paying independent firms (the most important of which was the Pittsburgh Wire Company) not to make nails. Ultimately, of course, this practice served only to aggravate the situation, for any small manufacturer could turn a handsome profit by selling nails just under the association price and then allowing himself to be bought off. All that was needed to enter the industry was an investment of $10,000 for nail machines, because small finishing works could easily obtain a supply of wire from rolling mills that did not themselves produce nails and that remained outside the association.[40] Attempts were made to organize these outside mills, but rod makers who devoted a large proportion of their output to specialty lines (they included Washburn and Moen, the second largest rod producer in the nation) were comparatively secure in their position. Before they would relinquish their independence of action, they demanded from the nail mills what were considered unrealistic concessions. As a result, attempts to organize the rod makers met with repeated failure, and outside mills continued to sell rods and wire to independents and even to add nail machines to their own works. Washburn and Moen, for example, acquired the capacity to produce 240,000 kegs of nails per year, and the Cleveland Rolling Mill Company, 200,000.[41]

By the fall of 1896 the Wire-Nail Association was on the verge of failure. Inflated prices had so reduced sales that annual production dropped approximately 1 million kegs below its 1895 level, a reduction of about one-fifth. The burden of payments to nonmembers was increasing enormously, but so were the amounts of nails being made outside the association. Desperate for sales, association manufacturers cut prices on their other wire products to wholesalers who agreed to buy nails from them, disrupting conditions in those markets, too.

[40] Edgerton, "The Wire-Nail Association," pp. 49-58; *Iron Age,* June 25, 1896, p. 1490, December 3, 1896, pp. 1106-7; U.S. Commissioner of Corporations, *Report on the Steel Industry,* Part I, p. 72.
[41] *American Manufacturer and Iron World,* April 17, 1896, p. 559; AISA, *Directory,* 1898.

The price of barbed wire, in particular, plunged to its lowest level ever, dropping to $1.85 per 100 pounds, 15 percent below its 1894 average (a drop of 15 percent in real terms as well).[42]

The final break came in November 1896, first in Chicago and then throughout the East. On December 1, the association met for the last time, set up a new "card of extras" fixing the relative prices of different sizes of nails, and then disbanded. Immediately the base price of nails dropped $1.15 per keg, stabilizing at around $1.40. The actual price decline was even greater, for in establishing the new nail card, manufacturers had reduced the amounts of extras chargeable for small sizes of nails (in order to force out of business small manufacturers who specialized in the higher-priced sizes). Allowing for this difference and also for changes in the general price level, the real fall in prices was about 64 percent.[43]

The effect of the pool's collapse on the price and output behavior of the rolling mills (like their response to the depression itself) can be explained in terms of our model. In 1893 the impact of depression on this rapidly growing, capital-intensive part of the industry had been to stimulate a price war that the manufacturers were unable to end, except, temporarily, by forming a pool. In 1896 the collapse of the Wire-Nail Association brought a repetition of the 1893 experience. The high prices charged by the pool had helped its members maintain discipline, but they had also attracted a flood of new firms to the industry. Many of these entrants were small, but some were rolling mills whose capital-intensive methods of production, like those of many members of the association, tempted them to struggle to operate at full capacity whenever falling prices threatened them with losses. Moreover, the very newness of some of these firms and the chaotic conditions in the industry following the collapse of the pool encouraged manufacturers to risk cutting prices.

We can obtain some idea of the effect of this second decline on

[42] Edgerton, "The Wire-Nail Associaton," pp. 56-8; U.S. Industrial Commission, *Report on Trusts and Industrial Combinations*, pp. xcii-xcviii; *Iron Age*, January 5, 1899, p. 42.

[43] Edgerton, "The Wire-Nail Association," pp. 56-8; U.S. Industrial Commission, *Report on Trusts and Industrial Combinations*, pp. xcvii-xcviii; *Iron Age*, December 3, 1896, pp. 1106-9; AISA, *Statistics of the Iron Trades 1896*, p. 89; 1897, p. 29; 1898, p. 28; Warren and Pearson, *Prices*, p. 13.

Table 3.3. *Trends in per-unit and total gross profits in the wire-nail industry*

Year	Estimated cost per gross ton[a]	Price per gross ton	Margin per gross ton	Output (gross tons)	Margin multiplied by output
1889	$47.16	$63.56	$16.60	108,700	$1,804,000
1890	47.73	64.03	16.30	140,000	2,282,000
1891	41.83	53.65	11.82	183,700	2,171,000
1892	39.58	50.12	10.54	210,700	2,221,000
1893	35.67	46.85	11.18	227,500	2,543,000
1894	31.02	38.34	7.32	253,700	1,857,000
1895	32.73	51.22	18.49	260,800	4,822,000
1896	32.72	69.37	36.65	210,700	7,722,000
1897	28.20	34.81	6.61	400,800	2,649,000
1898	28.06	34.70	6.64	331,200	2,199,000

[a]Excludes cost of converting wire into nails, freight charges, administrative and sales expenses, and fixed costs.
Source: Cost: See Note 44. Price: 8-d nails at Chicago, from AISA, *Statistics of the Iron Trades,* 1896, p. 89; 1902, p. 33. Output: *Ibid.,* 1896, p. 45; 1898, p. 51; 1900, p. 29.

industry profits by estimating the average yearly cost of producing a ton of nails, subtracting this value from the market price, multiplying the difference by total industry output, and deflating by the wholesale price index.[44] As this calculation reveals (Table 3.3), gross industry "profits" fell drastically between 1896 and 1897, and dropped

[44] In making this calculation I assumed that it took approximately 2,400 pounds of billets to make 1 gross ton of wire. I also assumed that the cost (including only fuel, labor, maintenance, and supplies) of transforming billets into wire decreased from approximately $15 in 1888 to $8.75 in 1902-6 and that this decline was distributed linearly over the period 1888-904. The former figure was based on R. H. Wolff's testimony in 1888 before the Senate Subcommittee on the Tariff that it cost $5-$6 to transform billets into rods and $8-$9 to draw the rods into wire (his estimates were corroborated by the scattered comments of other manufacturers). The 1902-6 figure was based on the finding of the Commissioner of Corporations that the cost of rod rolling at that time was $3.50 per ton. I assumed that the ratio of rod-rolling to wire-drawing costs had not changed since 1888. It is important to note that these estimates do not include many elements of cost – conversion of wire into nails, freight charges, administrative and sales expenses, depreciation, taxes, or interest. U.S. Senate, *Testimony Taken by the Subcommittee on the Tariff, 1878-1888,* pp. 110-15, 135-6, 145-6; U.S. Commissioner of Labor, *Sixth Annual Report,* pp. 183-93; U.S. Commissioner of Corporations, *Report on the Steel Industry,* Part III, p. 262.

again in 1898. In the latter year they even dipped below their 1892 level. When one considers the tremendous increase in investment that had occurred in the interim (the capacity of the industry had more than doubled between 1892 and 1898, and the capacity of the capital-intensive rolling-mill branch had more than quadrupled),[45] the effect of the competition on profits is evident. Earnings were so low in 1897 that J. P. Morgan refused to participate in a scheme to consolidate the industry. As one of the Morgan partners wrote J. W. ("Bet-A-Million") Gates, president of Consolidated Steel & Wire,

I have now in my possession and have carefully considered the reports of the chartered accountants relating to all the companies whose properties have been offered for sale to a new company proposed to be formed . . . I need hardly to say that I am not only surprised but disappointed with the result, especially for the year 1897 . . . The books of most of these companies show a good profit for 1895 and 1896 [under the pool] and some of the companies were very successful in 1897; but the aggregate profits for 1897 were surprisingly small in comparison with previous years and with what it was expected.

In view of the poor showing that is made as a whole for 1897, the proposed investment is not desirable and outsiders will not be disposed to take it . . . [T]he difference between 1897 and previous years is demonstration that some arrangement whereby prices can be maintained is absolutely essential to success.[46]

After failing in several attempts to revive the pool and fix prices, the manufacturers (led by Gates, without any help from Morgan) began to work toward a consolidation. But even as the negotiators were meeting in New York to set the terms of the consolidation, competition within the industry continued unabated. Cables sent from the Salem Wire Company's central office to its sales agents in the field show the workings of the downward price spiral in which the manufacturers found themselves enmeshed. Management repeatedly urged salesmen to meet whatever prices the competition quoted:

[45] AISA, *Directory,* 1892 to 1898.
[46] U.S. Supreme Court, *The United States of America, Appellant v. United States Steel Corporation, et al.: Transcript of Record* (Washington, D.C.: U.S. Government Printing Office, 1917), Vol. I, pp. 339-40. It should also be noted that Consolidated Steel & Wire neglected to publish its annual report for 1897. *Chicago Securities,* 1896, pp. 169-70; 1897, pp. 176-7; 1898, pp. 182-3.

Meet the situation as you find it we need orders for immediate shipment. We want you to make every effort to secure orders at competing prices. Don't send out notices about cut rates. All that is necessary is to advise trade if price is not satisfactory to advise you before they buy.

Keep up a firm front but meet the competition regardless of agreements. Need orders badly.

Make up your mind to get more than our share of the business if possible.[47]

Rumors reached the Salem Wire Company's central office in early March 1898 that the H. P. Nail Company had cut prices as low as $1.40 delivered at Cleveland, and Salem's managers reluctantly ordered its sales force to meet this price if necessary: "We want you to keep a look out for them and while we do not want to sell nails at that figure, if we can possibly avoid it, as it means absolute cost to us, or less, yet we must keep our mills in operation."[48] At the same time, the sales force was informed that Salem would go no lower than $1.40: "This price is less than the cost of manufacture today based on price of rods."[49] But by the end of the month, competition had forced the company to quote lower. "We are advised today that Pgh Wire Co and probably Oliver are quoting 1.35 Pgh for Eastern trade and have just advised you to meet it."[50] A few days later the Salem Wire Company agreed to join a consolidation, the American Steel and Wire Company of Illinois.[51]

Formed by Gates, American Steel and Wire encompassed the Consolidated Steel & Wire Company, three more of the top eight firms, and a handful of smaller producers. It was said to control as much as 75 percent of the wire and wire-rod production of the nation. Its wire-nail capacity of 9,300,000 kegs, however, was still only 55 percent of the total, and remaining outside the combination were some formidable competitors, including Washburn and Moen (wire-nail capacity 240,000 kegs per year), New Castle Wire Nail Company (1,250,000 kegs), Oliver Wire Company (960,000 kegs), Cleve-

---

[47] Baker Mss. 596, Salem Wire Company, Vol. I, pp. 50, 55, 58, 88, 101.
[48] *Ibid.*, p. 67.
[49] *Ibid.*, p. 96; see also pp. 101-2, 143.
[50] *Ibid.*, p. 163.
[51] *Ibid.*, pp. 173, 178.

land Rolling Mill (200,000 kegs), Pittsburgh Wire (570,000 kegs), and several other important rolling mills.[52]

The very existence of this competition prevented any significant advance in prices. Hence, 1898, in many respects, saw a repetition of the previous year's experience. At a time when the rest of the nation was recovering from depression, nail makers were not participating in the general prosperity. John Stevenson, Jr., of the New Castle Wire Nail Company later described his feelings at this state of affairs: "Gates used to joke me, 'You had better surrender and come in with us.' That was all there was about it. I felt like a kind of Ishmaelite, with everybody's hand against everybody else, and there was no profit for any of us, or very little, and I know there was none for me; I will tell you that."[53]

Even a firm like Washburn and Moen, with a large proportion of its product devoted to specialty items, suffered. Letters from the superintendent of the firm's Waukegan, Illinois, plant and from its general superintendent in Worcester, Massachusetts, show that the sales force managed to attract abundant orders throughout 1898, but not at remunerative prices. As the firm's monthly accounts show, average receipts for the first six months of 1898 were still at depression levels – about $300,000 per month below the 1892 average, even though in the interim the firm had built a giant new plant and virtually all its mills were running to capacity. By the middle of 1898 the company seems to have run short of cash, and it became difficult to obtain approval of expenditures for capital equipment. When, for example, Waukegan Superintendent Lewis Brittan sought permission to buy a more efficient type of coal grate, General Superintendent F. H. Daniels hemmed and hawed: "Regarding the McKenzie Grate. I do not know quite what to say. Talk it over with Mr. Boynton [the Chicago manager] and let me know his views and then I will take it up with Mr. Moen [the general manager] and then advise you. We

[52] *Iron Age*, December 23, 1897, pp. 20-1, March 10, 1898, p. 19; *American Manufacturer*, March 18, 1898, pp. 378-9, March 25, 1898, p. 415; *Commercial and Financial Chronicle*, March 12, 1898, p. 519; March 26, 1898, pp. 615-6; Lloyd Wendt and Herman Kogan, *Bet A Million! The Story of John W. Gates* (New York: Bobbs-Merrill, 1948), pp. 146-51; AISA, *Directory*, 1898.

[53] U.S. Supreme Court, *The United States v. United States Steel, et al.: Transcript of Record*, Vol. III, p. 1070.

are awfully shy of spending money but if that Grate will save us coal we can, of course, afford to use it at the expense named."[54]

Swayed by the pressures of competition, on the one hand, and generous offers for their plants, on the other, the manufacturers one after another sold out to Gates. During the last two months of 1898, American Steel and Wire absorbed the Pittsburgh Wire Company and Cincinnati Barbed Wire Fence, both important nail makers. By January 1899 the remainder of the firms had joined the movement. The result was the American Steel and Wire Company of New Jersey, including practically all the wire, wire-rod, and wire-nail mills in the country, and exercising a virtual monopoly over the nation's barbed-wire production.[55] Its organization put to an end competitive turbulence in the industry, and prices recorded a strong advance. As *Iron Age* remarked in its trade summary for the year 1899, "The market for the past year has been without the usual commercial features developing from competition among manufacturers."[56]

In the wire-nail industry, the sequence of events conformed closely to the predictions of the model developed earlier in this chapter. Severe depression interrupted a period of rapid expansion, triggering a price war that manufacturers were unable to end except by forming a consolidation. Among capital-intensive rail producers, however, the sequence of events was very different. This branch of the steel industry did not experience rapid growth on the eve of the Panic of 1893. Consequently, as the model would predict, competition during the depression was more restrained, and there was no serious move to consolidate the manufacturers.

The period of greatest expansion in rail production was the late

---

[54] Unfortunately, it is impossible to tell anything about the firm's overall financial condition from its brief monthly accounts. Baker Mss. 596, Washburn and Moen Mfg. Co. 1868-99, Vols. 31, 109-110. Daniels' remarks were quoted in a letter from Brittan to the McKenzie Furnace Company, July 11, 1898, Vol. 109, p. 661.

[55] For a detailed treatment of the negotiations and financial details, see Joseph M. McFadden, "Monopoly in Barbed Wire: The Formation of the American Steel and Wire Company," *Business History Review*, LII (Winter 1978), pp. 465-89. See also *Commercial and Financial Chronicle*, November 12, 1898, p. 1002; *Iron Age*, January 5, 1899, p. 41, January 12, 1899, pp. 19-21; U.S. Industrial Commission, *Report on Trusts and Industrial Combinations*, pp. xcvii-xcviii.

[56] *Iron Age*, January 4, 1900, pp. 60-1.

Table 3.4. *Production of Bessemer steel rails*

Year	Production (gross tons)	Year	Production (gross tons)
1880	852,196	1890	1,867,837
1881	1,187,770	1891	1,293,053
1882	1,284,067	1892	1,537,588
1883	1,148,709	1893	1,129,400
1884	996,983	1894	1,016,013
1885	959,471	1895	1,299,628
1886	1,574,703	1896	1,166,958
1887	2,101,904	1897	1,644,520
1888	1,386,277	1898	1,976,702
1889	1,510,057	1899	2,270,585
		1900	2,383,654

Source: AISA, *Statistics of the Iron Trade*, 1896, p. 66; 1898, p. 56; 1900, pp. 27, 36.

1870s and early 1880s. Even then, however, patents and the large amount of capital required to build a plant of efficient size restricted entry, so that in 1887, at the end of this period of expansion, fourteen firms accounted for 90 percent of total output.[57] These firms were far from equally matched, and the late 1880s and early 1890s were years of readjustment rather than expansion. By 1893, the ranks of rail producers had dwindled to seven, partly as a result of mergers and partly because the smaller firms dropped out of the competition. During these years, output actually declined. The 1887 production of 2,101,904 gross tons of rails was not surpassed again until 1899 (Table 3.4), and even during the boom year of 1892 manufacturers produced only 1,537,588 gross tons of rails. Meanwhile, the enormous amount of capital required for rail production continued to discourage entry. Aside from the Colorado Fuel and Iron Company, whose location protected it from competition, the only new entrant in this period (Duquesne Steel) was quickly vanquished and absorbed by Carnegie.[58]

[57] Temin, *Iron and Steel in Nineteenth-Century America*, pp. 169-82; U.S. Commissioner of Corporations, *Report on the Steel Industry*, Pt. I, pp. 68-72; *Iron Age*, February 11, 1897, p. 18.
[58] The seven remaining firms were Bethlehem, Cambria, Carnegie, Colorado, Illinois, Lackawanna, and Pennsylvania. *Ibid.*; Temin, *Iron and Steel in Nineteenth Century America*, pp. 182-3; AISA, *Statistics of the Iron Trades* 1907, p. 106; Bridge, *The Inside History of the Carnegie Steel Company*, pp. 174-80.

By the depression of the nineties, therefore, the rail industry was essentially in equilibrium. The firms that remained in the industry were large in size and few in number; all but Colorado Fuel and Iron were established enterprises whose officers had grown used to each other's dealings.[59] Their customers, the nation's railroads, had developed regular buying habits, generally apportioning their orders among the steel mills located along their tracks.[60] As a result, stable oligopolistic patterns of market behavior had taken shape, aided by institutions designed to regulate competition in the industry. The most important of these, the Rail Association, was formed in 1887 to control production and prices. Organized as a pool, the association allocated a percentage of total output to each firm in the industry on the basis of capacity. Those manufacturers who exceeded their allotments paid a tax on their surplus tonnage; those who fell short were granted a subsidy.[61]

Whereas similar institutions in rapidly growing industries usually failed under the pressure of high fixed charges and reduced demand, the rail pool was remarkably successful, even during the long depression of the nineties. Early in the decade the pool had set the price of rails at $30 per ton. After the panic, in response to the drop in demand, it lowered the price in successive steps between 1893 and 1895. Then, when business conditions showed a hint of improvement in 1895, it raised the price to $28 (a price it enforced for the next sixteen months). Both the reductions and the increases were executed with the utmost precision. Successive pricing goals were never separated by more than a two-month transition period, and each price was maintained for at least six months (Figure 3.6).[62]

This is not to say that the pool did not encounter problems. Given

---

[59] Although Carnegie was undoubtedly the most efficient producer, the others seem to have possessed compensating advantages in their home territories. Later in the decade, Carnegie would fail in an attempt to force some of the Eastern mills out of production. U.S. Supreme Court, *United States of America, Appellant v. United States Steel Corporation, et al.: Brief for the United States* (Washington, D.C.: U.S. Government Printing Office, 1917), Vol. II, pp. 271, 300.

[60] U.S. House, *Investigation of United States Steel Corporation*, Vol. I, pp. 308, 375.

[61] There was also a related association to administer patents. Temin, *Iron and Steel in Nineteenth-Century America*, pp. 182-3; *Iron Age*, April 9, 1896, p. 875; February 11, 1897, p. 18; U.S. Commissioner of Corporations, *Report on the Steel Industry*, Pt. I, pp. 68-72.

[62] Temin, *Iron and Steel in Nineteenth Century America*, pp. 185-7.

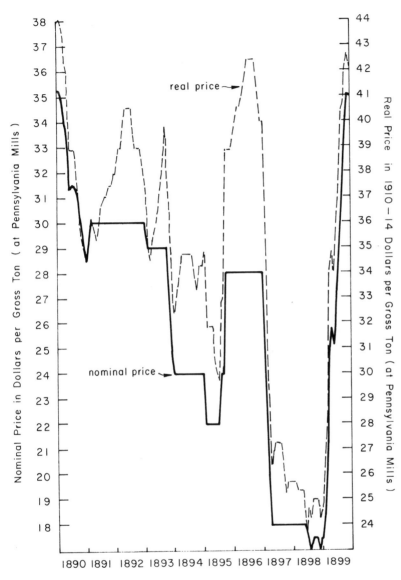

Figure 3.6. Nominal and real prices of steel rails, 1890–9. Data from AISA, *Statistics of the Iron Trades*, 1899, p. 66; Warren and Pearson, *Prices*, p. 13.

the state of business, the prices it set were apparently too high, for they encouraged the entry of new firms to the industry and the return of older establishments to the rail market. As a result, the organization found itself spending increasing amounts of its resources to buy off competitors and keep the additional capacity out of production. By 1896, such payments totaled a staggering $1,000,000.[63] To make matters worse, the inflated price of rails had so reduced consumption that many members could not sell their allotments and depended on payments from the pool for revenues. Even as important a corporation as Illinois Steel kept its Union works idle for most of the depression and often ran its other plants on billets.[64]

Division of this shrinking pie became an increasingly serious problem as pool members jockeyed for position. Then, in 1895, the difficulty was compounded when the association seriously overestimated demand for the following year. Allotments were based on a projected consumption of 2,200,000 tons of rails, but actual shipments in 1896 amounted to only 800,000 tons. All that was needed to precipitate the collapse of the association was a pretext, and Illinois Steel provided it the following February. Prevented by state law from officially participating in the pool, Illinois had a secret understanding with Carnegie to divide the latter's share. In response to some real or imagined violation of this pact, Illinois slashed its price for rails. The

---

[63] In 1895 the Rail Association concluded an agreement with the Johnson Company of Lorain, Ohio, which had just completed construction on a new rail mill. The Johnson Company promised not to make standard rails for steam railroads and in return was granted half the nation's tonnage of girder rails for electric street railways. Other competitors were paid in cash not to produce rails. These included the Colorado Fuel and Iron Company, the Cleveland Rolling Mill Company, the Maryland Steel Company, the Ohio Steel Company, and an Indianapolis mill (probably the Premier Steel Company). U.S. Supreme Court, *United States v. United States Steel, et al.: Transcript of Record: Government Exhibits*, pp. 1034-5, and *Brief for the United States*, Vol. II, pp. 67-8; Wallace E. Belcher, "Industrial Pooling Agreements," *Quarterly Journal of Economics*, XIX (November 1904), pp. 117-18; *Iron Age*, February 11, 1897, pp. 18-19.

[64] *Iron Age*, January 4, 1894, p. 10; March 22, 1894, p. 557; January 3, 1895, pp. 3-4; February 21, 1895, pp. 377-78; January 2, 1896, pp. 26-7; December 31, 1896, p. 1314; February 11, 1897, pp. 18-19; Belcher, "Industrial Pooling Agreements," pp. 117-18; Kenneth Warren, *The American Steel Industry, 1850-1970: A Geographical Interpretation* (Oxford: Clarendon Press, 1973), pp. 96-9.

breach was quickly discovered by the rest of the firms, and an all-out price war ensued.[65]

On the surface it seemed as if the Rail Association had met the same fate as the wire-nail pool and other similar organizations of common-grade producers. But that was not really the case. The collapse of the rail pool resulted mainly from the severe miscalculations of the pool's officers, not from any predisposition toward price cutting.[66] Take, for example, the case of Illinois Steel. With its large burden of bonded indebtedness, the firm certainly had high and pressing fixed charges to meet. Yet, even though it scarcely paid any dividends after 1892, even though it ran a deficit in every year of the depression except 1895, Illinois refrained from cutting prices until 1897. It took this action only when it became clear that the losses it suffered owed increasingly not to the depression but to the miscalculations of the pool.[67] Under the leadership of President J. W. Gates, also president of Consolidated Steel & Wire, the firm took a desperate gamble. It cut prices with the aim of expanding sales and reducing unit costs, hoping in this manner to eliminate its losses.

The gamble paid off, as falling prices stimulated sales. Illinois Steel ended 1897 in the black and did even better in 1898.[68] Moreover, the

[65] *Iron Age,* February 11, 1897, pp. 18-19; June 22, 1911, p. 1532; Warren, *The American Steel Industry,* pp. 117-18; Goodale, *Chronology of Iron and Steel,* p. 227.

[66] Of course, the Wire-Nail Association had also "miscalculated" and raised prices too high, but this miscalculation had been necessary to maintain discipline among the members and had been part of the pact from the very beginning. By contrast, the Rail Association had initially *lowered* prices in accordance with the fall in demand after the Panic and had only raised them again in 1895 in the mistaken belief that business conditions were improving.

[67] After charging off $1,467,372 for depreciation in the value of its raw-material stocks, Illinois ran a deficit of $349,472 in 1893. In 1894 the firm had net earnings of $30,607 after interest payments, leaving a deficit of $318,865. In 1895 Illinois had a much better year, ending up in the black with a $914,403 surplus. But in 1896 the firm was back in the red with a deficit of $349,399. *Commercial and Financial Chronicle: Investors' Supplement,* January 1895, p. 141; April, 1895, p. 143; *Commerical and Financial Chronicle,* February 16, 1895, pp. 299-300; February 15, 1896, pp. 316-17; February 26, 1896, p. 559; February 13, 1897, p. 327; U.S. Commissioner of Corporations, *Report on the Steel Industry,* Part I, pp. 117-21.

[68] Despite the necessity of writing off a large sum for the depreciation in value of its raw-material stocks, Illinois Steel earned enough to wipe out the past year's deficit and end 1897 with a surplus of $20,625. By November 1898, its surplus had risen to $664,907. *Commercial and Financial Chronicle,* February 12, 1898, p. 372; November 12, 1898, p. 1009.

increased consumption benefited other firms as well. For example, Carnegie's total output of rails had amounted to only about 300,000 tons in 1896. From January 1 through February 10, 1897, the firm had logged a mere 30,000 tons in orders, but in the next thirteen days, as a result of the break in prices, Carnegie sold nearly 600,000 tons of rails – a full year's production. Profits also began to improve for the Pennsylvania Steel Company, which had lost money steadily throughout the depression and had even suffered failure and reorganization. Lackawanna Steel was able to pay off its predepression debts, and Lackawanna, Bethlehem, and Cambria all declared better than normal dividends.[69] At the same time, firms that had entered the industry under the pool's pricing umbrella quickly retreated. One of the new entrants, Johnson Steel, shifted its capacity to light rails for street railroads, whereas the other, the Ohio Steel Company, never completed construction of its rail mill. With the exception of Bethlehem Steel, the older establishments that had returned to the rail market under the pool switched their production back to billets, rods, or whatever else they had been making.[70]

In the case of the rail industry, then, price cutting served the purpose of stimulating consumption and eliminating extra competition. Once it had accomplished that goal, the price war was fairly easily ended. In December 1898, Illinois and Carnegie negotiated a truce. Within the next year the entire rail pool was reconstituted, and prices

[69] It is doubtful that there was any significant change in market shares as a result of the competition. Carnegie and Illinois together accounted for 84 percent of the orders that the *Railroad Gazette* was able to trace in the three months following the break in the pool. This represented a substantial increase in their share of the market, which normally would have been 50-60 percent. According to *Iron Age*, however, the *Gazette* findings were incomplete. In particular, a number of sales by the Bethlehem, Pennsylvania, and Lackawanna companies had not been counted. *Iron Age*, February 11, 1897, p. 19; May 20, 1897, p. 23; U.S. Supreme Court, *United States v. United States Steel, et al: Transcript of Record: Government Exhibits*, Vol. III, pp. 1074-92, and *Brief for the United States*, Vol. II, pp. 73-5, 78-82; *Commercial and Financial Chronicle*, March 20, 1897, p. 566; October 30, 1897, p. 824; February 26, 1898, p. 427; April 2, 1898, pp. 662-3; January 21, 1899, p. 128; March 4, 1899, p. 428; March 25, 1899, p. 568; July 8, 1899, pp. 77-8; September 23, 1899, p. 647; and *Investors' Supplement*, October 1897, p. 156.

[70] *Iron Age*, May 9, 1895, pp. 973-6; U.S. Industrial Commission, *Preliminary Report on Trusts and Industrial Combinations*, 56th Cong., 1st Sess., 1900, House Doc. 476, "Testimony," p. 982; U.S. Supreme Court, *United States v. United States Steel, et al.: Brief for the United States*, Vol. II, p. 202.

rose – in striking contrast to the experience of the wire-nail industry.[71] Not surprisingly, although rumors of consolidations occasionally surfaced, there was no serious move to combine the nation's rail
producers. Instead, rail makers busied themselves over the next few
years with putting their own internal affairs in order. Cambria and
Bethlehem raised new capital for improvements by reorganizing their
corporate structures in 1898 and 1899. Lackawanna built a modern
steel plant in Buffalo, New York, and, in 1902, similarly reorganized
its finances. In September 1898, Illinois Steel merged with a number
of allied concerns to form the Federal Steel Company, which was
completely self-sufficient with respect to iron ore, fuel, and transportation. Carnegie continued to lease additional iron-ore properties
and, in 1899, capped its already far-flung transportation network
with the purchase of the Lake Superior Iron Company and its fleet of
barges. At about the same time, a legal dispute with Henry Clay
Frick led to a reorganization of the Carnegie interests and their
merger with the Frick Coke Company, resulting in March 1900 in
the formation of the Carnegie Company of New Jersey.[72]

Neither the Carnegie Company nor Federal Steel was a horizontal
combination of the type found in the tin-plate and wire-nail industries. Nor, for that matter, was the United States Steel Corporation,
organized in 1901. Although it is true that the Steel Corporation
took in three major rail producers (Carnegie, Federal, and the National Steel Company, a new combination of lesser crude-steel manufacturers), other important firms, including Cambria, Bethlehem,
Lackawanna, Pennsylvania, and Colorado Fuel and Iron, remained
permanently outside. U.S. Steel was formed primarily to protect the
interests of promoters who had invested in Federal Steel, in National
Steel, and in the major finished-steel consolidations: American Steel
and Wire, American Tin Plate, American Sheet Steel, American Steel

---

[71] *Ibid.*, p. 271; *Iron Age*, December 1, 1898, p. 37.
[72] *Commercial and Financial Chronicle*, August 27, 1898, p. 427; September 24,
1898, p. 633; July 8, 1899, p. 77; U.S. Commissioner of Corporations, *Report on
the Steel Industry*, Pt. I, pp. 76-8, 85-9, 95-6; Warren, *The American Steel Industry*,
pp. 99-102; U.S. Industrial Commission, *Preliminary Report on Trusts and Industrial Combinations*, "Testimony," p. 982; *Moody's Manual*, I (1900), p. 29; Victor
S. Clark, *History of Manufacturing in the United States* (1929 ed.; New York: Peter
Smith, 1949), Vol. III, pp. 21, 43.

Hoop, American Bridge, and National Tube. The finished-steel combinations generally did not make their own billets and were dependent on Federal, National, Carnegie, and a few other crude-steel producers for their raw materials. Unhappy with this dependence, American Steel and Wire and National Tube began to integrate backward into steel production. Fearful of losing such major customers, Federal Steel threatened to integrate forward into wire production, and Carnegie announced plans to construct a major tube works. These challenges seemed to investors to portend another period of instability in the steel industry, an eventuality they hastened to forestall by merging both finished- and crude-steel producers into one giant consolidation. U.S. Steel was only incidentally a combination of rail producers.[73]

In both the wire-nail and rail branches of the steel industry, production was capital-intensive, and the burden of fixed investments gave firms an incentive to run full. If anything, the incentive was likely to be greater for rail than for nail producers, because the former had more opportunity to capture economies of speed.[74] As we saw in Chapter 2, rails were produced by a continuous process from blast furnace to Bessemer converter to rolling mill. Any slackening of the pace of manufacture, short of a full shutdown of blast furnaces, meant that steel had to be cooled and reheated, sharply raising unit costs. No comparable energy savings were possible in nail manufacture. Although rods were rolled by a continuous process, they were allowed to cool before being drawn into wire. Similarly, billets were cooled before they were rolled into rods (wire makers, in fact, rarely made their own steel).

Yet, despite the greater incentive to run full, rail manufacturers (in sharp contrast to their counterparts in the wire-nail industry) main-

---

[73] See Edward Sherwood Meade, "The Genesis of the United States Steel Corporation," *Quarterly Journal of Economics*, XV (August 1901), pp. 517-50; U.S. Supreme Court, *The United States v. United States Steel, et al.: Brief for the United States*, Vol. I, pp. 40-5, Vol. II, pp. 315-17; U.S. Commissioner of Corporations, *Report on the Steel Industry*, Part I, pp. 100-6; *Iron Age*, January 24, 1901, pp. 27-8, January 31, 1901, p. 29.

[74] Unfortunately it is not possible to compare the capital-output ratios for these two branches of the steel industry, because Census figures lumped them together.

tained a remarkable pricing discipline throughout most of the depression of the nineties. This was true even though some of the manufacturers suffered serious financial losses. Only when the Rail Association set prices and production quotas that were clearly out of line with demand did industry discipline break down. Even then it was easily reestablished.

The different behavior of the wire-nail and rail manufacturers during the depression of the nineties can be explained by the timing of investment in the two industries. Unlike the rail industry, the wire-nail industry experienced its period of most rapid growth on the eve of the Panic of 1893. As a result, prices were already in a state of flux when depression struck. Regular marketing patterns had not yet taken hold; firms knew little about their rivals' strength and efficiency. Hence, manufacturers had good reason to hope that they could increase their share of the market by cutting prices. When the demand for nails dropped after the Panic and firms found themselves losing money at their current production levels, they slashed prices to increase sales, triggering a price war that proved very difficult to end. Although the nail manufacturers formed a pool in 1895 that, for a time, earned handsome profits for its members, success was fleeting, and the venture left the industry in worse shape than before. Indeed, the additional investment that the pool's high prices stimulated meant that the collapse of the association brought a repetition of the 1893 experience. This time the manufacturers turned to consolidation for relief.

The rail industry, by contrast, had experienced its period of expansion much earlier and was essentially in equilibrium when the Panic of 1893 erupted.[75] Established marketing habits had developed, and the manufacturers all knew each other's capabilities. Rather than cut prices and risk certain retaliation, firms accepted the discipline of the pool. It was this reluctance to cut prices that made collusion possible, not the reverse. Moreover, firms were willing to accept the discipline

---

[75] The rail industry's earlier period of expansion was interrupted by a recession in the mid-1880s; the result, as our model would predict, was a price war. However, because firms in the rail industry were then very unevenly matched, prices soon fell below variable costs for some of the firms, resulting in shutdowns that relieved much of the pressure on prices. *Iron Age*, November 8, 1883, pp. 14-15; November 22, 1883, p. 15; December 27, 1883, p. 14.

of the pool only so long as its pricing and output decisions seemed reasonable – that is, so long as they approximated the firms' own profit-maximizing calculus. Here, again, collusion was successful only insofar as its goals approached the market solution. When pool prices proved badly out of line in 1896, industry discipline completely broke down.

The result was a price war, but one whose consequences were radically different from those of the simultaneous struggle in the wire-nail industry. Whereas wire-nail producers quickly found themselves worse off as a result of the competition, rail manufacturers generally improved their financial condition. Furthermore, the rail competition, unlike the price war in wire nails, was easily ended. Once rail makers established a reasonable price structure, they were able to reconstitute the pool. The agreement held, and as the economy recovered, prices rose. There was no real need, and no serious move, to consolidate the industry.

The contrasting experiences of the wire-nail and rail branches of the steel industry offer suggestive confirmation for the model developed in this chapter. High fixed costs alone were not sufficient to explain the incidence of price competition during the depression of the nineties. Indeed, as the example of the rail industry demonstrated, they could even work in the opposite direction: to inhibit price competition rather than incite it. In order to predict whether or not a capital-intensive industry was susceptible to price warfare, another variable had to be added to the analysis: the rate of new investment. The industries most likely to erupt into price wars were those in which fised costs were high and in which expansion had been rapid and recent.

4. Quantitative and qualitative evidence on the great merger movement

My explanation for the great merger movement can now be stated explicitly. Manufacturers formed consolidations to escape the severe price competition that developed during the depression of the nineties in certain types of industries: capital-intensive, mass-production industries in which firms were closely matched and in which expansion had been rapid on the eve of the Panic of 1893. In these industries, not only did firms have extensive capital investments, but also they were new firms and thus most likely to be pressured by high fixed charges. As a result, they were particularly susceptible to the temptation to cut prices and struggle for a greater share of the market when falling demand sent prices tumbling below total costs. Moreover, in such industries manufacturers were also most likely to risk cutting prices. Firms were new; marketing patterns and customer loyalties were not yet established; the ability of competitors to respond to price cuts was not yet known. The very newness of the firms, the fact that the industry was in a state of flux, made price warfare all the more likely.

The quantitative evidence

This rapid growth hypothesis satisfactorily accounts for the different behaviors of wire-nail producers and rail producers during the 1890s and for the formation of a consolidation in the former industry but not in the latter. The extent to which it also explains the pattern of consolidations in the manufacturing sector as a whole can be assessed using data collected by the U. S. Census Office and the list of consolidations Ralph L. Nelson compiled for his study of industrial mergers. In order to test the theory, I divided the industries defined in the Census into two groups: those in which no consolidations were formed and those that experienced a significant level of consolidation activity (I excluded from the analysis industries that experienced only

87

a small amount of activity, on the grounds that the consolidating firms constituted too small a portion of total industry capacity to show up in the statistics).[1] This grouping constituted the dependent variable in the analysis – a dichotomous variable attaining a value of 1 if there was significant consolidation activity in the industry and a value of 0 if no consolidation was formed.

Independent variables were drawn from the U.S. Census of Manufactures.[2] Because data on the actual proportion of fixed in total costs faced by firms in each industry were not available, I adopted two alternative estimates: (1) the ratio of the value of capital invested in the industry to the value of annual output; (2) an approximation of the proportion of fixed in total costs, the ratio [k(value of capital invested)]/[k(value of capital invested) + (cost of

[1] There were 180 industries with no consolidations and 52 with significant consolidation activity; 57 industries were excluded from the analysis. An industry was dropped if the ratio of the capitalization of its consolidations to the total amount of capital invested in the industry was less than 0.25 and the ratio of the number of firms consolidating to the total number of establishments in the industry was less than 0.10. Also excluded were industries dominated by major combinations formed before 1895 (the year Nelson's list begins) that did not experience much subsequent merger activity, industries for which data were missing, and industries with ten or fewer establishments. Occasionally I combined two or more industries into one when this was necessary to make use of data from both the Eleventh Census and Twelfth Census, or when consolidations cut across categories.

  Nelson listed consolidations with capitalizations of $1,000,000 or more and acquisitions worth at least $35,000. He limited his study to the manufacturing and mining sectors. From Nelson's list I selected all horizontal consolidations formed in the manufacturing sector between 1895 and 1904 that involved at least five firms and all acquisitions in which one firm purchased six or more of its competitors. By eliminating mergers that involved only a small number of concerns, I hoped to exclude two types of combinations from the analysis: acquisitions of one or two weak firms by a much stronger competitor, and consolidations involving firms among which price competition had already been significantly reduced by means of patents or other similar devices. What I am trying to explain is the horizontal combination of a large number of previously competing firms, for it is this that one must understand in order to assess the long-run implications of the great merger movement. Inclusion of other types of mergers might obscure statistical relationships, because there is no reason to assume that the motivation for their formation was the same. This, in fact, was the major problem with Jesse W. Markham's study, "Survey of the Evidence and Findings on Mergers," *Business Concentration and Price Policy*, Universities-National Bureau Committee for Economic Research Conference (Princeton University Press, 1955), pp. 141-82. Ralph L. Nelson, *Merger Movements in American Industry, 1895-1956* (Princeton University Press, 1959), pp. 8, 13-15, 22-3, 53; Nelson's unpublished list of consolidations.
[2] See U.S. Census Office, *Twelfth Census: Manufactures*, Pt. I (Washington, D.C.: U.S. Government Printing Office, 1902), pp. 3-53.

labor and materials to produce one year's output)], where k is some constant proportion (I tried 0.10, 0.05, and 0.01 – the first to approximate an interest rate plus depreciation, the others to allow for the possibility that firms seriously underestimated their fixed costs). The second measure is based on the assumption that fixed charges are directly proportional to the amount of capital invested in an enterprise. It simply substitutes an estimate of fixed costs for the true (but unavailable) figure in the formula for the proportion of fixed in total costs. The first measure eschews the formula in favor of a ratio that captures the way manufacturers at the time thought about the problem of fixed charges. Whenever businessmen talked about the burden of their investments, they used the capital turnover ratio as a measure – the amount of time it took to earn revenues equivalent to the value of their investment, in other words, the capital-output ratio.[3]

In order to measure an industry's rate of expansion, the second major independent variable, I calculated the percentage increase in the money value of its capital from 1889 to 1899, from 1879 to 1899, and from 1879 to 1889. Unfortunately, deflated estimates of capital and output were not available for individual industries. Therefore, I chose to measure growth in terms of the rate of increase of capital instead of output, because the former should have been less distorted by changes in relative prices.[4]

The first step in the quantitative analysis was to perform a differ-

[3] See, for example, the testimony of Hugh J. Chisholm before the U.S. Industrial Commission, *Report on Trusts and Industrial Combinations*, 57th Cong., 1st Sess, 1901, House Doc. 182, p. 435, and the testimony of David S. Cowles, Arthur C. Hastings, and George F. Steele in U.S. Congress, House, *Pulp and Paper Investigation Hearings*, 60th Cong., 2d Sess., 1909, Doc. 1502, Vol. II, pp. 893-4, Vol. V, pp. 3099, 3166. A problem with the capital-output ratio, however, is that its value was affected by changes in relative prices. The Twelfth Census was taken in the midst of the great merger movement, after some of the new combines had already raised their prices, which fact might diminish our ability to associate a high capital-output ratio and consolidation activity. On the other hand, some of the consolidations may have overvalued their investments. Here a further caution is necessary. The Census data on capital investment are not altogether reliable, for firms were permitted to report their investments however they carried them on their books. Some firms valued their investments at original cost, some at current market value, and so on. For a discussion of this and other problems relating to the Census's capital statistics, see *Twelfth Census: Manufactures*, Part I, pp. lxi-lxii, xcvii-xcix.

[4] But see the discussion of the Census's figures on invested capital and the timing of the Census in the previous note. If the timing of the Census did in fact bias the analysis, we should observe a relationship between the date a consolidation was

Table 4.1. *Difference-of-means test using proxies for high fixed costs and rapid growth*

Variable[a]	Difference of means[b]	Sign in predicted direction?	One-tailed *t*-test probability
CAPOUT	0.28 year	yes	0.001
FIXED1	0.025	yes	0.005
FIXED2	0.015	yes	0.006
FIXED3	0.004	yes	0.007
GROWTH1	28.66%	yes	0.001
GROWTH2	18.37%	yes	0.025
GROWTH3	4.76%	yes	0.312

[a]Definitions of variables:

CAPOUT   = value of capital invested/value of annual output

FIXED1   = (0.1 × value of capital invested)/(0.1 × value of capital invested + annual cost of materials + annual wage bill)

FIXED2   = same as FIXED1, except the constant is 0.05

FIXED3   = same as FIXED1, except the constant is 0.01

GROWTH1 = [(value of capital invested in 1899 − value of capital invested in 1889)/(capital invested in 1899 + capital invested in 1889) × 0.5] × 100

GROWTH2 = [(value of capital invested in 1899 − value of capital invested in 1879)/(capital invested in 1899 + capital invested in 1879) × 0.5] × 100

GROWTH3 = [(value of capital invested in 1889 − value of capital invested in 1879)/(capital invested in 1889 + capital invested in 1879) × 0.5] × 100

[b]Difference between the mean of the industries that experienced significant consolidation activity and that of those that experienced no consolidation activity.

ence-of-means test to see if industries that experienced consolidations differed from those that did not in the way the model would predict. The results, reported in Table 4.1, generally support the model. In-

organized and our ability to predict its occurrence statistically. For example, if consolidations inflated their capital-stock figures, the growth variables using the year 1899 should be more successful in identifying consolidations formed before the Census was taken than after. A discriminant analysis shows that this was not the case. Correct and incorrect predictions were divided proportionally among consolidations formed before 1899, in 1899, and after 1899. The same result was obtained when I tested the predictive ability of the capital-output ratio.

dustries with consolidations tended to have higher means than those without on all proxies for the proportion of fixed in total costs, and the differences in the means of the two groups were all statistically significant.[5] The same was true for two of the three proxies for growth: the percentage increase in the capital stock between 1889 and 1899 and that between 1879 and 1899. In the case of the third proxy for growth, the percentage increase in the capital stock between 1879 and 1889, the difference in the means of the two groups of industries was in the predicted direction but was not statistically significant. Rather than contradicting the model, however, this result actually helps confirm it. As the case of the rail producers demonstrated, industries that experienced their period of most rapid growth in the late 1870s and early 1880s had already begun to develop stable oligopolistic relations, both between producers and consumers and among producers, by the time depression struck in 1893. These industries were much less susceptible to outbreaks of price warfare than those in which expansion had been more recent.

I also conducted a series of difference-of-means tests to assess the validity of other elements of the explanation developed in Chapter 3. The results are recorded in Table 4.2. In addition to having a higher proportion of fixed in total costs and experiencing more rapid growth in the late 1880s and early 1890s, industries that underwent consolidations tended to have larger establishments, both in terms of the amount of capital invested and in terms of the number of workers employed.[6] These results fit the conclusion of Chapter 2 that serious price competition was more likely to be a problem in industries in which adoption of the strategy of mass production had stimulated the growth of large firms.

Large, mass-production firms tended to be vertically integrated,

---

[5] For an explanation of the difference of means test, see Hubert M. Blalock, Jr., *Social Statistics* (rev. 2d ed.; New York: McGraw-Hill, 1979), pp. 224-32.
[6] This last result, however, was biased in favor of the hypothesis by the fact that the Twelfth Census was taken in the midst of the consolidation movement. The Census Office defined an establishment as "one or more mills owned or controlled by one individual, firm, or corporation, located either in the same city or town, or in the same county, and engaged in the same industry." *Manufactures*, Pt. I, p. lxii. Whenever a consolidation combined two or more firms with plants in the same vicinity, it raised the average size of an establishment in its industry. Unfortunately, the Census did not record information on the basis of plants or firms.

Table 4.2. *Difference-of-means test: additional variables*

Variable[a]	Difference of means[b]	Sign in predicted direction?	One-tailed t-test probability
SIZE1	$148.87 thousand per establishment	yes	0.001
SIZE2	36.03 workers per establishment	yes	0.000
ENERGY1	1.46 horsepower per employee	yes	0.006
ENERGY2	155.53 horsepower per establishment	yes	0.001
VERT1	0.085	yes	0.040
VERT2	0.623	no	—
MARGIN	-0.048	yes	0.000
PROFIT	-0.147	yes	0.000

[a]Definition of variables:
SIZE1 = value of capital invested/no. of establishments
SIZE2 = no. of workers/no. of establishments
ENERGY1 = (total horsepower × no. of establishments)/(no. of workers × no. of establishments reporting horsepower)
ENERGY2 = total horsepower/no. of establishments reporting horsepower
VERT1 = annual cost of raw materials/annual cost of materials
VERT2 = annual value of output/(annual value of output − annual cost of materials)
MARGIN = [annual value of output − (annual wage bill + annual cost of materials + annual miscellaneous expenses)]/annual value of output
PROFIT = [annual value of output − (annual wage bill + annual cost of materials + annual miscellaneous expenses)]/value of capital invested
[b]Difference between the mean of the industries that experienced significant consolidation activity and that of those that experienced no consolidation activity.

and this, along with their capital- and energy-intensive production processes, should have encouraged manufacturers to struggle to run their plants full – to take advantage of what Alfred D. Chandler, Jr., has called economies of speed. Tables 4.1 and 4.2 show that industries that experienced consolidation tended to be more capital- and energy-intensive than those that did not. But the evidence concerning vertical integration is ambiguous. I included two proxies for vertical integration in the analysis. First and simplest was the ratio of raw to total (raw plus manufactured) material input.[7] My assumption was that the greater the proportion of raw (as opposed to manufactured) input an industry employed, the greater the degree of vertical integration. The second proxy, the ratio of value of product to value added, was proposed by M. A. Adelman. Adelman suggested that if an industry were perfectly integrated all sales would involve final goods; if the degree of vertical integration were incomplete, however, there would be sales of intermediate goods as well. Hence, the more an industry was subdivided into component processes, the greater the value of total sales (value of annual output) relative to value added.[8] The problem with both these measures, unfortunately, was that they were extremely sensitive to the way an industry was defined by the Census—to the "stretch" of products it included. The closer an industry to primary production, and the more restricted its range of products, the greater its apparent degree of integration.[9] Given the problems with these measures, their contradictory performances on the difference-of-means test is not surprising.

Table 4.2 shows that profit margins earned on each dollar of sales were lower in industries that experienced consolidation than in those that did not. Because earnings per unit of output (as opposed to earnings on capital) should have been lower in industries in which the mass-production strategy prevailed (where profits were earned on volume) than in those characterized by product differentiation (where profits were earned on high margins), this provides further confirmation for the model. Low earnings, however, were also a function of the intense competition that occurred during the 1890s in industries that experienced consolidations. Table 4.2 shows that profit rates on capital were on the average lower in consolidating indus-

---

[7] I am referring to the Census categories "principal materials purchased in a raw state" and "principal materials purchased in partially manufactured form." These categories exclude materials that do not become a part of the product itself, e.g., fuel and mill supplies.

[8] M. A. Adelman, "Concept and Statistical Measurement of Vertical Integration," *Business Concentration and Price Policy*, Universities-National Bureau Committee for Economic Research Conference (Princeton University Press, 1955), pp. 281-322.

[9] On this point see Irston R. Barnes's critique of Adelman's article, *ibid.*, pp. 322-30.

tries than in the rest of the manufacturing sector in 1899, a result that is also consistent with the model.

Logit analysis[10] permits a more direct test of the model by allowing us to combine the various independent variables into a single analysis and also to measure interaction effects. This latter advantage is especially important. According to the model, it was not simply high fixed costs and rapid growth acting independently that produced the price warfare leading to the great merger movement, but rather the combined effect of both factors operating together – in other words, an interaction effect. Table 4.3 reports the results of a logit estimation that tested the relationship between the dichotomous dependent variable (whether or not an industry experienced consolidation) and a series of independent variables (the proxies that performed best on the difference-of-means test and an interaction term).

As the t-ratios in Table 4.3 indicate, the two variables representing the mass-production strategy (SIZE1 and MARGIN) were significantly related to consolidation activity. Thus, consolidations tended to occur in industries with large firms – firms whose profits were earned on volume of output rather than on high margins.[11] The proxy for fixed costs (CAPOUT) was also significantly related to consolidation activity. The growth variable was not, however, and the interaction term just missed significance at the 0.05 level. This last result was a function of colinearity between the interaction term and the growth variable. Once the latter was excluded from the analysis

[10] Normal linear regression analysis is not appropriate in cases in which the dependent variable is dichotomous, because the distribution of the error terms violates the assumptions of the regression model. This can be dealt with by employing logit analysis, which involves estimation of the following equation:

$$\ln[\text{Prob}(y = 1)/\text{Prob}(y = 0)] = XB$$

where X is a vector of explanatory variables, B is a vector of coefficients to be estimated, $\text{Prob}(y = 1)$ is the probability that an industry will consolidate, $\text{Prob}(y = 0)$ is the probability that an industry will not consolidate, and $\ln[\text{Prob}(y = 1)/\text{Prob}(y = 0)]$ is the natural log of the odds ratio.

For a discussion of this technique, see Eric A. Hanushek and John E. Jackson, *Statistical Methods for Social Scientists* (New York: Academic, 1977), Chapter 7; and George G. Judge et al., *The Theory and Practice of Econometrics* (New York: Wiley, 1980). I used the logit program contained in Kenneth J. White's statistical package, *Shazam: An Econometrics Computer Program*, Version 3.2.

[11] The independent variables for vertical integration and energy intensity did not prove statistically significant, once the other variables were included in the regression.

Table 4.3. *Logit estimation 1ᵃ (maximum-likelihood method)*

Independent variables[b]	Estimated coefficient	Approximate t-ratio
CAPOUT	1.22	2.21
GROWTH1	-0.000702	-0.16
INTERACT	0.0109	1.92
MARGIN	-8.64	-3.03
SIZE1	0.00498	2.79

Constant = -1.20; likelihood ratio test = 62.30 with 5 df.
[a]The dependent variable is a dichotomous indicator of whether or not an industry experienced consolidation.
[b]The variable INTERACT is an interaction term defined as the product of the proxy for growth (GROWTH1) and a dichotomous variable that attained a value of 1 if an industry's capital-output ratio (CAPOUT) was above the mean for the manufacturing sector, and 0 if below. The main independent variables are defined in Tables 4.1 and 4.2.

(Table 4.4), the interaction term also proved to be significantly related to consolidation activity,[12] although when the interaction term was excluded, the growth variable still performed poorly.

The logit estimations show that rapid growth alone was not a good predictor of consolidation activity, but that rapid growth in combi-

---

[12] For the interaction term I used the product of the proxy for growth and a dichotomous variable that attained a value of 1 if an industry's capital-output ratio was above the mean for the manufacturing sector, and 0 if below. I also tried the following interaction terms with similar results: (1) the product of the proxy for high fixed costs and a dichotomous variable that attained a value of 1 if an industry's growth rate exceeded the mean, and 0 if not; (2) a dichotomous variable that attained a value of 1 if both an industry's growth rate and its capital-output ratio were above the mean, and 0 for all other cases; (3) the product of the proxies for growth and fixed costs; (4) the residual of this product, after the effects of the two main variables were taken out; (5) a number of discrete indices that assigned various weights to high fixed costs and rapid growth. With the exception of the residual (which was not significantly related to consolidation activity), all the interaction terms were highly significant when included in a bivariate logit equation (their t-ratios were higher, in fact, than those in similar equations for CAPOUT and GROWTH1 alone). Unfortunately, all but the residual had correlations with either CAPOUT or GROWTH1 (or both) ranging from 0.53 to 0.83. (The highest correlation between any two of the main variables was only 0.31.)

Table 4.4. *Logit estimation 2 (maximum-likelihood method)*

Independent variable	Estimated coefficient	Approximate t-ratio
CAPOUT	1.24	2.26
INTERACT	0.0104	2.39
MARGIN	-8.65	-3.03
SIZE1	0.00496	2.77

Constant = -1.22; likelihood ratio test = 62.27 with 4 df.

nation with high fixed costs was a good predictor (our model). In other words, the growth variable had no significant independent effect. The proxy for fixed costs, however, did have an independent effect on consolidation activity, suggesting that circumstances other than rapid growth may sometimes have combined with high fixed costs to produce the price competition that led to mergers. For example, some consolidations occurred in industries in which production was capital-intensive but growth rates were low or negative. These were dying industries in which declining demand left manufacturers saddled with unnecessary and outdated capacity. Thus, Virginia Iron, Coal and Coke and the Empire, Republic, and Susquehanna iron and steel companies were combinations of outmoded rolling mills and blast furnaces. Similarly, National Steel (one of the consolidations included in the U.S. Steel merger) took in billet plants whose lack of finishing capacity and raw material resources had rendered them obsolete.[13]

---

[13] *Iron Age*, January 28, 1897, p. 11; January 12, 1899, p. 30; January 19, 1899, p. 20; January 26, 1899, pp. 32-3; February 9, 1899, pp. 21-2; April 6, 1899, pp. 18-19; June 1, 1899, p. 13; *Moody's Manual of Industrial and Miscellaneous Securities*, I (1900), pp. 412-414, 429-33, 449-54; U.S. Commissioner of Corporations, *Report on the Steel Industry, Part I: Organization, Investment, Profits, and Position of the United States Steel Corporation* (Washington, D.C.: U.S. Government Printing Office, 1911), pp. 136-8; AISA, *Directory*, 1888 to 1898; U.S. Supreme Court, *United States of America, Appellant v. United States Steel Corporation, et al.: Brief for the United States* (Washington, D.C.: U.S. Government Printing Office, 1917), Vol. II, p. 202.

The qualitative evidence

Further statistical evidence will be presented later. To this point, however, we can conclude that the quantitative data support in a general way the hypothesis developed in Chapter 3. They show that consolidations tended to occur in industries in which the mass-production strategy prevailed, and especially in capital-intensive industries that had undergone rapid expansion on the eve of the depression of the nineties.

Qualitative evidence, drawn from the secondary literature on consolidations, further confirms the hypothesis. Surveying the literature on industries that underwent consolidation at the turn of the century, one is struck by the number that either were newly created or had been radically restructured not long before the Panic of 1893. Recall the transformations wrought by the wood-pulp revolution in the paper industry, by continuous rod rolling in the wire industry, and by the McKinley tariff in the tin-plate industry. The experiences of these three industries were repeated in many others. For instance, all the remaining finished-steel consolidations [American Sheet Steel (1900), American Steel Hoop (1899), National Tube (1899), and American Bridge (1900)] occurred in industries that had undergone tremendous expansion during the late 1880s and early 1890s as a result of the falling price of crude steel, on the one hand, and the development of new products or production processes, shifts in demand, or increases in tariff protection, on the other. In the case of the National Tube consolidation, for instance, the tariff seems to have been the significant factor. According to the respected steel-industry engineer Julian Kennedy, high tariffs stimulated an excessive influx of capital into the industry, causing the severe competition that led to the formation of the combine:

The tariff on tubes was $40 per ton, which was practically a Chinese wall, and the tube people were small in number for a while and their profits got very abnormal and very fancy, and a great many other people jumped into the tube business. It is a business that is not necessarily very highly organized, and men could get in very quickly and with a small amount of capital, if necessary; so a great many tube plants started.[14]

[14] U.S. Congress, House, *Hearings before the Committee on Investigation of United States Steel Corporation* (Washington, D.C.: U.S. Government Printing Office, 1912), Vol. VII, pp. 5075-6.

Additional examples abound. The American Bicycle consolidation (1899) was organized in an industry that had mushroomed out of nowhere as a result of the bicycle craze of the 1890s. The Glucose Sugar Refining Company (1897) was formed in an industry that had begun its spurt of rapid growth after 1884, when a government investigating committee published a report that glucose was a healthful sweetener, counteracting the prejudice that had hitherto restricted the product's sales. In the new plate-glass industry, a major expansion late in the 1880s led to severe competition and to the formation of the Pittsburgh Plate Glass consolidation in 1895. The two fertilizer combinations, American Agricultural Chemical (1899) and the Virginia-Carolina Chemical Company (1895), emerged in an industry that had recently been revolutionized by the discovery of new cheap sources of superphosphate rock and by the simultaneous spread of a process to manufacture (rather than mine) superphosphates. Likewise, the American Woolen Company (1899) consolidated the manufacturers of worsted textiles, whose branch of the wool industry derived from recent innovations in combing machines, changes in the tariff, and the growing popularity of lighter-weight men's clothing.[15]

Nor was the sequence of expansion, depression, and consolidation peculiar to the 1890s; a similar pattern characterized industries that underwent mergers in the earlier period as well. In the paper industry, the American Straw Board combination was formed in 1889 in a branch of the industry that had developed rapidly in the 1880s as a consequence of the same search for raw materials that uncovered the utility of wood pulp. Depressed business conditions during the mid-1880s provoked price warfare among the straw-board manufacturers, spurring them to form a consolidation. In the oatmeal industry, expansion was rapid once Ferdinand Schumacher broke down the American prejudice against eating oats, and the fierce competition that resulted led to the formation of the American Cereal Company in 1888. Corn-starch production grew swiftly after the Civil War,

[15] Arthur S. Dewing, *Corporate Promotions and Reorganizations* (Cambridge: Harvard University Press, 1914), pp. 75-8, 249-53; U.S. Industrial Commission, *Report on Trusts and Industrial Consolidations,* pp. lviii, 226-7, 689-90; Williams Haynes, *American Chemical Industry, Vol. I: Background and Beginnings* (New York: D. Van Nostrand, 1954), pp. 345-9; Arthur Harrison Cole, *The American Wool Manufacture* (Cambridge: Harvard University Press, 1926), Vol. II, pp. 152-7.

and especially in the early 1880s, as Western mills producing cheap grades of starch entered the market. Price warfare developed in the mid-1880s, and in 1890 manufacturers organized the National Starch Manufacturing Company, a consolidation. One final example: After crop failures in Europe stimulated a heavy export demand for whiskey, production underwent such an enormous expansion that U.S. distilleries had a total capacity four times the size of the domestic market. When a falloff in export demand exacerbated the effects of the economic turbulence of the mid-1880s, manufacturers formed the Whiskey Trust (1887), later incorporated as the Distilling and Cattle Feeding Company.[16]

Quantitative analysis showed that consolidations tended particularly to occur in rapidly growing industries in which production processes were capital-intensive, with the result that firms were likely to face high and pressing fixed charges. Unfortunately, the secondary literature does not add much information on this point, because cost structures have rarely been treated. One important exception is Alfred S. Eichner's study of consolidation in the sugar industry, an industry that also had recently been transformed by technological innovation. According to Eichner, fixed charges on the large investment required for sugar refining were high, and this, in combination with the competitive structure of the industry, created a situation in which most firms were by the mid-1880s producing at a loss. The result was the sugar trust in 1887, later reorganized as the American Sugar Refining Company.[17] Likewise, fixed costs were an important cause of competition leading to consolidation in the cast-iron pipe industry. A number of large, capital-intensive pipe producers entered the Southern market in the 1880s. Because their fixed charges were a high proportion of total costs, the penalty for losing out on munici-

[16] *Paper Trade Journal*, February 9, 1905, pp. 115, 120; John A. Guthrie, *The Economics of Pulp and Paper* (Pullman: State College of Washington Press, 1950), p. 32; Arthur F. Marquette, *Brands, Trademarks and Good Will: The Story of the Quaker Oats Company* (New York: McGraw-Hill, 1967), pp. 20-44; Dewing, *Corporate Promotions and Reorganizations*, pp. 51-5; J. W. Jenks, "The Development of the Whisky Trust," *Trusts, Pools and Corporations*, ed. William Z. Ripley (rev. ed.; New York: Ginn & Co., 1916), pp. 25-35.

[17] Alfred S. Eichner, *The Emergence of Oligopoly: Sugar Refining as a Case Study* (Baltimore: Johns Hopkins Press, 1969), pp. 50, 93-101. See also the discussion of the salt industry in Chapter 3.

pal contracts for pipe was steep. Vigorous competition for contracts resulted, stimulating formation of the Addyston Pipe pool in 1894 and the U.S. Cast Iron Pipe and Foundry consolidation in 1899.[18]

The whiskey industry provides an even more striking example of the way in which high fixed costs could increase competitive pressures. Distilleries were capital-intensive, and in order to make use of refuse grain, they usually supported herds of cattle. Shutdowns or curtailments were consequently very expensive; the distilleries either had to sacrifice their livestock or purchase feed grains on the market. These added costs exacerbated the pressure to run full when prices fell below costs, fueling the competition that led to the organization of the trust.[19]

Although the secondary literature is vague on the issue of cost structure, there is abundant evidence that industries that formed consolidations tended to have suffered severe price competition during the depression of the nineties – competition so severe and so persistent that repeated attempts at collusion failed to stop it. In industries as diverse as copper, whiskey, leather, oatmeal, cordage, cotton yarn, rubber, sugar, smelting, and window glass, manufacturers tried to organize associations to restrict production and support prices. When these weak gentlemen's agreements failed, many of them tried more tightly structured organizations, such as selling agencies (which took control of sales away from the manufacturers) or pools (which apportioned sales among firms and assessed fines for exceeding allocations). But the contracts that underpinned these organizations were not enforceable in court, and the incentive to cheat was, we have already seen, high. As a result, even the tightest agreements rarely succeeded. Often, as in the case of the Wire-Nail Association, they

---

[18] The Addyston Pipe pool is the main exception to my argument that pools in expanding mass-production industries were unlikely to be successful. The pool was organized in 1894 and lasted until the courts ruled it illegal in 1899. Almarin Phillips, *Market Structure, Organization and Performance: An Essay on Price Fixing and Combinations in Restraint of Trade* (Cambridge: Harvard University Press, 1962), pp. 99-103. See also George Bittlingmayer, "Decreasing Average Cost and Competition: A New Look at the Addyston Pipe Case," *Journal of Law and Economics*, XXV (October 1982), pp. 201-79; and "Price Fixing and the Addyston Pipe Case," *Research in Law and Economics*, V (1983), pp. 57-128.

[19] Jenks, "The Development of the Whisky Trust," pp. 22-45; U.S. Industrial Commission, *Preliminary Report on Trusts and Industrial Combinations*, 56th Cong., 1st Sess., 1900, House Doc. 476, "Digest of Evidence," pp. 75-84.

left the industry in a worse state than before.[20] Also unsuccessful were several more devious attempts to restrict production. Sugar refiners, for instance, sought to convince insurance companies not to write policies for plants that operated at night. Window-glass manufacturers negotiated contracts with the glass-workers union, restricting the hours of production and the amount of glass that each worker was allowed to produce.[21]

Collusive devices generally failed to bring the price warfare to a halt. Nor was survival of the fittest a viable option, for competitors were much too evenly matched for price cutting to force shutdowns or even curtailments in production. Unfortunately, most of the evidence for the closeness of this competition is necessarily indirect. For example, many accounts of industries that experienced consolidation fail to mention leading entrepreneurs or firms – the list includes woolens, window glass, plate glass, chemicals, fertilizer, whiskey, leather, salt, malt, cotton yarn, steam pumps, rubber goods, linseed oil, and cast-iron pipe.[22] Moreover, even where entrepreneurs do figure in the

[20] One exception was the Gunpowder Trade Association. Here, price-fixing agreements were supported by purchases of stock in competing firms. Williams Haynes, *American Chemical Industry, Vol. VI: The Chemical Companies* (New York: D. Van Nostrand, 1949), p. 128; Orris C. Herfindahl, *Copper Costs and Prices: 1870-1957* (Baltimore: Johns Hopkins Press, 1959), pp. 73-9; Jenks, "Development of the Whisky Trust," pp. 25-7; U.S. Industrial Commission, *Preliminary Report on Trusts and Industrial Combinations,* "Digest of Evidence," p. 76, and *Report on Trusts and Industrial Combinations,* pp. xlvi-xlviii; Dewing, *Corporate Promotions and Reorganizations,* pp. 17-18, 114-18, 306-10; Marquette, *Brands, Trademarks and Good Will,* pp. 39-44; Glen D. Babcock, *History of the United States Rubber Company: A Case Study in Corporate Management* (Bloomington: Indiana University Graduate School of Business, 1966), pp. 59-66; James E. Fell, Jr., *Ores to Metals: The Rocky Mountain Smelting Industry* (Lincoln: University of Nebraska Press, 1979), pp. 201-22; Pearce Davis, *The Development of the American Glass Industry* (New York: Russell & Russell-Atheneum, 1970), pp. 127-30, 175-80; Thomas K. McCraw, "Rethinking the Trust Question," *Regulation in Perspective: Historical Essays* (Cambridge: Harvard University Press, 1981), p. 6.
[21] Eichner, *The Emergence of Oligopoly,* pp. 59-62; Davis, *The Development of the American Glass Industry,* pp. 127-30.
[22] Cole, *The American Wool Manufacture,* Vol. II; Davis, *The Development of the American Glass Industry;* Haynes, *American Chemical Industry,* Vol. I; Theodore J. Kreps, *The Economics of the Sulfuric Acid Industry* (Stanford University Press, 1938); Jenks, "The Development of the Whisky Trust;" Dewing, *Corporate Promotions and Reorganizations,* pp. 16-48, 203-26, 269-333; M. J. Fields, "The International Steam Pump Company: An Episode in American Corporate History," *Journal of Economic and Business History,* IV (1931-2), pp. 637-64; Babcock, *History of the United States Rubber Company;* Whitney Eastman, *The History of the Linseed Oil Industry in the United States* (Minneapolis: T. S. Denison & Co., 1968); Phillips, *Market Structure, Organization and Performance,* pp. 99-118.

accounts, they were not always able to maintain a competitive advantage. For instance, despite the fact that Colonel A. A. Pope was the father of the American bicycle industry, the Pope Manufacturing Company's profits were seriously eroded by the influx of new competitors in the mid-1890s. As Pope himself later testified,

The business had been very profitable up to 1895, and in that and the following years a great number of new people embarked in the business. Many of them had no adequate capital . . . They were pressed for money, and they or their competitors were compelled to throw their machines on the market and get cash out of them, even if they got no profit. It is true that the strongest concerns still made some money every year, but with the constant and increasing cutting of prices a condition was approaching in which it was feared that even the strongest could make no profit. There was no cohesion in the trade as there is in some older trades. Competition was of the cut-throat order.[23]

In the case of sugar manufacture, the Havemeyer family owned the largest, most efficient refinery in the industry. Yet the firm's vulnerability to price cutting by other large refiners convinced the family to help organize a consolidation. Similarly, when Ferdinand Schumacher, the oatmeal industry's pioneer and most productive producer, found his profits whittled down by competition, he agreed to join the American Cereal Company, later renamed Quaker Oats.[24]

Direct evidence about the closeness of the competition is provided by John Moody's 1904 study, *The Truth About Trusts*. To supplement his list of consolidations, Moody compiled information on the competitive advantages (patents, trademarks, raw-material supplies, tariffs, etc.) that might affect the financial performance of the combines. If we eliminate those advantages that clearly came only with consolidation (e.g., monopolization of vital raw-material resources), and those that (like tariffs) would have benefited all the firms in an industry before consolidation, we find that only fifteen out of ninety-seven consolidations occurred in industries in which one firm might have had a definite edge over the rest.[25]

[23] U.S. Industrial Commission, *Report on Trusts and Industrial Combinations*, pp. 689-90. See also Dewing, *Corporate Promotions and Reorganizations*, pp. 249-56.
[24] Eichner, *The Emergence of Oligopoly*, pp. 70-84; Marquette, *Brands, Trademarks, and Good Will*, pp. 20-44.
[25] These fifteen combines had "elements of monopoly" characterized by Moody as "important," "large," "strong," or "pronounced." John Moody, *The Truth About Trusts: A Description and Analysis of the American Trust Movement* (New York: Moody Publishing, 1904).

Further evidence of the competitive balance within these industries comes from the fact that price competition rarely divided firms into winners and losers. Rather, as in the case of tin-plate and wire-nail producers, the competition inflicted damage on them all. The majority of the manufacturers interviewed by the Industrial Commission at the turn of the century claimed that "ruinous" competition had led them to form consolidations. The following testimony by John Pitcairn, president of the Pittsburgh Plate Glass Company, was typical:

> For several years prior to the consolidation which took place in 1895, there was absolutely no profit in the plate-glass business. The new glass factories which had been built a few years prior to the consolidation had made no profits whatsoever and had paid no dividends.[26]

At the same time, despite widespread complaints about competition "so vigorous that profits of nearly all competing establishments were destroyed,"[27] witnesses also had to admit that there had been relatively few failures in their industries. Thus, in the case of the Pittsburgh Plate Glass combination, Pitcairn could only assert that massive failures "probably" would have resulted if the competition had been allowed to continue.[28]

This combination of severe competition with few failures puzzled investigators. But it makes sense in terms of our model. High fixed costs meant that there was a wide range of prices within which firms would produce at a loss. At the same time, if firms were evenly matched, it was unlikely that prices could be cut to levels that would force competitors out of production. Instead, prices might stick at a level too low to earn firms an adequate return but too high to precipitate shutdowns.

This situation may not have shown up in the firms' account books as losses, for the simple reason that firms did not typically take all their fixed charges into consideration, either because they undercapitalized their assets or because they failed to make allowances for depreciation. This point helps us sort out some contradictory information on the severity of the competition. For example, in the case of

---

[26] U.S. Industrial Commission, *Report on Trusts and Industrial Combinations*, p. 233.
[27] U.S. Industrial Commission, *Preliminary Report on Trusts and Industrial Combinations*, "Review of Evidence," p. 9.
[28] U.S. Industrial Commission, *Report on Trusts and Industrial Combinations*, p. 241.

the tin-plate industry, manufacturers testified that consolidation had been necessary to halt price cutting that had gone so far that perhaps fifteen firms were on the brink of ruin. According to Daniel G. Reid, first president of the American Tin Plate combination,

the competition between the old companies had become so strong, the business was fast drifting into a condition where there was little, if any, profit. There were a number of mills losing money and very few of them making any . . . I am quite sure that if the consolidation had not gone through there would have been 15 companies closed and seven or eight thousand men out of work.[29]

Yet, in statements to the financial community, whose investments the firm wanted, Reid asserted that in 1898 American's constituents had earnings amounting to $2 million, equivalent to a rate of return of 11 percent on the consolidation's preferred stock (approximately the value of its assets), and that even when prices were lowest, a profit of $0.35 per box could be earned.[30] If most of the constituents had registered positive profits, however, they did so on the basis of accounting procedures that did not make any allowance for depreciation. This is an important qualification. W. H. Griffiths claimed to have earned 20 percent profits at his Washington Steel and Tin Plate Mills in late 1898, but other evidence suggests that these earnings came in large measure at the expense of his capital. George Greer, district manager of the American Tin Plate Company, wrote the Industrial Commission that the Washington works was "in practically the worst condition of all the mills in the Pittsburgh district." Shortly after consolidation, in fact, the entire plant was scrapped.[31] The Washington mill, moreover, was not an isolated case. The American Tin Plate Company wrote off $1.5 million in depreciation in 1899 and began to dismantle plants. It closed at least nine works and reduced production at several more before it was absorbed into the United States Steel Corporation in 1901, at which point nine more plants were shut down. According to U.S. Steel's officers, most

[29] U.S. Industrial Commission, *Preliminary Report on Trusts and Industrial Combinations*, "Testimony," pp. 866-7.
[30] *Iron Age*, February 16, 1899, p. 17; *Commercial and Financial Chronicle*, December 24, 1898, p. 1307.
[31] U.S. Industrial Commission, *Preliminary Report on Trusts and Industrial Combinations*, "Testimony," pp. 900, 923.

of these plants were "badly run down and in poor physical condition."[32]

The struggle to run full during the depression had accelerated the normal depreciation of tin-plate machinery. The practice of the time was to finance replacements (and improvements) out of revenues, or, where these were not sufficient, by borrowing. But with resources strained to the limit by price competition, funds for replacement of worn-out equipment were scarce. By 1898, as a result, manufacturers were "getting on the ragged edge" and becoming desperate about the future. As John Stevenson, Jr., of the New Castle, Pennsylvania, tin-plate interests later testified,

Q. Was there any profit in [the industry] at that reduced price? . . .
A. Yes, sir; there was a profit to the mills.
Q. But to the mills generally was there a profit?
A. Well, they were getting on the ragged edge, a good many of them. They were very much distressed about it.
Q. Was the business in a healthy condition at this time?
A. I would call it getting demoralized . . . They had bankruptcy staring them in the face, you know, or thought they did . . .
Q. I only want your judgment as an experienced man as to whether this condition was widespread or confined to only one plant.
A. No; it was widespread. We were feeling the pinch ourselves.[33]

In the case of the newsprint industry, a similar inconsistency in the data can be just as easily resolved. On the one hand, the American Pulp and Paper Association, the manufacturers' trade organization, asserted that the International Paper Company had been born of a fear of bankruptcy: "The impending ruin of at least four of the big companies, and the prospect of ruin by the other mill owners, forced the consolidation."[34] On the other hand, according to the Newspaper

[32] D. E. Dunbar, *The Tin-Plate Industry: A Comparative Study of Its Growth in the United States and in Wales* (Boston: Houghton Mifflin, 1915), pp. 91-2; American Iron and Steel Association (hereafter AISA), *Directory to the Iron and Steel Works of the United States*, 1898 and 1901; U.S. Congress, House, *Investigation of United States Steel Corporation*, Vol. VI, p. 4363.

[33] U.S. Supreme Court, *The United States of America, Appellant v. United States Steel Corporation, et al.: Transcript of Record* (Washington, D.C.: U.S. Government Printing Office, 1917), Vol. III, pp. 1062-3.

[34] *Paper Trade Journal*, Convention No., February 6, 1908, pp. 41, 45.

Publishers' Association, at least one of the large firms (Rumford Falls) had earned generous profits before the combination.[35]

The publishers went on to remark, however, that the Rumford Falls mill "was in such poor shape when acquired by the trust that an enormous outlay was necessary to bring it into condition."[36] In other words, to the extent that the firm recorded profits, they had been earned at the expense of its capital. Quite possibly the same was true of Rumford's competitors as well. Even under normal circumstances pulp and papermaking equipment depreciated rapidly owing to its constant exposure to water and corrosive chemicals;[37] the pressures to run full that manufacturers experienced during the depression of the nineties could only have accelerated the process of deterioration. A correspondent for the *Paper Trade Journal* made this point in 1898: "When it becomes necessary, in order to make any show whatever on the profit side of the account to run machines for all they are worth, one or both of two evils will occur: Any accident that may befall the machine while running . . . involves a big loss. The other is, that this kind of fast driving will involve a greater amount of wear and tear."[38] That the large newsprint manufacturers were not able to maintain their mills and keep them up to date during the depression is indicated by the massive sums of money that the International Paper Company poured into repairs and improvements immediately following its formation. The consolidation was unable to finance all the necessary repairs and improvements out of its organizational capital or current earnings, and by 1904 it had accumulated a floating debt of $4 million for this purpose.[39]

Some of the smaller newsprint firms that went into the consolidation had definitely been losing money. According to John Norris, business manager of the *New York Times*, the Herkimer Paper Com-

---

[35] U.S. Industrial Commission, *Report on Trusts and Industrial Combinations*, pp. 414-17, 420.

[36] *Ibid.*

[37] Louis Tillotson Stevenson, *The Background and Economics of American Papermaking* (New York: Harper & Brothers, 1940), p. 87.

[38] *Paper Trade Journal*, April 16, 1898, p. 325.

[39] International was capitalized with $22,400,000 in preferred stock (probably about the value of its assets), $17,400,000 in common, and $10,000,000 in bonds. U.S. Congress, House, *Pulp and Paper Investigation Hearings*, Vol. I, pp. 193-4, Vol. II, p. 1027.

pany had been running in the red for years. The Jay Paper Company failed on the eve of the consolidation, and the Piercefield Paper and Mining Company, a new entrant, had failed in early 1897. Because it was new, Piercefield had been forced to cut prices in order to establish its product on the market. But the *Paper Trade Journal* offered a more general explanation for the firm's distress:

> The price of newspaper is to-day too low, and there are offerings made in the market which are not warranted by any well founded figures as to the cost of product. There is no immediate relief in sight, and it is a serious question as to how much longer the trade can stand the pressure.[40]

Additional factors and the role of promoters

In newsprint, tin plate, wire nails, bicycles, window glass, copper, and many of the other industries that formed consolidations at the turn of the century, the price wars that erupted during the depression of the nineties were severe and long-lasting. Manufacturers tried a variety of collusive devices to stop the competition, but to no avail. Nor did market forces offer much relief: Firms were too closely matched for price cuts to force capacity out of production, and there was a wide range of prices within which firms would continue to produce at a loss. Not even the return of prosperity, beginning in 1897, put a halt to the competition, and manufacturers organized consolidations to gain relief.

This conclusion that consolidations were formed to escape competition is a departure from much of the current scholarly thought on the subject. Since World War II, economic historians have tended to downplay the importance of the market-control motive in the great merger movement. Some have emphasized instead the drive for efficiency—to capture economies of scale, integrate vertically, better coordinate the flow of production, and obtain capital more cheaply. Others have singled out institutional factors: changes in the way the Supreme Court interpreted the Sherman Act, or the maturation of the

---

[40] *Paper Trade Journal,* January 30, 1897, p. 88; February 13, 1897, p. 124; *Paper World,* January 1898, p. 6; U.S. Industrial Commission, *Report on Trusts and Industrial Combinations,* p. 420.

nation's capital markets and the appearance of promoters ready and able to finance mergers.[41]

Whatever the merits of these alternative explanations, the evidence for discounting the market-control motive has been flimsy at best. In "The Beginnings of 'Big Business' in American Industry," for example, Chandler's conclusion was that combinations in extractive industries were not typically formed to control prices; he based this conclusion on little more evidence, in some cases, than the combines' subsequent moves to integrate vertically and improve efficiency.[42] This reasoning backward from outcome to cause is also characteristic of Jesse W. Markham's "Survey of the Evidence and Findings on Mergers." Markham calculated the percentage of mergers that achieved significant market power, found that it was small (about 20 percent), and concluded from this figure that most mergers were not formed to escape competition or obtain monopoly power. Not only was Markham's reasoning backward, but his figure was far too low. Markham made a number of questionable assumptions that reduced the numerator of his equation. He also padded the denominator by including very small mergers.[43] My own calculation, restricted to mergers of at least five previously independent firms (the consolidation movement proper), suggests that the market control motive cannot be so facilely dismissed. At the very minimum, more than half of the consolidations formed between 1895 and 1904 absorbed over 40 percent of their industries and nearly a third absorbed in excess of 70 percent (see Chapter 1).

That the market-control motive cannot be ruled out on the basis of

---

[41] In the first group find Alfred D. Chandler, Jr., "The Beginnings of 'Big Business' in American Industry," *Business History Review*, XXXIII (Spring 1959), pp. 1-31, and Lance Davis, "The Capital Markets and Industrial Concentration: The U.S. and the U.K., A Comparative Study," *Economic History Review*, Second Series, XIX (August 1966), pp. 255-72. In the second, Chandler, *The Visible Hand: The Managerial Revolution in American Business* (Cambridge: Harvard University Press, 1977), pp. 331-4, George J. Stigler, "Monopoly and Oligopoly by Merger," *The Organization of Industry* (Homewood, Ill.: Richard D. Irwin, 1968), pp. 95-107, and Markham, "Survey of the Evidence and Findings on Mergers."

[42] See, for example, pp. 21-2. Chandler abandoned this line of argument by the time he came to write *The Visible Hand*.

[43] See George W. Stocking's critique of Markham's estimates in the same volume, pp. 196-9. Most other scholars who have downplayed the market-control motive have not bothered to refute it.

market-share evidence was also Ralph L. Nelson's conclusion in *Merger Movements in American Industry*. Nelson then went on to reject a number of alternative explanations that have been proposed for the consolidation movement – including the theory that mergers were formed to increase efficiency through vertical integration or economies of scale and the hypothesis that they were stimulated by changing Supreme Court interpretations of the Sherman Act. According to the latter view, the Supreme Court had signaled in the case of *United States v. E. C. Knight Company* and in the *Addyston Pipe & Steel* decision that pools and similar price-fixing associations were in violation of the Sherman Act, but that consolidations were not, setting off a scramble to adopt the sanctioned form of organization. Although there is undoubtedly some validity to this argument, Nelson pointed out that the timing of the Court's decisions was "not clear enough to permit a simple cause-and-effect explanation." The *Addyston* decision was not handed down until 1899, after many consolidations had already been formed. Nelson's doubts about the efficacy of this explanation are borne out, moreover, by the fact that consolidations continued to participate in pools, selling agencies, and gentlemen's agreements after their formation. U.S. Steel, for instance, retained its memberships in the plate- and structural-steel pools at least until 1904.[44]

As for the argument that mergers were organized primarily to improve efficiency, Nelson expressed two basic objections. First, the overwhelming majority of mergers were horizontal rather than vertical, suggesting that market control was a more important motive than vertical integration. Second, consolidations were organized in many different industries with widely varying types of production processes. It is difficult to believe, Nelson argued, that significant economies of scale could have characterized them all.[45] Further support for Nelson's objections is provided by the statements of businessmen at the time. In testimony before the Industrial Commission, manufacturers repeatedly explained that they had joined consolidations because "ruinous" competition during the depression of

---

[44] Nelson, *Merger Movements in American Industry*, pp. 71-89, 134-6; U.S. Congress, House, *Investigation of United States Steel Corporation*, Vol. III, pp. 1715-19.

[45] Nelson, *Merger Movements in American Industry*, pp. 100-4.

the nineties had left them but one choice: bankruptcy or combination. When prompted by questioners, they usually detailed the improvements in efficiency that consolidations made possible. But, as the following testimony by the president of the International Silver Company makes clear, considerable prompting was sometimes necessary:

Q. Will you explain to us what special sources of saving and special advantages there were in bringing the different plants engaged in the same line of work together into one organization?

A. One advantage must be that the administration of 12 or 15 companies would be brought under one head. If there were factories that had more room than the output demanded, you could bring them under one and consolidate them better.

Q. You would say that those were the two chief sources of savings?

A. Yes; I should say that those were the two chief sources of saving. The closing of stores and agencies in the different cities that a good many of the plants had would also be a saving.

Q. In the first place a saving would come from better organization for administration. In that way, I suppose, you save the salaries of a good many high-priced officers?

A. Yes; you have all your buying under one head; a thousand and one ways in which money could be saved.

Q. By putting all under one head you can save, of course, the salaries of several different buyers. Can you also buy to better advantage by buying in large quantities?

A. Undoubtedly, yes.

Q. Can you give any estimate as to the percentage of saving that probably would come from buying in that way?

A. No.[46]

None of the manufacturers mentioned access to capital markets as a reason for consolidation.

Nelson dismissed most of the explanations recent scholars have offered for the great merger movement, with one big exception: changes in the stock market. Although he was not able to reject the market-control thesis, he nonetheless attributed greater explanatory

[46] U.S. Industrial Commission, *Preliminary Report on Trusts and Industrial Combinations*, "Testimony," p. 1050. The questioner, J. W. Jenks, was an academic who believed combination to be inevitable and who was interested in collecting information on the efficiencies to which it might give rise. By the second round of testimony, the manufacturers were better prepared for Jenks's questions. Nonetheless, most continued to assert that the primary reason for consolidation was excessive competition. See also *Report on Trusts and Industrial Consolidations*.

importance to developments in the capital markets. The recent emergence of a market for industrial securities had made consolidations possible by providing a means of financing the purchase of merging firms' assets. Moreover, rising stock prices made the promotion of (and participation in) consolidations an attractive proposition. As confirmation for his hypothesis, Nelson found that merger activity correlated positively with indices of stock-market prices and of trading activity.[47]

Undoubtedly there is some validity to this argument. But it cannot provide a complete explanation for the consolidation movement, as Nelson himself admitted.[48] Why, given the general development of a market for industrial securities, did certain industries (but not others) experience consolidation? Nelson was unable to answer this question. Yet, interestingly enough, his own data support the rapid-growth explanation developed in this study. Refuting the theory that consolidations were caused by a slowing in the nation's rate of economic growth,[49] Nelson discovered that in industries that experienced a large number of mergers, the pattern was typically acceleration rather than retardation of growth!

At the same time, however, one must recognize that the rapid-growth model cannot provide a complete explanation for the merger movement either. Granting that manufacturers sought to escape competition by forming consolidations, their ability to do so depended on a legal environment that made that solution permissible and on the existence of capital markets capable of floating the necessary stock and bond issues. Moreover, even granting further the general correctness of the rapid-growth explanation, it would be silly to conclude that all consolidations fit the model. We have already seen that some

[47] Nelson, *Merger Movements in American Industry*, pp. 89-100, 106-26.
[48] *Ibid.*, pp. 125-6.
[49] This theory was originally proposed by Myron W. Watkins. See *Industrial Combinations and Public Policy: A Study of Combination, Competition and the Common Welfare* (Boston: Houghton Mifflin, 1927), pp. 3-27. Nelson also convincingly refuted Joe S. Bain's hypothesis that the mergers were stimulated by the transportation revolution, which brought firms for the first time into competition within a national market. See "Industrial Concentration and Anti-trust Policy," *The Growth of the American Economy*, ed. Harold F. Williamson (2nd ed.; Englewood Cliffs, N.J.: Prentice-Hall, 1951), pp. 616-30. Nelson presented no evidence one way or another on the fixed-cost hypothesis. See *Merger Movements in American Industry*, pp. 71-89.

mergers resulted from conditions of economic distress that had causes other than the combination of high fixed charges and rapid growth. Undoubtedly, others, formed for the purpose of promoters' profits or in anticipation of monopoly gains, were not rooted in economic distress at all. Moreover, once the merger movement got under way, it is likely that the very idea of consolidation took on a contagious aspect, resulting in combinations that otherwise might never have been formed.

We can obtain some idea of the numbers and types of consolidations which do not fit the model by returning to the quantitative evidence and employing a technique called discriminant analysis. Performed by computer, discriminant analysis selects the linear combination of independent variables that best distinguishes between groups of cases, in this instance between the group of industries that experienced consolidation and the group of industries that did not. Using the variables that performed best on the logit estimations (I left out the capital-output ratio to exclude the independent effect of high fixed costs), the resulting "discriminant function" (written in standardized form) is $D = 0.59(\text{INTERACT}) - 0.39(\text{MARGIN}) + 0.64(\text{SIZE1})$. The larger absolute magnitudes of the coefficients of the variable SIZE1 and the interaction term point to their greater explanatory power in distinguishing between the two groups of industries.[50]

This discriminant function can be used to divide all the industries into two categories: those that the equation indicates were likely to undergo consolidation and those that it indicates were not. The basic procedure is to determine the value of the discriminant function for each industry in the group that experienced consolidation activity, calculate the group's average score and standard deviation, do the same for industries that did not experience consolidation, and then use this information to assign each industry a probability of belonging to one group or the other. When we do this, we find that 37 (71%) of the 52 industries that actually experienced mergers were

[50] For an explanation of the technique see Norman H. Nie et al., *SPSS: Statistical Package for the Social Sciences* (2nd ed.; New York: McGraw-Hill, 1975), pp. 434-67; C. Hadlai Hull and Norman H. Nie, *SPSS Update: New Procedures and Facilities for Releases 7 and 8* (New York: McGraw Hill, 1979), pp. 184-99.

Table 4.5. *Results of discriminant analysis*

	Predicted group	
Actual group[a]	Consolidation-prone	Not consolidation-prone
Significant consoli- dation activity	37 (71%)	15 (29%)
No consolidation activity	31 (17%)	149 (83%)

Total number of industries classified correctly: 186 (80%)
[a]See footnote 1, p. 88 for the definitions of the categories.

correctly classified as consolidation-prone, whereas 149 (83%) of the 180 industries in which no consolidations occurred were properly identified as unlikely to experience consolidation. Overall, 80 percent of the 232 industries studied were classified correctly (Table 4.5). In other words, the great majority of the industries fit the model.[51]

Here it is necessary to caution that too much significance should not be attached to the 80 percent figure. If an uninformed observer were to guess that none of the industries experienced consolidations, he would be wrong only 22 percent of the time, because 180 of the 232 industries experienced no consolidations. He would not, how-ever, identify any of the consolidating industries correctly, whereas the discriminant analysis correctly identified 37 (or 71%) of the in-dustries that experienced consolidation. A somewhat more knowl-edgeable observer might randomly assign 52 industries to the con-solidating category, but on the average he would select only 12 of them correctly [52 × (52/232)]. The discriminant-analysis program again performed much better, selecting 37 of the industries correctly.

If we use the discriminant-analysis program and the variable for

[51] Simply dividing the cases into two groups on the basis of the absolute magnitudes of the logit predictions did not do a very good job of distinguishing consolidating and non-consolidating industries. Eighty-one percent of all the industries were pre-dicted correctly this way, but only 33 percent of those with consolidations. Inspec-tion of the logit results revealed, however, that the predicted values for the two groups of industries tended to cluster around different points, suggesting that a probabilistic calculation, such as that performed by the discriminant analysis pro-gram, was more appropriate for the task of prediction.

the profit rate on capital to test the relationship between economic distress and consolidation activity, we find that 41 of the 52 industries with consolidations were correctly classified on the basis of low profit rates alone, and only 11 were classified incorrectly.[52] In other words, relatively few consolidations seem to have been formed when manufacturers were not motivated by the desire to escape serious competition, whether caused by a combination of rapid expansion and high fixed costs or by some other situation.

It is unlikely, therefore, that many consolidations were formed solely for the purpose of promoters' profits; real economic hardship underlay most manufacturers' willingness to sell out. This did not mean, however, that the role of promoters in the great merger movement was insignificant. A quick survey of the reports of the Industrial Commission suggests that promoters were most important in mergers that brought together relatively large numbers of firms, that is, when organizational problems were likely to have been greatest. The Industrial Commission collected information on methods of organization for twenty-three of the consolidations from our list. Of the ten that combined ten or more firms, only two were formed without the aid of promoters, whereas promoters did not participate in as many as seven of the thirteen consolidations involving less than ten firms.[53]

Evidence from the case studies bears out this generalization. In the case of the newsprint industry, in which there were fewer than ten major competitors, promoters played a secondary role in the organization of the International Paper Company. As the consolidation's president told the Industrial Commission in 1901, "There was no promoter, underwriter, or any other party engaged directly or indirectly in the formation of the International Paper Company, except the owners, and the attorneys who were engaged to do the legal work, the committees making no charge for their services. Not a dollar was paid for promoting."[54] Chisholm's statement was some-

---

[52] However, only 107 (57 percent) of those industries that did not experience consolidation were classified correctly, indicating that low profits characterized many industries that did not experience consolidation as well.

[53] I excluded from the calculation reorganizations of earlier consolidations and the mergers organized by the American Tobacco Company to increase its dominance over all forms of tobacco manufacture. U.S. Industrial Commission, *Preliminary Report* and *Report on Trusts and Industrial Combinations*.

[54] *Ibid.*, p. 432.

thing of an exaggeration, because the manufacturers did engage the services of a banking firm to help finance the merger. Nonetheless, all the important decisions (the firms to be included in the consolidation, the method of valuation) were made by the manufacturers themselves.[55]

The experience of the tin-plate industry presents a striking contrast. After their repeated attempts to stop the downward-spiraling price competition failed, the manufacturers sought the aid of Judge William H. Moore, already famous for his work in promoting the Diamond Match and Nabisco combinations, to organize a consolidation. Moore's intervention was very important for the success of this venture. With nearly forty firms in the industry, the manufacturers were simply too numerous to organize themselves, especially as years of severe competition had left them intensely suspicious of one another. They needed an impartial arbiter to overcome their mutual distrust, to "get them together," in the words of Daniel G. Reid, first president of the consolidation.[56] Even as late as September 1898, when the organization was on the verge of consummation, manufacturers were still trying to outdo each other, loading themselves up with heavy contracts at low prices for delivery far into the future — just in case the combination failed.[57] Falling prices and meager profits made all the mills less recalcitrant, but it was Moore's reputation and skillful diplomacy that helped him accomplish the tricky task of evaluating the individual works. By maintaining absolute secrecy in his dealings with each producer and using hefty bonuses of common stock as sweeteners, Moore managed to satisfy most of the manufacturers. The American Tin Plate Company was incorporated in New Jersey in December 1898. It was enormously overcapitalized, but it controlled 90 percent of the industry.[58]

[55] *Paper Trade Journal,* November 27, 1897, p. 925; December 4, 1897, p. 945; January 1, 1898, p. 1; January 28, 1899, p. 61; February 4, 1899, p. 81; October 26, 1899, p. 684; David C. Smith, *History of Papermaking in the United States (1691-1969)* (New York: Lockwood Publishing, 1970), pp. 166-70, 185; Lyman Horace Weeks, *A History of Paper-Manufacturing in the United States, 1690-1916* (New York: Lockwood Trade Journal Co., 1916), pp. 302-4.

[56] U.S. Industrial Commission, *Preliminary Report on Trusts and Industrial Combinations,* p. 866.

[57] *Metal Worker, Plumber, and Steam Fitter,* September 10, 1898, p. 55.

[58] For testimony on Moore's methods, see U.S. Industrial Commission, *Preliminary Report on Trusts and Industrial Combinations,* pp. 959-67. See also U.S. Commissioner of Corporations, *Report on the Steel Industry,* Pt. I, pp. 133-6.

Undoubtedly, the number of mergers formed at the turn of the century would have been significantly fewer had not the maturation of the nation's capital markets given rise to financiers with the skill and resources to promote consolidations. Nevertheless, the appearance on the scene of these promoters should be regarded as a development that facilitated the consolidation movement, not its root cause. Manufacturers joined combinations mainly as a result of economic distress, and the most important source of this distress was the severe competition that occurred in capital-intensive industries that had experienced abnormally rapid expansion on the eve of the Panic of 1893. As a consequence of both growth capacity and fall in demand, many manufacturers found themselves facing losses after the Panic. As pressures mounted to meet interest payments on their debts, maintain dividends, and even amass working capital, so did the temptation to cut prices, with the aim of increasing sales. Moreover, the very newness of these industries, the fact that prices were already in a state of flux, encouraged manufacturers to believe they could get away with price cuts. Unfortunately for the manufacturers, in most cases the cuts were quickly detected, whereupon competitors retaliated, and the industry was plunged into a price war that proved extremely difficult to end. As the capital markets rebounded from the depression of the nineties, manufacturers seized the opportunity to form consolidations, finally bringing the price wars to an end.

This explanation for the great merger movement has an important implication: Consolidation was by no means an inevitable component in the rise of large-scale industry, but rather the consequence of a particular conjunction of events. Without the interaction of growth and depression, mass-production industries most likely would have proceeded to adjust to their long-run equilibrium positions (along the lines indicated by the preliminary model in Chapter 3). In such cases, as the example of the steel-rail industry illustrated, the dangers of price warfare were greatly reduced, and there was little inclination to form consolidations. In fact, pools and other types of collusive associations could successfully regulate prices and output for the industry as a whole, so long as their goals were not too far out of line with market forces.

This conclusion raises some intriguing questions. If the great merger movement was not an inevitable consequence of the rise of large-scale industry, what were the effects of its occurrence? How did consolidations bring to an end the price wars of the 1890s? To what extent did they permanently alter the competitive structure of American industry?

5. What changed?

The impact of consolidations on competitive behavior

For steel and newsprint manufacturers, the depression that followed the Panic of 1907 had strikingly different effects from the downturn in 1893. In both industries the earlier crisis had stimulated price warfare so severe that repeated attempts to end the competition proved fruitless. Manufacturers had tried banding together in pools, gentlemen's agreements, and selling agencies, but all these devices failed to stem the decline in prices. Finally they turned to consolidation for relief. By contrast, after the Panic of 1907, manufacturers successfully prevented outbreaks of price competition from recurring, and with only a minimum of organization. In November of 1907, Judge Elbert H. Gary, chairman of the United States Steel Corporation, called the nation's steelmakers together to talk about the state of the market – the first of the famous Gary dinners. Over the course of the next year the manufacturers met every few months to continue their discussions. These meetings, although certainly qualifying as collusive behavior, were much less formal and coercive than the elaborate pools of the 1890s. Yet, unlike the earlier pools, the Gary dinners were remarkably successful in preventing price cutting. Until January 1908, for example, manufacturers held the price of common-grade tin plate steady at its predepression level of $3.90 per box. Then, in response to the decline in demand, U.S. Steel announced a reduction to $3.70 per box, and this price was maintained without apparent difficulty for the rest of the year. Similarly, despite the Panic, the price of wire nails held at $2.23 per keg until U.S. Steel reduced it to $2.13 in April 1908. Manufacturers were able to maintain this price for a full year, again with little or no apparent difficulty.[1]

---

[1] In real terms, the price of tin plate fell 2% between 1907 and 1908, and the price of wire nails fell 1%. Between 1893 and 1894 the real price of wire nails declined 17%, and between 1894 and 1895 (because of changes in the tariff, these are the relevant dates) the price of tin plate dropped 22%. The point is not simply that list prices fell further after 1893 than 1907 but that the earlier Panic stimulated price

In the newsprint branch of the paper industry the situation was much the same. Although the demand for paper fell sharply in 1907 and 1908, papermakers did not cut prices as they had fourteen years before. Instead, led by the International Paper Company, they uniformly restricted production so as to maintain prices at predepression levels. Stunned by this shift in behavior, their customers, the nation's newspaper publishers, clamored for an antitrust investigation. In hearings before a special congressional committee, the publishers amassed evidence suggesting that meetings had occurred at which newsprint manufacturers agreed informally to a division of the market. Nonetheless, the publishers were unable to convince congressional investigators that a combination in restraint of trade actually existed. The fact that the manufacturers had met and discussed prices seemed inconsequential in and of itself. How could such a loose and informal association prevent price competition when much more highly structured organizations had failed in the past?[2]

Obviously, the Panic of 1893 and the Panic of 1907 were not strictly comparable. But the latter event resulted in a decline in demand similar to the drop that had immediately triggered price cutting in 1893. That the 1907 Panic did not have this effect in two industries as different as steel and paper suggests that a fundamental transformation had taken place. Because both industries underwent major consolidations at the turn of the century, the question arises whether or not the new type of horizontal combination lay at the root of the change in competitive behavior. Could consolidations use their newly won market power to prevent price cutting by their rivals?

cutting, whereas the later one did not. Trade journals reported few incidents of price cutting in 1907 and 1908, but many in 1893 and 1894. There was a flurry of price cutting in 1909, but a punitive response by U.S. Steel speedily reestablished industry discipline. American Iron and Steel Association (hereafter AISA), *Statistics of the American and Foreign Iron Trades: Annual Report of the Secretary*, 1907, p. 38; 1910, pp. 44, 50; U.S. Congress, House, *Hearings before the Committee on Investigation of United States Steel Corporation*, (Washington, D.C.: U.S. Government Printing Office, 1912), Vol. VII, p. 5563; U.S. Congress, House, *Tariff Hearings before the Committee on Ways and Means, 1896-1897*, 54th Cong., 2d Sess., 1897, Doc. 338, Vol. II, pp. 2136-7.

[2] See U.S. Congress, House, *Pulp and Paper Investigation Hearings*, 60th Cong., 2d Sess., 1909, Doc. 1502; and *Pulp and Paper Investigation Report*, 60th Cong., 1st Sess., 1908, Rept. 1786.

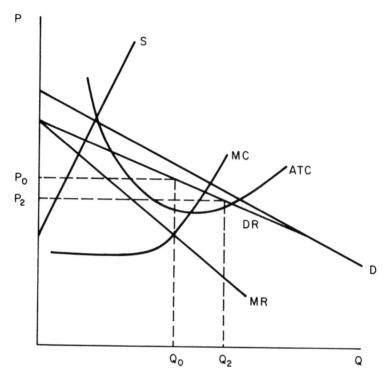

Figure 5.1. Dominant-firm strategy.

The dominant-firm strategy

In theory, the answer is that they could – at least in the short run. By pursuing what is known as the dominant-firm strategy, a consolidation could remove all incentive for price cutting by allowing the independent firms to sell as much output as they wished at whatever price the dominant firm set. The logic of this strategy can be followed with the aid of Figure 5.1.[3] Imagine an industry consisting of one giant multiplant firm (the product of a consolidation) and a number of much smaller independent firms. For the sake of simplic-

---

[3] The figure and the following discussion are based on F. M. Scherer, *Industrial Market Structure and Economic Performance* (2nd ed; Chicago: Rand McNally, 1980), pp. 232-6.

ity, assume that each independent firm possesses only one plant, that all of these plants are identical in size and efficiency, and that each produces the same homogeneous product as the consolidation.[4] Following the dominant-firm strategy, the combine bases its price and output decisions on a residual-demand curve such as DR, derived by subtracting from the market-demand curve D the amount of output the independent firms would like to supply at each price (shown as supply curve S). Once the combine makes a decision, the independents behave as price takers in the model of perfect competition. They take the consolidation's price as a given and produce at the level of output that equates marginal revenue and marginal cost. As can be seen from Figure 5.2, the independents have no incentive to cut prices, for this would only reduce profits. For example, a reduction in prices from P_0 to P_1 would reduce output from q_0 to q_1 and per-unit profits from ab to cd.

Compare this result with the analysis in Chapter 3. In the preconsolidation case, in which all the firms in the industry were the same size, each concern had an incentive to cut prices and increase its share of the market at the others' expense. In the current case, by contrast, this temptation can be completely removed. In other words, a simple change in the size distribution of firms, such as resulted from the consolidation movement, was sufficient to transform a potentially unstable oligopoly to a stable one – so long as the consolidation adopted the dominant-firm strategy.[5]

Evidence exists that at least some consolidations did, in fact, pursue dominant-firm pricing. George J. Stigler has argued, for example, that U.S. Steel adopted this type of pricing strategy in the early twentieth century and that it proved eminently profitable.[6] Randall

---

[4] These assumptions are similar to those made in Chapter 3 and have the same justification.

[5] As developed by Scherer, the foregoing theory implies that the independent firms were so small relative to the market that they were incapable of affecting the price of their output. In actuality, firms in industries with consolidations were unlikely to be that small. Nonetheless, consolidations could prevent the independents from cutting prices by allowing them to sell as much output as they wished at the current market price. The important question is whether and under what conditions a consolidation would find it profitable to pursue such a strategy, as will be discussed later.

[6] George J. Stigler, "The Dominant Firm and the Inverted Umbrella," *The Organization of Industry* (Homewood, Ill.: Richard D. Irwin, 1968), pp. 108-12.

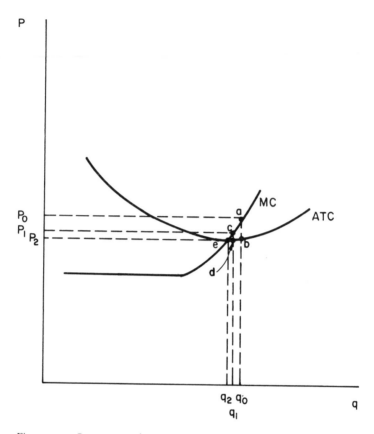

Figure 5.2. Cost curves for an independent firm.

Mariger has shown that what previously had been regarded as preda-tory pricing behavior by Standard Oil was consistent with a domi-nant-firm model.[7] Further, the statements of businessmen at the time confirm elements of the dominant-firm model. According to John Pitcairn, president of the Pittsburgh Plate Glass Company, the three independent firms that had been left outside when the combination was organized in 1895 had been on the verge of bankruptcy. By 1900, however, they were earning good profits, because "the consoli-

[7] Randall Mariger, "Predatory Price Cutting: The Standard Oil of New Jersey Case Revisited," *Explorations in Economic History*, 15 (October, 1978), pp. 341-67.

dated company reduced the production of its factories, and the independent companies were enabled to run their factories at full capacity."[8] F. B. Thurber, president of the U.S. Export Association, told the Industrial Commission that the independent sugar refineries generally followed American Sugar's prices. "And," he added, "there has been enough of an outlet, in view of the demand, for the output of all except the American Sugar Refining Company, which, however, has had sufficient outlet to keep, perhaps two-thirds of their capacity going."[9] Finally, Charles C. Clarke, an independent distiller, articulated explicitly the workings of dominant-firm pricing: "A trust can control prices . . . provided they allow their competitors to get what trade they want and simply take what is left."[10]

Granted that some consolidations, at least, adopted dominant-firm pricing, the question arises as to the conditions under which such a strategy was likely to be profitable: (1) How important were the consolidation's costs compared with those of its rivals? (2) Were consolidations as likely to maintain dominant-firm pricing during downswings in the business cycle as during upswings? In answer to the first question, note that in Figure 5.1 the dominant firm's short-run profit-maximizing price is P_0. But at price P_0, the independent firms are earning positive profits. If we assume, as in Chapter 3, that there are no barriers to entry into the industry, then the presence of these profits will stimulate new investment. The increase in capacity, in turn, will shift the independents' supply curve, and therefore the combine's residual-demand curve, downward. The consolidation's share of the market will be reduced. This result can be avoided if the consolidation forsakes its short-run profit-maximizing position and sets the price of its output at P_2 – the so-called limit price. Here the independents produce output q_2 and earn zero per-unit profits. No new capital is attracted to the industry.

[8] U.S. Industrial Commission, *Report on Trusts and Industrial Combinations*, 57th Cong., 1st Sess., 1901, House Doc. 182, p. 227.
[9] U.S. Industrial Commission, *Preliminary Report on Trusts and Industrial Combinations*, 56th Cong., 1st Sess., 1900, House Doc. 476, "Testimony," p. 14; see also pp. 107-8, 149; Alfred S. Eichner, *The Emergence of Oligopoly: Sugar Refining as a Case Study* (Baltimore: Johns Hopkins Press, 1969), pp. 158-61, 208-18.
[10] U.S. Industrial Commission, *Preliminary Report on Trusts and Industrial Combinations*, "Testimony," p. 189.

The consolidation thus faces a choice. It can set its price at the short-run profit-maximizing level (P_0), at the limit value (P_2), or somewhere in between. The actual decision will depend on a number of factors, including the rate at which new firms are likely to enter the industry and the value of present as opposed to future earnings. But above all, the decision will depend on the consolidation's costs of production as compared with those of its rivals. If the combine's plants are no more efficient than those of the independents, it can be shown that the combine will maximize its long-run profits (in terms of the dominant-firm strategy) by setting prices above the limit value. But in this case new entrants will stream into the industry, and the consolidation's share of the market will be steadily reduced until it no longer has the power to set prices for the industry.[11] If, on the other hand, the combine's costs are lower than those of the independents (perhaps as a result of economies of multiplant operation), a different result obtains. The dominant firm will typically hold prices at the limit value, where it and no one else is able to earn positive profits. No new entrants will be attracted to the industry. The dominant firm may even for a time cut prices below the limit value in order to drive some of its rivals out of business. In this case, rather than suffering erosion, its market power over the long run may actually be enhanced.[12]

The key data needed to assess the long-run viability of the dominant-firm strategy, therefore, are the combine's costs compared with those of its rivals. Evidence on this subject will be presented later, but first it is necessary to address the question of the consolidation's behavior in the short run, under conditions of depression. Figure 5.3 illustrates the problem. Suppose demand is initially at D_0. On the basis of residual-demand curve DR_0, the consolidation's profit-maximizing price is P_0. The limit price, as before, is P_2; so the con-

[11] In order to show this, one must again make some simplifying assumptions, e.g., that the rate of entry into the industry is directly proportional to the difference between the market price and the limit price. See Darius W. Gaskins, Jr., "Dynamic Limit Pricing: Optimal Pricing under Threat of Entry," *Journal of Economic Theory*, III (1971), pp. 306-22; N. J. Ireland, "Concentration and the Growth of Market Demand: A Comment on Gaskins' Limit Pricing Model," *ibid.*, V (1972), pp. 303-5; Scherer, *Industrial Market Structure and Economic Performance*, pp. 236-9.
[12] Gaskins, "Dynamic Limit Pricing;" Scherer, *Industrial Market Structure and Economic Performance*, pp. 238-9.

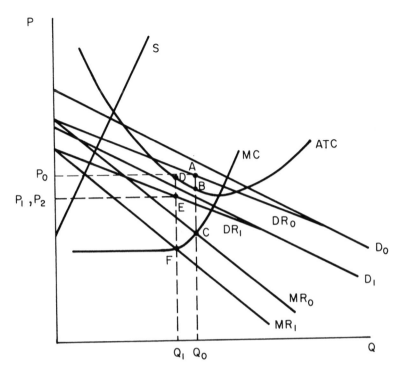

Figure 5.3 Effect of a decline in demand on the dominant-firm strategy.

solidation is likely to charge a price greater than or equal to P_2, but less than or equal to P_0 (as this particular case is drawn, the consolidation is no more efficient than the independent firms, and so it will likely charge a price above P_2). Now suppose that depression reduces the demand for the industry's product to D_1. The combine's residual-demand curve falls to DR_1. Its profit-maximizing price approaches and, depending on the severity of the depression, may even fall below the limit price. In the event of a downward shift in demand, therefore, the consolidation is likely to cut prices.

This move will not trigger a price war. So long as the consolidation follows the dominant-firm strategy (i.e., so long as it allows the independents to sell as much output as they wish at whatever price it sets), competitors have no incentive to initiate price cuts. It is possible, however, that the consolidation itself might touch off a price war by cutting prices and attempting to increase its market share beyond what it would receive by pursuing dominant-firm pricing. In the case displayed in Figure 5.3, for example, the combine has no advantage in costs over the independent firms. If it follows the dominant-firm strategy and sets prices at P_1 (equal in the example to the limit price), the combine produces output Q_1 and loses an amount equal to DE on each unit of output it makes. By contrast, the independent firms produce at their least-cost level of output and do not lose any money (Figure 5.2). Just as with the high-fixed-cost firms discussed in Chapter 3, the combine may be tempted secretly to cut prices in order to increase its share of the market at its rivals' expense. As before, this action will be more likely the greater the chance of getting away with the price cut without detection, and the greater the burden of fixed charges.

Short-run response to depression in the newsprint industry

This type of price warfare did, in fact, occur in the newsprint industry when an economic downturn combined with a steady stream of new entrants to reduce the International Paper Company's share of the market below the level it was willing to tolerate. For a time after the consolidation was organized in January 1898, the newsprint industry had gained respite from the downward trend in prices that had prevailed for most of the decade. In the absence of competition, the price of newsprint rose – according to reports in the *Paper Trade Journal*, from about 1.6 to 2.15-2.25 cents per pound.[13] Not all responsibility for the rise can be attributed to the consolidation; economic recovery combined with the rebellion in Cuba to stimulate the demand for paper. But whatever the cause, it is certain that prices rose above the limit value, for new firms rushed into the industry. Major enterprises were announced almost immediately. Although the long gestation period required for construction delayed most entries for several years, as early as 1900 two pulp mills (the Pejebscot and

---

[13] *Paper Trade Journal*, February 19, 1898, p. 143; June 4, 1898, p. 459; January 7, 1899, p. 9; U.S. Industrial Commission, *Report on Trusts and Industrial Combinations*, p. 416.

the Oswego Falls) had integrated forward into paper production, and the Great Northern Paper Company (soon to be International's most formidable competitor) had already put its first paper mill into production. Over the next five years seventeen more firms entered the market. Most of these were small, but one (the St. Regis Paper Company) had a newsprint capacity of 105 tons of paper per day. In addition, the Great Northern and Berlin Mills companies added gigantic mills to their works, the former increasing its capacity from 60 to 310 tons of paper per day, and the latter from 37.5 to 215 tons. As a result of all this new construction, International's share of Eastern newspaper capacity slipped to 64 percent in 1900 and to 48 percent in 1905 (Table 5.1).[14]

In the face of this growing competition, the International Paper Company adopted a three-pronged strategy. Its first move was to invest large sums of money to improve the productivity of its plants and put itself in a stronger competitive position. As we shall see later, this attempt was not altogether successful. Its second move was to promote cooperative relations among all the firms in the industry – to combine the independents into an informal cartel so that they could obtain "a good price" for their output and keep production "down to market requirements." This attempt to shift some of the burden of

[14] Many of the new firms were headed by entrepreneurs who had been active competitors in the 1890s. *Lockwood's Directory of the Paper, Stationery and Allied Trades*, 1900-1, 1905.

In computing International's share of the industry, I summed the capacities of all mills that produced at least some newsprint. Although this resulted in overstatement of International's newsprint capacity and of the capacity of the industry as a whole, the effect was to hide the true extent of International's decline. For the industry, the ratio of the capacity of mills devoted solely to newsprint to the capacity of mills used to make at least some newsprint increased from 0.31 in 1900 to 0.60 in 1905. For the International Paper Company, by contrast, the ratio decreased from 0.68 to 0.27 over the same period.

Confining the calculation to the Eastern newsprint market also understates the extent of International's decline. There was very little interregional competition in the 1890s, but interregional sales began to increase in importance in the first decade of the twentieth century. A combination of Eastern producers, International found itself facing growing Western (and Canadian) competition in the years after its formation. U.S. Congress, House, *Pulp and Paper Investigation Hearings*, Vol. I, pp. 45-6, 89-105, 231, 441-3, 458-62; Vol. II, pp. 941-2; Vol. III, pp. 2131-2; *Lockwood's Directory*, 1901-2, 1905, 1910; *Paper Trade Journal*, January 12, 1905, p. 3; Trevor J. O. Dick, "Canadian Newsprint, 1913-1930: National Policies and the North American Economy," *Journal of Economic History*, XLII (September 1982), pp. 659-87.

Table 5.1. *Changes in numbers and capacities[a] of independent Eastern newsprint firms*

	1900–5	1905–10
Number of new independents[b]	17	6
Total capacity of new independents	1,132,000	660,000
Number of independents that disappeared[c]	11	8
Capacity of independents that disappeared	439,000	341,000
Net change in the capacity of independents existing in first and last years	+835,000	+537,000
Total number of independents in last year	36	34
Total capacity of independents in last year	3,269,000	4,125,000
Capacity of the International Paper Company in last year	3,051,000	3,192,000

[a]Pounds of paper per day (includes only those of the firms' mills that made at least some newsprint).
[b]Number of firms listed as producing newsprint in last year but not in first.
[c]Number of firms listed as producing newsprint in first year but not in last.
Source: Lockwood's Directory, 1900–1, 1905, 1910.

restricting output to the independents was not successful either. Although International achieved some victories (e.g., it succeeded in restructuring newsprint contracts from the abuse-prone "production" basis to the "gross-weight" basis and in prohibiting Sunday operations),[15] the consolidation could not force the independent firms

[15] In the 1890s, most newsprint was sold on what was called the production basis. In effect, this meant that publishers paid only for the number of perfect sheets of paper that rolled off their presses, and manufacturers were liable for the mistakes of the pressmen as well as for their own. Shortly after its formation, International Paper introduced a new type of contract that called for payment on a gross weight basis: The manufacturer promised to provide paper that would run a predetermined number of sheets to the pound, and the publisher was billed for the total weight of the paper delivered. This type of contract was formally adopted at a meeting of the manufacturers in late 1900 and soon became standard throughout the industry.

At about the same time, International Paper won another victory when the manufacturers agreed to prohibit Sunday operations and to close their factories at 6:00 Saturday evenings. Because the workers' weekly earnings were not to be reduced, this was an important gain for labor. But it also resulted in a substantial curtailment

to accept a reduced share of the market – except when supply and demand conditions favored the endeavor. In late 1903, for instance, labor troubles and drought helped the consolidation orchestrate an industry-wide shutdown that eased the way for an advance in prices. When the demand for paper slumped during the summer of 1899, on the other hand, International's leadership was ineffective.[16]

For the most part, therefore, International relied on the third element of its three-pronged strategy: It simply refused to engage in price competition. Rather than meet the prices of the Great Northern Paper Company, International allowed its rival to capture enough contracts to fill its order books quickly. In that manner, International kept to a minimum Great Northern's ability to disrupt prices in the market. In 1901, for example, the combination scarcely contested Great Northern's bids to two major New York daily newspapers, the *Times* and the *World*. Contracts amounting to 65 percent of total U.S. newspaper consumption were up for renewal by the end of that year, and as a result of the *Times* and *World* deals, Great Northern had filled up its order books by early September.[17]

When it adopted this tactic, the International Paper Company was in essence pursuing the dominant-firm strategy: allowing its competitors to sell as much output as they wished and basing its own price and output decisions on a residual-demand curve. For the inroads competitors made on its sales, International attempted to compensate in two ways: by developing the export market for newsprint and by diversifying its product. In the former endeavor, the company was only moderately successful; International Paper sold abroad an aver-

of production. The *Paper Trade Journal* estimated that the Saturday night closing alone reduced output by more than 275 tons of paper per day – almost the capacity of the Great Northern Paper Company. The Sunday prohibition also reduced production, but to a somewhat lesser extent, because many of the mills had never run on Sundays. U.S. Industrial Commission, *Report on Trusts and Industrial Combinations*, pp. 433-5; U.S. Congress, House, *Pulp and Paper Investigation Hearings*, Vol. I, pp. 32-3, 451-5; *Paper Trade Journal*, January 3, 1901, p. 20; July 3, 1902, p. 6.

[16] *Ibid.*, December 3, 1903, p. 707, January 28, 1904, p. 112; U.S. Congress, House, *Pulp and Paper Investigation Hearings*, Vol. V, p. 3082; U.S. Industrial Commission, *Report on Trusts and Industrial Combinations*, p. 412; L. Ethan Ellis, "Print Paper Pendulum: Group Pressures and the Price of Newsprint," *Newsprint: Producers, Publishers, Political Pressures* (New Brunswick: Rutgers University Press, 1960), pp. 29-30.

[17] *Paper Trade Journal*, September 12, 1901, p. 323.

age of 28,000 tons of paper per year between 1900 and 1907, enough to keep busy a couple of its smallest mills. International fared somewhat better at diversification. It switched a number of its paper machines from production of newsprint to manila, integrated forward into paper-bag manufacture, and became a major competitor of the Union Bag and Paper Company – the consolidation that dominated that field. Manila production absorbed 60,000 to 65,000 tons per year of International's output, and various other grades absorbed another 20,000 tons. By means of diversification and exports, therefore, International Paper was able to assure an outlet for about 20 percent of its production.[18]

By pursuing dominant-firm pricing, developing exports, and diversifying its products, International managed to maintain prices at a generally profitable level through 1904, in large measure because business conditions were favorable to the endeavor. During that period, the output of new mills reached the market only gradually, and the demand for newsprint continued to run strong – strong enough to absorb the increase in output with little change in price.[19] But the favorable economic conditions that underlay this "noncompetitive era"[20] largely disappeared by the end of 1904. The demand for newsprint began to turn down. Then the giant new plant of the Berlin Mills Company entered production. To make matters worse, competitors proceeded to take more desirable contracts from International. The greatly expanded Berlin Mills Company captured the contract for the *Philadelphia Inquirer*, and the Great Northern Paper Company won the business of the *New York Herald*. In order to accommodate the *Herald*, Great Northern had to drop contracts with two smaller papers, the *St. Louis Post-Dispatch* and the *Philadelphia Press*. International took the former contract, but Berlin

[18] U.S. Congress, House, *Pulp and Paper Investigation Hearings*, Vol. II, pp. 1071, 1165; *Paper Trade Journal*, July 1, 1899, p. 135; July 8, 1899, p. 167; August 31, 1899, p. 425.
[19] The earnings (not net of depreciation) of the International Paper Company averaged 9.5 percent on the company's preferred stock (approximately the value of its assets) in this period. U.S. Congress, House, *Pulp and Paper Investigation Hearings*, Vol., II, p. 1211.
[20] This phrase appeared in a 1907 trade-journal article that was reprinted, *ibid.*, Vol. I, p. 247.

Mills obtained the latter. The consolidation had been reduced to competing with its rivals for castoffs.[21]

The inroads competitors made on International's sales had by then become too great to ignore. When the demand for newsprint deteriorated further during the recession of 1905, International abandoned all pretence of dominant-firm pricing and began to compete actively for business. Determined to hold onto its customers, the corporation voluntarily reduced prices on contracts already in force. Frederick Roy Martin of the Providence, Rhode Island, *Journal* later recounted how representatives of the International Paper Company surprised him by unilaterally offering a reduction in price:

We were told that the market price had dropped, and they decided on March 1, 1905, to reduce our price without any suggestions from us to $2.05 [per hundred pounds]. On October 12 they decided voluntarily to reduce the price for the rest of the year to 2 cents [per pound], and they led us to sign a five-year contract with them . . . the price to be set each year [at the market rate].[22]

John D. Plummer of the Springfield, Massachusetts, *Union* told of a similar experience:

We had a contract which ran and expired in the middle of the summer [of 1905], and the International Paper Company, for some reasons that I have never been able to discover, came around in the summer and said that if we would make a new contract for that time, extending through the balance of that year and covering the next year, and have it expire on the first of January, they would make us a price of 2 cents [per pound].[23]

Simultaneously, International Paper courted publishers who were under contract with other manufacturers. In order to lure the *New York Times* away from the Great Northern Paper Company, the combine promised to supply the publisher with newsprint from its best-equipped mill at a price that would be either (1) the lowest price International offered any of its customers or (2) the cost of manufacture and delivery plus a profit of $7.50 per ton, whichever the *Times* preferred. International estimated that the actual billing price under this contract would average close to 1.9 cents per pound, but if for

[21] *Paper Trade Journal*, December 22, 1904, p. 8, November 2, 1905, p. 6.
[22] U.S. Congress, House, *Pulp and Paper Investigation Hearings*, Vol. I, pp. 535-6.
[23] *Ibid.*, p. 534.

any reason the price exceeded 2 cents, the *Times* would have the option of canceling the contract. International made similar deals with the *New York Journal* and the *Chicago Daily News*.[24]

International's price cuts triggered retaliatory cuts by its rivals, and by the middle of 1905 newsprint manufacturers found themselves engaged in a price war reminiscent of what had followed the Panic of 1893. In the ensuing scramble for business, contract terms slipped back to the "production" basis, and newsprint prices dropped sharply from 2.25 cents per pound to 1.85 cents, nearing the level they had reached during the depths of the depression of the nineties, although the general price level was still considerably higher.[25] Once again some of the manufacturers found themselves producing at a loss. According to one of its officers, "The Berlin Mills Company, together with many others, has its back to the wall in this matter of paper prices and cannot retreat further . . . The company has not been getting anything like a fair profit."[26] The St. Regis Paper Company lost an average of $1.60 on each ton of paper it sold in January 1906. Its net earnings for the fiscal year ending April 30, 1906, were down more than $100,000 from the previous year. After dividends, only $99.08 remained as surplus, and no deduction for depreciation had been made.[27] The industry was clearly experiencing its worst competition since the depression of the nineties. As the *Paper Trade Journal* reported in early 1906, "Conditions in the news market have been anything but satisfactory for more than a year . . . Competition has been indulged to the limit, and each manufacturer has bid lower than the others when contracts of any size were in the market."[28]

From the standpoint of the International Paper Company, the new strategy was a qualified success. Certainly sales increased. Interna-

---

[24] *Ibid.*, pp. 17-22.

[25] *Ibid.*, pp. 32-3, 202, 235-6, 451-5, 458; *Paper Trade Journal*, January 4, 1906, p. 20.

[26] *Ibid.*, September 26, 1907, p. 8.

[27] U.S. Congress, House, *Pulp and Paper Investigation Hearings*, Vol. I, pp. 572-8; Vol. II, pp. 941-2, 974; Vol. III, pp. 1763-7.

[28] *Paper Trade Journal*, March 22, 1906, p. 3. Data collected by a House committee investigating the paper industry show that most firms seem to have earned some profits in this period (not allowing for depreciation) but that margins were considerably reduced. See U.S. Congress, House, *Pulp and Paper Investigation Hearings*, Vol. II, pp. 837-8, 893-4, 974-6, 1017-19, 1079, 1103, 1422-5; Vol. III, pp. 1586-7, 1630-40, 1673, 1693, 1698-9, 1860-1, 1872-3, 1877-8, 1920-2, 1941.

tional's board of directors reported in late November 1905 that the firm's product was sold out for the next eighteen months and that the combine had produced more paper during the previous three months than in any corresponding period of its history.[29] The expansion of sales came at the expense of earnings, however. International's net profits (after taxes, insurance, and interest, but not depreciation) fell from $2.14 million in the fiscal year ending June 30, 1905, to $1.99 million in fiscal 1906, and decreased again to $1.62 million in fiscal 1907. Because the firm produced 473,526 tons of paper in fiscal 1907, this meant that its net earnings amounted to only $3.42 per ton. Fiscal 1907 was a prosperous year for the economy in general and for the newsprint industry in particular, but International Paper had so burdened itself with low-priced, long-term contracts during the previous bout of price warfare that it barely earned the $3.00 per ton that its officers estimated as necessary to cover depreciation.[30]

Ironically, pursuit of a strategy designed to forestall price competition had led the International Paper Company to trigger a price war itself. Dominant-firm pricing had succeeded in preventing the independents from undercutting the consolidation's prices, but the strategy's drawback was the stimulus to new entrants it provided. As a result, by 1904, International's market share had fallen to a level apparently too low to tolerate. When a recession further reduced the demand for its paper, the company retaliated by cutting prices in order to increase its share of the market. Repeating the experience of the 1890s, independent firms more than matched International's cuts. Prices fell, and many firms, including the International Paper Company, wound up worse off than before.

But there was an important difference between the price warfare of the 1890s and that triggered by the International Paper Company in 1905. The latter competition was easily ended. All the consolidation had to do was revert to dominant-firm pricing and the price warfare would subside. This, in fact, is what happened. As the demand for

[29] *Ibid.*, Vol. I, p. 201; Vol. II, pp. 859, 1425.
[30] Unfortunately, there is no information on International's profit margins for 1905 and 1906. *Ibid.*, Vol. I, p. 194; Vol. II, pp. 726-7, 1103; see also pp. 1017-19, 1425; and Vol. III, p. 1698.

paper began to rise in 1907, International shifted its strategy. In two stages, in the spring and the fall, International raised its price on new contracts to 2.5 cents per pound for large orders, and higher for less desirable business. At about the same time, the independent paper-makers met and raised their prices accordingly. Not only did prices increase, but contract terms returned to the gross-weight basis.[31]

Price cuts forge industry discipline

As a result of the consolidation movement, then, price warfare had become a device that dominant firms could control. This was an enormously significant development, for it meant that the threat of price warfare could be used to enforce cartel-like behavior – that is, to relieve the dominant firm of some of the burden of price maintenance, especially during periods of slack demand.

How well this could work can be seen most clearly in the case of the steel industry. At the time of its formation in 1901, U.S. Steel, like the International Paper Company, faced a barrage of new competition. The high prices charged by its predecessors had attracted a rush of new capital to the industry. For example, in early 1899 there were only three tin-plate rolling mills in competition with the American Tin Plate Company; their total capacity amounted to a mere 7,480 boxes of tin plate per week as compared with the consolidation's capacity of more than 200,000 boxes. By 1901, however, two dipperies had integrated backward into black-plate production, five completely new firms had entered the industry, and at least eight additional enterprises were in various stages of planning and construction. All told, the combined capacity of these projects amounted to almost half that of the American Tin Plate Company. In wire, the story was much the same. American Steel and Wire had incorporated all the rod mills in existence in 1899 except Illinois Steel (with which it signed a market-sharing agreement) and a handful of small works that concentrated on specialty products. But by early 1901, eleven additional firms had entered the rod market, six works were under construction, and one other enterprise was in the planning stage.

[31] *Ibid.*, Vol. I, pp. 91, 171, 214, 253-4, 451-5; Vol. III, pp. 1974-5; *Paper Trade Journal*, April 25, 1907, p. 38; May 16, 1907, p. 14.

Added together, the capacity of the newcomers would equal that of American Steel and Wire and Illinois Steel combined.[32]

Like International Paper, the Steel Corporation at first attempted to follow a dominant-firm pricing strategy: setting a price for its output, allowing the independents to fill their plants with orders at this or at a slightly lower price, and then satisfying the rest of the market itself. But U.S. Steel, like International Paper, decided after a time that independents were obtaining too large a share of the market. U.S. Steel's next response was similar to that of International: It attempted to organize the independent manufacturers into a cartel so as to spread the burden of the increased capacity. After the entrance of a number of new wire-nail concerns in late 1901, for instance, the wire manufacturers met and agreed to fix prices. But the failure of this and other similar efforts convinced the corporation's officers to shift tactics. In October 1902 (in an interval of slack demand), U.S. Steel's American Steel and Wire subsidiary announced that "for some time, owing to the varying conditions throughout the country, our schedule of prices has become more or less out of line." In order to "meet present conditions," American sharply reduced its prices for wire nails and other wire products. Other subsidiaries followed suit, with dramatic results. In tin plate, for example, nearly all the independent firms had been running full in October 1902, whereas the corporation's American Tin Plate subsidiary was turning out less than half its potential product. After the American Tin Plate Company slashed its prices, the situation was completely reversed. By January 1903, most of the independents' mills were idle. U.S. Steel was still operating only half its plants, but as the demand for tin plate rose in early 1903, the corporation put more mills back in production. By June 1903, only three of its plants were idle. In the meantime, U.S. Steel advanced quotations, the independents began to

[12] AISA, *Directory to the Iron and Steel Works of the United States*, 1901, 1904, 1908; *Iron Age*, September 6, 1900, p. 6; February 14, 1901, p. 31; *Metal Worker, Plumber and Steam Fitter*, January 7, 1899, p. 46; January 14, 1899, p. 33; February 4, 1899, p. 35; February 3, 1900, p. 34; March 30, 1901, p. 50; April 6, 1901, p. 47; September 7, 1901, p. 49.

resume production, and the corporation reverted to its dominant-firm posture.[33]

Over the next few years this pattern was repeated. The Steel Corporation maintained prices until its officers felt that competitors were obtaining too large a share of the business. Then (typically during downturns) U.S. Steel suddenly reduced its quotations.[34] As Figure 5.4 shows, over time, the periods of price maintenance grew longer and bouts of price cutting less frequent. In part, this was a result of U.S. Steel's success in forestalling further entry (to be discussed later), but it was also a result of the increase in discipline that U.S. Steel's periodic price cuts had fostered among the manufacturers. By mid-decade, the independent firms had, for all practical purposes, joined U.S. Steel in a cartel to restrain production and support prices.

It was this learning process that explained the achievements of the Gary dinners after the Panic of 1907. Historians have generally accepted the success of the dinners as a matter of course, without realizing what a remarkable feat it was that such a loose combination could curtail output and maintain prices when much more tightly structured combinations had failed under similar circumstances in the past. And circumstances were indeed similar. Not only did demand drop after the Panic of 1907, just as it had in 1893, but both depressions followed periods of growth. The model in Chapter 3 would lead us to predict outbreaks of price warfare in both instances. Yet serious price competition developed only after the earlier panic.

The absence of price competition in 1907 was a change attributable to two related developments: the shift in the size distribution of firms that had occurred as a result of the great merger movement and the learning process that this change in size made possible. A firm as large relative to its competitors as U.S. Steel could adopt the dominant-firm strategy and prevent price cutting by its rivals. It also had the power to switch price competition on and off and thereby teach its rivals a lesson. By 1907, U.S. Steel's policy of instigating price

[33] *Iron Age,* January 2, 1902, p. 37; January 16, 1902, p. 55; October 2, 1902, p. 47; November 6, 1902, p. 31; January 1, 1903, pp. 62, 103-4; January 7, 1904, p. 86. As we shall see, unlike the International Paper Company, U.S. Steel had an advantage in costs.

[34] See, for example, *ibid.,* January 7, 1904, pp. 129, 136-8; January 28, 1904, p. 60.

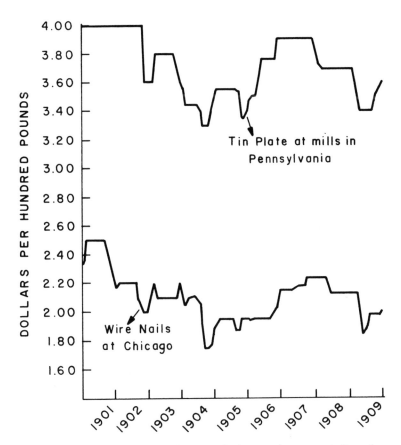

Figure 5.4. Prices of tin plate and wire nails, by months, 1901–8. Data from AISA, *Statistics of the Iron Trades,* 1910, pp. 46, 50.

competition during recessions seems to have convinced the independents to accept more of the burden of curtailment during downturns. The steel industry had one of the worst years in its history in 1908; yet, from the point of view of *Iron Age,* it was a year that redounded to the credit of the manufacturers: Cooperating under the leadership of Judge Gary, the manufacturers had together reduced output and avoided ruinous price cutting.[35]

[35] *Iron Age,* January 7, 1909, p. 36; see also pp. 38, 107, and January 2, 1908, pp. 36, 38-9, 70, 96. In the case of tin plate, U.S. Steel still seems to have borne a

Manufacturers of newsprint accomplished a feat similar to the Gary dinners at approximately the same time. Although the demand for newsprint fell sharply after the Panic of 1907, papermakers did not cut prices as they had when demand dropped in 1893. Nor did sole responsibility for adjusting output to demand devolve on the International Paper Company, as it had earlier in the century. Instead, led by International Paper, the manufacturers uniformly restricted production so as to maintain prices at their predepression levels. International began to curtail operations in early 1908; by May it had shut down twenty-four of its eighty-five machines. The St. Regis Company operated at two-thirds of capacity the first five months of 1908, and we know that the Great Northern Paper Company, Berlin Mills, Remington-Martin, Lisbon Falls Fibre, Pejebscot Paper, Gould Paper, and Cliff Paper all went on short time. Simultaneously, the newsprint firms staunchly refused to reduce quotations.[36]

Long-run consequences of the consolidation movement

The experiences of the steel and newsprint industries in the first decade of the twentieth century show that consolidations could and did alter the competitive environment in a dramatic way. By pursuing the dominant-firm strategy, a consolidation could remove all incentive for price cutting by competitors. Moreover, its large size enabled it both to start and to stop price warfare, a power that it could use to force rivals to accept some of the burden of curtailment during depressions.

We know that consolidations possessed these powers in the years immediately following their organization, but what about over the long run? The analysis presented earlier in this chapter suggests that

disproportionate share of the curtailment after the Panic of 1907, but as *Iron Age* pointed out, "the trade of the independents is of a steadier nature, from quarter to quarter, than is that of the leading interest. This is naturally to be expected from the more miscellaneous nature of the independent business, while a large portion of the leading interest's business is in tin plates for the principal can producer." *Ibid.*, January 7, 1909, p. 43.

[36] U.S. Congress, House, *Pulp and Paper Investigation Hearings*, Vol. I, pp. 255, 336, 338-9, 341; Vol II, pp. 859, 941, 981-2, 1010-13, 1098-100, 1414-17; Vol. III, pp. 1584-5, 1632, 1781-2, 1867-9, 1892, 1932. No mill reported to the House Investigating Committee that it was running full.

the answer to this question depends on whether or not the combines' costs of production were lower than those of their competitors'. If a consolidation had an advantage in costs over its rivals, it could set prices at the limit value and maintain indefinitely both its market share and its ability to forestall price cutting by independents. If the consolidation was no more efficient than its rivals, it would gradually lose its position of dominance and, with this, its ability to set prices for the industry.

Everything we know about the process of forming consolidations indicates that the latter result was more common. When consolidations were organized at the turn of the century, they took in large numbers of plants built in the 1880s and early 1890s, plants whose equipment had been sorely taxed by years of competition. At the same time, the high prices they charged immediately after their formation attracted an influx of new competitors – rivals equipped with the most efficient, up-to-date machinery. Although the consolidations responded by improving their equipment and building new, modern plants of their own, one would expect that their possession of so much older capacity kept their average total costs high, especially as old plants were often taken into the consolidations at inflated prices.[37] Only if there were substantial benefits to combination (economies of scale or speed, economies of multiplant operation, or pecuniary economies resulting from monopoly power in labor or resource markets) could this disadvantage be offset.

The newsprint industry once again provides an example. In response to the influx of new competition after its formation, International Paper moved to improve the productivity of its plants. Between 1899 and 1904, the company undertook major renovations at eight of its mills,[38] but much of its capacity was still outmoded in comparison with its rivals. The most significant technological development in paper manufacture in this period was the trend toward wider, faster, more efficient Fourdrinier paper machines. Although

[37] Under normal circumstances the high variable costs associated with an older plant should be offset by low fixed charges, but the method of financing consolidations kept fixed charges on old plants high.

[38] According to the testimony of company officers, *ibid.*, Vol. II, p. 1213; see also pp. 1027, 1072; and Vol. V, p. 3071; *Paper Trade Journal*, July 8, 1899, p. 167; August 31, 1899, p. 425; December 8, 1904, pp. 3, 17.

there is no information on the speeds attained by particular machines, *Lockwood's Directory* recorded the widths of the Fourdriniers used in each newsprint mill. This width measurement can serve as a crude index of production costs. In 1905 the International Paper Company had only six machines that were 135 inches or wider (one 135-inch machine, one at 136, two at 145, one at 147, and one at 162). The average width of the ninety-one machines in its newsprint mills was 98 inches, and fifty-five of them were less than 100 inches wide (a width considered desirable ten years before). Great Northern, on the other hand, had eight 152-inch Fourdriniers and two 136-inch machines; the Berlin Mills Company's new plant contained four 164-inch machines; and the average width of the machines in the other seventeen new enterprises was 116 inches (six had Fourdriniers at least 135 inches wide).[39]

Differences in the widths of machines were reflected in production costs. In 1907, the mill cost of producing a ton of paper at the International Paper Company's most efficient plant was $27.59. At the company's most inefficient plant, the cost was $37.10 per ton, and the average for all its mills was $33.57. By way of comparison, among its competitors, the Gould Paper Company had production costs of $29.57 per ton; St. Regis, $30.56; Remington-Martin, $31.89; Pejebscot, $35.27; Lisbon Falls, $37.05; Cliff Paper Company, $41.66 (the last two were older mills).[40] When dividends and interest payments are added to costs, International's position looks even worse. Its $45,000,000 in stock and $16,000,000 in bonds amounted to a capitalization of $39,000 per ton of daily capacity. By contrast, Great Northern's stock and bond issues were equivalent to $26,000 per ton, those of St. Regis, $23,000 per ton, and those of Remington-Martin, $14,000 per ton.[41]

[39] *Lockwood's Directory*, 1905.

[40] It should be noted that these figures are not strictly comparable, for the firms did not employ uniform accounting procedures. Unfortunately, we have no information on the mill costs of the Great Northern and Berlin Mills companies. U.S. Congress, House, *Pulp and Paper Investigation Hearings*, Vol. II, pp. 849, 860, 898-903, 911-12, 915, 924, 931-2, 944-7, 966, 974-5, 1010-13, 1017-19, 1074-83, 1100-1, 1414-20, 1422-5; Vol. III, pp. 1586-7, 1592-3, 1763-7; Vol. V, pp. 3096, 3099-100, 3102-4.

[41] These figures are for 1905. *Ibid.*, Vol. I, pp. 193-4; Vol. II, p. 1422; Vol. III, p. 1764.

Dominant-firm theory suggests that a consolidation such as the International Paper Company, with no advantage in costs over the most efficient independent firms, would set prices above the limit value, allow rival concerns to fill up their order books, and tolerate a steady influx of new firms into the industry. This, as we have seen, is essentially what happened. With the exception of a brief episode of price cutting in 1905, which temporarily halted entry and encouraged industry discipline after the Panic of 1907, the International Paper Company adopted dominant-firm pricing and suffered a steady erosion of its share of the market.[42]

Scattered information on market shares and earnings suggests that many consolidations experienced a fate similar to or worse than that of International Paper in the decade following the great merger movement. To give just a few examples, United States Envelope's share of the market fell from 90 to 50-60 percent between 1899 and 1904; American Hide and Leather fell from 75 to 55 percent over the same period; International Silver fell from 75 to 40 percent between 1898 and 1904; the Glucose Sugar Refining Company fell from 85 to 45 percent within four years of its formation in 1897.[43] Some consolidations, such as United States Leather, National Cordage, American Malting, and the Distilling and Cattle Feeding Company, suffered failure and reorganization – sometimes more than once. Many others, such as American Window Glass Company and American Thread, never earned satisfactory profits.[44] The most favorable assessment of the success rate of turn-of-the-century consolidations, Shaw Livermore's 1935 study, shows that about half of the combinations were

---

[42] The period after 1907 was characterized by a steady shift in newsprint production from the United States to Canada. With its market share dwindling rapidly, International Paper belatedly, in 1924, began to spend large sums of money to acquire Canadian competitors and woodlands. Ellis, "Print Paper Pendulum," pp. 125-33; Dick, "Canadian Newsprint," pp. 659-87.

[43] John Moody, *The Truth About Trusts: A Description and Analysis of the American Trust Movement* (New York: Moody Publishing, 1904), pp. 225-6, 254-6, 278-9; Arthur S. Dewing, *Corporate Promotions and Reorganizations* (Cambridge: Harvard University Press, 1914), pp. 82-9, 526.

[44] *Ibid.*; U.S. Industrial Commission, *Preliminary Report on Trusts and Industrial Combinations,* "Topical Digest of Evidence," pp. 76-84; Shaw Livermore, "The Success of Industrial Mergers," *Quarterly Journal of Economics,* L (November 1935), pp. 68-96.

unsuccessful. Livermore collected information on 136 mergers that were powerful enough at the time of their formation "to influence markedly conditions in the industry." After examining their earnings records over the period 1901 to 1932, he categorized 50 of the mergers (37 percent) as failures, 10 (7 percent) as failures that were subsequently rejuvenated, 16 (12 percent) as marginal or "limping" concerns (he included the International Paper Company in this category), and only 60 (44 percent) as successes.[45]

It is likely that the unsuccessful mergers had failed to obtain an advantage in costs over their rivals,[46] but what about the comparatively profitable combines? Some of the enterprises on Livermore's list of successes were combinations of only a small number of firms, and as a result, their chances of upgrading their facilities to meet new competition were probably good. Of the 51 successful mergers for which this type of information is available, 11 (22 percent) combined less than 5 firms (and hence did not even meet this study's definition of consolidation); another 17 (33 percent) involved only 5 to 9 firms.[47]

Mergers of relatively few firms may have maintained their positions through superior efficiency. So may have combinations that involved greater numbers of competitors. But it is also possible that the success of these combines, especially the larger ones, derived from something other than superior efficiency – the exploitation of artificial barriers to entry, for example. Unfortunately, data that bear directly on this issue are difficult to come by. Nonetheless, scattered information from a variety of sources is available, and for U.S. Steel there is one good (though limited) set of data on costs: the records of

---

[45] These totals differ from the ones in Livermore's article because I restricted the focus to the manufacturing sector and eliminated double counting of reorganizations. The criteria Livermore used to measure success are not altogether clear, but he seems to have considered a firm successful if its profit rate (net earnings after deduction of fixed charges divided by total stockholders' equity) equaled or exceeded that for manufacturing firms in general. *Ibid.*

[46] Of course, there are other possible reasons for the poor performance of consolidations. But Arthur S. Dewing's study of unsuccessful mergers suggests that one of the most important causes of failure was lack of advantage in costs. Dewing, *Corporate Promotions and Reorganizations*, pp. 562-6.

[47] Livermore, "The Success of Industrial Mergers," pp. 90-4; Moody, *The Truth About Trusts*; Ralph L. Nelson's unpublished list of consolidations.

the Federal Trade Commission (FTC) investigation of the steel industry during World War I.[48]

The FTC data show that, as in the case of the International Paper
Company, there was significant variation in the costs of production
at the Steel Corporation's many plants. For the month of August
1918, U.S. Steel's expense in producing standard open-hearth rails
(mill costs only) ranged from $32.46 to $48.27 per gross ton. Its cost
of producing sheet bars ranged from $31.30 to $54.98 per gross ton,
wire rods from $36.41 to $78.10, and black plate for tinning from
$89.12 to $99.17.[49] Unlike the International Paper Company, however, U.S. Steel had, on average, an advantage over its competitors –
at least so far as the mill costs of the foregoing products were concerned. Not only did U.S. Steel possess the great majority of the most
cost-efficient plants in the industry, but its average costs undercut
those of all its rivals (reporting to the FTC), except for one sheet-bar
producer and one black-plate producer.[50]

[48] The records include actual monthly cost sheets for all plants owned by U.S. Steel
and for many independent firms for the period October 1917 until the end of the
war. The records are stored in the National Archives Building in Washington, D.C.,
Record Group 122, Federal Trade Commission File 8900. I am indebted to archiv-
ists Jerry N. Hess and T. Gedosch for their efforts in helping me locate these
documents and to Lane Moore for pointing out their existence.

[49] These figures do not include transportation charges, administration and sales expenses, depreciation, or an allowance for interest on invested capital. The mean,
median, and standard deviation of U.S. Steel's mill costs for each type of product (in
dollars per gross ton) were:

	No. of plants	Mean	Median	Standard deviation
Open-hearth rails	7	36.54	43.39	5.20
Sheet bars	11	39.41	37.50	7.81
Wire rods	23	52.11	49.91	10.49
Black plate	14	93.52	93.09	2.51

[50] The FTC's study is admittedly rather late for the purposes of this inquiry, but its
findings are similar to those of an earlier investigation conducted by the Bureau of
Corporations. The bureau collected data on costs of production for the steel industry as a whole for the years 1902-6 and for the United States Steel Corporation
alone for the year 1910. According to the bureau, production costs did not change
significantly from 1902-6 to 1910, and so it is possible to compare these two sets of
figures. To give one example, for the years 1902-6 the average cost of producing
large Bessemer billets for the steel industry as a whole (including U.S. Steel) was
$16.80. For U.S. Steel alone, in 1910, the cost was $14.35. Unfortunately, it is
impossible to break down this comparison further because the bureau was careful
to protect the identity of the firms involved, and it destroyed (or returned to the
firms) all the documents it had collected. U.S. Commissioner of Corporations,
Report on the Steel Industry, Part 3, Cost of Production (Washington, D.C.: U.S.
Government Printing Office, 1913), pp. 320, 483.

Closer examination shows that much of U.S. Steel's advantage stemmed from lower raw-material costs. In fact, on the average, 73 percent of the differential in cost between U.S. Steel and the independent firms in wire-rod production, 86 percent in sheet-bar production, 44 percent in black-plate production (excluding one independent, whose advantage also derived from low raw-material costs), and 82 percent in open-hearth rails were accounted for by differences in costs of one basic raw material: steel.[51] Because U.S. Steel was the most fully integrated enterprise in the industry (it possessed vast iron-ore and coking-coal deposits, a transportation network to deliver these minerals to its plants, and mills for each stage of the process of converting raw ore to finished steel), we must ask whether this advantage in cost resulted primarily from economies of vertical integration or whether it derived from ownership of desirable raw material deposits.

It is unlikely that, by this period, vertical integration made possible any new savings in the production process itself. Certainly, substantial economies had derived from connecting pig-iron smelting with crude-steel manufacture,[52] but this degree of integration had generally been achieved by the industry long before formation of the United States Steel Corporation. There is no evidence that additional production economies resulted from further integration backward into ore mining; in fact, steel firms typically managed their ore holdings as separate businesses or even contracted out the management to

---

[51] The FTC figures understate U.S. Steel's advantage in raw materials because the corporation's cost figures included profits paid to subsidiary companies. According to the calculations of the Bureau of Corporations, these amounted to approximately $3.50 to $5.00 per ton of steel. It should be mentioned that differences in accounting practices and in the mix of products might have affected the rankings. Also, during the war, the disruption of shipping raised the cost of raw materials for those of U.S. Steel's integrated competitors who imported iron ore from Latin America. In the case of black plate, much of the differential above raw-material costs is attributable to some firms' specialization in high-grade roofing plates. *Ibid.*, p. 482; U.S. Federal Trade Commission, *War-Time Profits and Costs of the Steel Industry* (Washington, D.C.: U.S. Government Printing Office, 1925), pp. 28-43.

[52] Molten iron from the blast furnaces could be converted into steel and rolled into billets or rails without reheating. This saved $1.00 to $1.25 per ton of steel in the first decade of the twentieth century. U.S. Congress, House, *Tariff Hearings before the Committee on Ways and Means, 1908-1909*, 60th Cong., 2d Sess., 1909, Doc. 1505, pp. 1574-6; U.S. Congress, House, *Investigation of United States Steel Corporation*, Vol. VII, pp. 5100-01.

independent mining companies.[53] Nor is there any evidence of production economies from linking crude-steel and finished-steel operations. Billets were allowed to cool before they were rolled into products such as black plate for tinning. Often they were shipped for finishing to rolling mills long distances away.[54]

There were two possible motivations for vertical integration beyond the stages in which production economies could be achieved: (1) the drive to reduce uncertainty and assure the firm a ready source of raw materials (backward integration) and a ready outlet for its products (forward integration), so as to capture economies of speed, and (2) the desire to secure monopoly power and erect barriers to new competition.[55] Although the first motive undoubtedly affected U.S. Steel's officers, there is considerable evidence that the corporation's acquisition of ore lands was part of a complex strategy of market control. The elements of the plan have been amply documented in the literature.[56] At the time of its formation, U.S. Steel acquired, along with its constituent firms, massive iron-ore deposits in the Lake Superior region – the source of most of the ore used by the country's steel mills. Over the next few years U.S. Steel added greatly to its holdings, both through the purchase or lease of individual mining properties and the acquisition of steel firms with extensive

---

[53] Richard B. Mancke, "Iron and Steel: A Case Study of the Economic Causes and Consequences of Vertical Integration," *Journal of Industrial Economics*, XX (July 1972), p. 228.
[54] James W. McKie, *Tin Cans and Tin Plate: A Study of Competition in Two Related Markets* (Cambridge: Harvard University Press, 1959), p. 51.
[55] S. R. Dennison argued for the primacy of the first in "Vertical Integration and the Iron and Steel Industry," *Economic Journal*, XLIX (June 1939), p. 255. The second was the thesis of Donald O. Parsons and Edward John Ray in "The United States Steel Consolidation: The Creation of Market Control," *Journal of Law and Economics*, XV3 (April 1975), pp. 181-219. This latter explanation was discounted by Richard B. Mancke, who argued that ore properties fell in value in the late 1890s and that steel manufacturers acquired them simply because they recognized a good bargain. But Mancke dealt only with the period before the formation of U.S. Steel, and, as we shall see, there is substantial evidence for the market-control thesis after 1901. Mancke, "Iron and Steel," pp. 228-9.
[56] For a recent account, see Parsons and Ray, "The United States Steel Corporation." For full documentation, see U.S. Commissioner of Corporations, *Report on the Steel Industry, Part I, Organization, Investment, Profits, and Position of the United States Steel Corporation* (Washington, D.C.: U.S. Government Printing Office, 1911), pp. 259-63, 377-82; U.S. Congress, House, *Investigation of United States Steel Corporation*, Vol. VII, "Report," pp. 72-84.

ore resources. It was the avowed purpose of the corporation's officers to buy up everything "that is good, that is best, that is first class" in the region.[57] Other major steel producers were forced to follow suit, and by mid-decade most of the then commercially exploitable ore lands had been taken up. U.S. Steel held more than 50 percent of the ore in the ground; another 20 percent or so was in the possession of other big steel firms; most of the rest was controlled by James J. Hill, a railroad magnate, who had acquired the property in order to guarantee his Lake Superior district railroad an adequate tonnage. In 1906, U.S. Steel capped its string of purchases by leasing the Hill properties. The monopolistic intent of the corporation's action was clear, for the terms Hill extracted were onerous. Hill obligated U.S. Steel to mine a certain minimum tonnage annually (the amount increasing yearly over the next ten years), to ship this over his Great Northern Railroad, and to pay a royalty on the ore substantially in excess of the usual rate.[58]

By 1907, then, U.S. Steel controlled 70-75 percent of the iron ore in the Lake Superior region. These holdings enabled the corporation effectively to prevent the emergence of new, fully integrated competitors and to limit the expansion of existing rivals. As Charles M. Schwab testified before a congressional committee investigating the steel industry, "I do not believe there will be any great development in iron and steel by new companies, but rather development by the companies now in the business . . . For the reason that the possibility of a new company getting a sufficiently large supply of raw materials would make it exceedingly difficult if not impossible."[59] Events

---

[57] This statement by Judge Elbert H. Gary, chairman of U.S. Steel, is found in the minutes of the corporation's Executive Committee. *Ibid.*, p. 78.

[58] For the details of this arrangement, see *Iron Age*, October 11, 1906, pp. 950-1, 953-4; U.S. Commissioner of Corporations, *Report on the Steel Industry*, Part I, pp. 260-3. U.S. Steel paid above-market prices for other ore lands as well. See, for example, the Bureau of Corporations' analysis of U.S. Steel's acquisition of the Sharon and Donora mining properties, *ibid.*, pp. 282-6.

U.S. Steel's control of iron-ore resources was furthered by its ownership of two of the three railroads that served the Mesabi Range (the third was a branch of Hill's Great Northern Railroad). The Bureau of Corporations found that the freight rates U.S. Steel charged were excessive; the ratio of operating expenses to gross earnings was 36.5 percent for one of the roads and less than 30 percent for the other, as compared with an average of 66 percent for all U.S. railroads. U.S. Commissioner of Corporations, *Report on the Steel Industry*, Pt. I, pp. 374-7.

[59] U.S. Congress, House, *Investigation of United States Steel Corporation*, Vol II, p. 1291.

proved Schwab correct. As Gertrude Schroeder's study of the twenti-
eth-century steel industry shows, there was little new entrance from
that time on. Virtually all the firms that rose to prominence in the
next fifty years were mergers or reorganizations of existing concerns – concerns that already had acquired ore resources.[60]

Control of ore resources also helped U.S. Steel limit the entry of
less vertically integrated competitors, for independents that did not
have their own raw-material sources could be squeezed between rising costs and falling prices for their output. Throughout the first
decade of the twentieth century, U.S. Steel set prices so as to raise the
cost of crude steel relative to finished products and, more important
(because high steel prices might stimulate the entry of additional
capacity), the cost of iron ore relative to steel (Figure 5.5).[61] Moreover, U.S. Steel's periodic price cuts heightened both the squeeze and
the independents' uncertainty about raw-material supplies. For example, at the same time that U.S. Steel slashed prices on its finished
products in late 1902, the crude-steel market was booming. The
result, as *Iron Age* observed, was "that those interests in the iron and
steel industry not self contained – those not having recourse to resources within their own control for obtaining raw materials – have
suffered from the narrow margin between raw materials and the
finished products, not only reducing the profit, but in some instances
even entailing a loss."[62] For independent tin-plate and sheet producers, the squeeze was so serious that they began negotiating a plan
to pool their resources and construct a steel plant. According to *Iron*

[60] Gertrude G. Schroeder, *The Growth of Major Steel Companies, 1900-1950* (Baltimore: Johns Hopkins Press, 1953). When the federal government filed its dissolution suit against U.S. Steel, the corporation canceled the Hill lease, opening up
additional Lake Superior ore lands to its competitors. Some rivals also tapped ore
resources in the South and West and in Canada and Latin America, though the
location of these ores put firms that used them at a disadvantage in main American
markets. U.S. Steel attempted to limit access to these sources of ore as well by
buying up property. Its most important acquisition in outlying areas was the Tennessee Coal, Iron, and Railroad Company in 1907.
[61] The spread of open-hearth steel production reduced U.S. Steel's power somewhat,
for open-hearth furnaces (unlike Bessemer converters) could use a mixture of scrap
and ore. But, as F. M. Scherer has shown, if there are two inputs that are at least to
some extent substitutable, and if the price of one is raised above the competitive
level, producers will be forced to use a suboptimal combination of resources. *Industrial Market Structure and Economic Performance*, p. 302.
[62] *Iron Age*, January 1, 1903, p. 38.

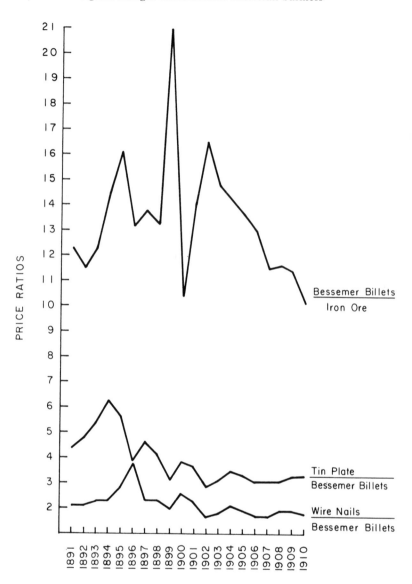

Figure 5.5. Price ratios for steel outputs and inputs, 1891–1910. Data from AISA, *Statistics of the Iron Trades,* 1896, p. 89; 1902, p. 33; 1910, p. 50; *Iron Age,* January 4, 1900, p. 61; U.S. Congress, House, *Investigation of U.S. Steel,* Vol. VII, pp. 5555, 5562; Parsons and Ray, "The United States Steel Consolidation," p. 197.

Age, "The relative high prices of sheet and tin plate bars, together with the recent reduction in prices of tin plates and sheets, have put the independent manufacturers in the position that some action to protect their interests has become imperative."[63]

The vise in which the independent manufacturers found themselves caught was not simply an accident of market forces but the result of conscious policy by U.S. Steel. In the words of the not unsympathetic *Iron Age,* U.S. Steel aimed "to forestall competition by holding up prices on raw materials and forcing down prices on finished products."[64] In late 1902, just about the time U.S. Steel cut its prices on finished-steel commodities, the corporation announced that it would no longer sell raw materials to firms with which it competed – a move calculated to increase the market prices of these materials. This policy was later modified to allow subsidiaries to sell surplus billets to independents, but even then the corporation sold billets only at a price that would give its own finishing mills a substantial advantage in costs.[65]

By buying up raw-material resources, raising the price of iron ore relative to steel, and creating uncertainty in the pig-iron and billet markets, U.S. Steel was able to choke off new entry at the same time that it earned handsome profits. After deductions from net earnings for depreciation and replacement allowances, sinking funds, and a 7 percent dividend on its preferred stock, U.S. Steel earned, on the average, 9.1 percent per year from 1902 to 1910 on its approximately $500 million of common stock – earnings that were all the more striking in light of the Bureau of Corporations' conclusion that all of U.S. Steel's common stock represented water.[66] Yet whereas investment had rushed into the industry in the period before 1901, in

---

[63] *Ibid.,* p. 92. See also *Metal Worker,* January 3, 1903, p. 54; January 10, 1903, p. 38; January 31, 1903, p. 50.

[64] *Iron Age,* January 7, 1904, pp. 92, 97.

[65] *Ibid.,* January 1, 1903, p. 43; U.S. Congress, House, *Investigation of United States Steel Corporation,* Vol. VI, pp. 3857, 3938, 4059, Vol. VII, "Report," pp. 107-9. The annual summaries of pig-iron market reports, published in *Iron Age* each January, show that U.S. Steel and other major steel producers also intervened on occasion in pig-iron markets to support prices. On this point, see also U.S. Congress, House, *Investigation of United States Steel Corporation,* Vol. VII, "Report," pp. 97-100.

[66] *Ibid.,* Vol. V, pp. 3517-41; U.S. Commissioner of Corporations, *Report on the Steel Industry,* Pt. I, p. 37.

Table 5.2. *Changes in numbers and capacities of independent tin-plate firms*

	1898–1901	1901–4	1904–7
Number of new firms (firms listed as producing tin plate in the last year but not in the first)	7	8	1[a]
Capacity of new firms	55,620[b]	47,500[b]	11,000[b]
Number of firms that disappeared (firms listed as producing tin plate in the first but not in the last year, including those that merged into U.S. Steel)	0	2	3
Capacity of firms that disappeared	0[b]	21,880[b]	7,900[b]
Net changes in capacity of firms listed in first and last years	+600[b]	+680[b]	+10,300[b]
Total capacity of independent firms in last year	63,100[b]	89,400[b]	102,800[b]
Capacity of U.S. Steel in last year	220,900[b]	232,100[b]	265,800[b]

[a]This was not a new mill, but the acquisition of a mill built in 1902 that failed while in the process of starting up.
[b]Boxes of tin plate per week.
Source: AISA *Directory,* 1898, 1901, 1904, 1908.

the years that followed, the pace of entry slowed, and after a time virtually halted. In the tin-plate branch of the industry, four independent rolling-mill enterprises were completed in 1902, three in 1903, and two in 1904. Between 1904 and 1908, no new independent works were constructed (Table 5.2). In wire (Table 5.3), only two enterprises came into production in 1902, one in 1903, and two (one small and one medium-size works) in 1906. In both the tin-plate and wire industries, moreover, many of the mills that had been under construction when U.S. Steel was formed were never completed, and other enterprises ran into financial difficulties. Plans for a huge wire-rod works in New Castle, Pennsylvania, were abandoned. Two independent rod-rolling firms went bankrupt, five disappeared from the

Table 5.3. *Changes in numbers and capacities of independent wire-rod firms*

	1898–1901	1901–4	1904–7
Number of new firms (firms listed as producing wire rods in the last year but not in the first)	14	3	2
Capacity of new firms	1,000,000[a]	465,000[a]	115,000[a]
Number of firms that disappeared (firms listed as producing rods in the first but not the last year, including those that merged into U.S. Steel)	4	6	2
Capacity of firms that disappeared	63,500[a]	540,000[a]	43,000[a]
Net changes in the capacity of firms listed in first and last years	+11,000[a]	+30,000[a]	−43,000[a]
Total capacity of independent firms in last year	1,074,350[a]	1,029,350[a]	1,000,350[a]
Capacity of U.S. Steel in last year	1,510,000[a]	1,688,000[a]	1,725,000[a]

[a]Gross tons per year.
Source: AISA *Directory*, 1898, 1901, 1904, 1908.

list of rod producers, and another converted one of its two rod mills to bar production. In tin plate, four enterprises were never completed, four disappeared from the ranks of tin-plate manufacturers, and one mill went bankrupt and was later put into operation under new ownership. Of the remaining firms, U.S. Steel absorbed three wire-rod and two tin-plate enterprises, including the mills of its two most formidable rivals: the Union and Sharon steel companies.[67]

[67] Just before the organization of U.S. Steel, the American Tin Plate Company absorbed the Champion Tin Plate Company (capacity 5,500 boxes of tin plate per week) and contracted for the entire output of the Sharon Tin Plate Company (capacity 20,400 boxes). In late 1902, the Sharon and Union Steel companies agreed to a merger. The new concern, fully integrated from iron ore to finished

The effect of this retardation in entry can be seen in the statistics of U.S. Steel's share of total production. In 1901, the Steel Corporation produced 77.7 percent of the nation's output of wire rods. By 1902 its share had fallen to 71.6 percent, but it remained at about that level from 1902 through 1908, climbing as high as 73.1 percent and never falling below 67.9 percent. The corporation's share of wire-nail production declined from 68.1 percent in 1901 to 64.8 percent in 1902, but the combine regained lost ground, and between 1903 and 1908 it produced, on the average, 68.2 percent of the country's wire nails. In tin plate, the corporation held its own after an initial drop. Though its proportion of output fell as low as 71.4 percent by 1902, for the next six years it remained at or above that level, on one occasion going as high as 76.4 percent.[68]

The problem of barriers to entry

As the examples of the steel and paper industries have shown, by pursuing the dominant-firm strategy a consolidation could remove all incentive for price cutting by its rivals. Moreover, by occasionally instigating price warfare itself, a consolidation could discipline its competitors and teach them to shoulder some of the burden of curtailment during depressions. These were significant powers. But in the

product, was immediately acquired by U.S. Steel. Its rod capacity was 325,000 gross tons per year. The corporation also acquired the Trenton Iron Company (rod capacity 18,000 gross tons per year). AISA, *Directory*, 1901, 1904, 1908; *Iron Age*, January 17, 1901, p. 19; January 31, 1901, p. 19; February 14, 1901, p. 31; November 27, 1902, pp. 26-7; December 8, 1902, pp. 49-50; January 7, 1904, p. 87; December 8, 1904, p. 37; July 26, 1906, p. 232; *Metal Worker*, January 12, 1901, p. 43; December 12, 1903, p. 42; December 10, 1904, p. 58; April 15, 1905, p. 59; September 29, 1906, pp. 66-7; U.S. Commissioner of Corporations, *Report on the Steel Industry*, Part I, pp. 252-6.

[68] U.S. Congress, House, *Investigation of United States Steel Corporation*, Vol. I, pp. 222-4. Over the next ten years, U.S. Steel's market shares began to drop as fear of antitrust prosecution caused the corporation to relinquish the Hill ore lease and to allow its proportion of sales to fall toward a politically safer 50 percent. The slip in U.S. Steel's market share did not make the industry more competitive, however. The steel industry remained the province of a few large, vertically integrated firms, secure in their dominance of the nation's ore resources. Not until recently has this tight oligopoly been challenged.

absence of barriers to entry, these powers could be preserved over the long run only if the dominant firm possessed an advantage in costs.

In the majority of cases, consolidations probably were no more efficient than their rivals. Therefore, they did not pose any long-term threat to the competitive structure of the American economy – so long (and here is the rub) as no barriers to entry were permitted to be erected. In practice, however, the managers of a dominant firm recognized that they could both maintain their market share and set prices above the limit value if they could remove the threat of future competition. U.S. Steel was a case in point. Under the guidance of Judge Gary, the Steel Corporation adopted a successful policy of forestalling entry by limiting access to vital raw materials. In this manner it managed both to protect its market share and to earn handsome profits.

But to what extent can we generalize from the U.S. Steel example? To what extent were the successes of other combines attributable less to superior efficiency than to artificial barriers to new competition? In *The Visible Hand*, Alfred D. Chandler, Jr., suggests that U.S. Steel's experience was not representative. True, he admits, successful consolidations tended to be vertically integrated. True, they erected barriers to entry. But, he argues (and this is the crucial point), the height of these barriers was a function of a consolidation's relative efficiency. According to Chandler, the real advantage of vertical integration, backward and forward, was the opportunity it offered manufacturers in industries that were characterized by economies of speed. So long as combines developed the appropriate management structures, vertical integration enabled them better to regulate the flow of output from raw material to buyer, increase the volume of production, capture economies of speed, and thereby place themselves in a superior competitive position. Only by completely duplicating the combine's vertically integrated structure could competitors obtain a foothold in the industry. But, of course, the enormous amount of capital this duplication required constituted a powerful discouragement to new competition.[69]

[69] Alfred D. Chandler, Jr., *The Visible Hand: The Managerial Revolution in American Business* (Cambridge: Harvard University Press, 1977), pp. 315-44.

In the absence of data on relative costs, Chandler provides two types of evidence for his thesis. The first consists of case studies. Thus, Chandler uses the example of the National Biscuit Company to show how consolidations achieved success. A merger of three regional consolidations, Nabisco at first copied the policies of its predecessors and concentrated on destroying or buying out competitors. Quickly, however, the firm's officers shifted strategy. According to their 1901 annual report,

Experience soon proved to us that, instead of bringing success, either of these courses, if persevered in, must bring disaster. This led us to reflect whether it was necessary to control competition . . . We soon satisfied ourselves that within the company itself we must look for success.
We turned our attention and bent our energies to improving the internal management of our own business, to getting the full benefit from purchasing our raw materials in large quantities, to economizing the expense of manufacture, to systematizing and rendering more effective our selling department, and above all things and before all things, to improving the quality of our goods and the condition in which they should reach the consumer.[70]

After 1900, Nabisco centralized production in a few large plants, advertised to differentiate its products, and built global marketing and purchasing organizations. By looking "within the company itself," according to Chandler, Nabisco reduced unit costs and simultaneously erected barriers to new competition.[71]

Chandler's second type of evidence is quantitative. He used the list of successful and unsuccessful consolidations compiled by Livermore, broke it down by industrial categories, and added data on the degrees of vertical integration achieved by the combinations. The results seemed to confirm Chandler's thesis: Successful mergers were most numerous in industries characterized by economies of speed. Furthermore, most of the successful mergers were vertically integrated.[72]

There are, however, two problems with this analysis. First, Chandler did not systematically collect data on vertical integration for consolidations that failed. Therefore, it is impossible to conclude from his data that successful consolidations differed from the unsuc-

[70] *Ibid.*, p. 335.
[71] *Ibid.*
[72] *Ibid.*, pp. 337-44.

cessful in their degree of vertical integration.[73] Second, even if vertical integration was responsible for their success, we do not know why. Did integration result in the superior efficiency Chandler claims? Or did it close off opportunities for newcomers?

Although a full resolution of these issues is beyond the scope of this study, it should be noted that abundant documentation exists to show that consolidations – successful and unsuccessful alike – made attempts to protect their positions by securing monopoly control over a resource or market. Like U.S. Steel, some sought to limit competitors' access to raw materials. In the newsprint industry, for instance, International Paper attempted to buy up large tracts of woodlands in order to support the price of its product. Similarly, in nonferrous metals, dominant firms such as American Smelting & Refining and Anaconda Copper gradually gained control of vital ore deposits. Where raw materials or the threat of new competition were likely to come from abroad, combines such as American Linseed and the International Paper Company agitated for tariff barriers. Where the problem was closer to home, others made deals with buyers or suppliers to prevent them from conducting business with competitors. The American Sugar Refining Company, for example, offered rebates to grocers who promised not to market rivals' sugar. Similarly, National Cordage and the American Tin Plate Company contracted to buy up all the output of machinery manufacturers, on condition that they would not equip competitors. And United Shoe Machinery structured its leasing agreements so that shoe manufacturers had to rent an entire line of machinery from the combine.[74]

[73] Actually, it is impossible to conclude anything about the degree of vertical integration. Chandler distinguished only between those consolidations that confined themselves to manufacturing and those that had their own branch sales offices and/or their own purchasing organizations and/or controlled sources of raw or semifinished materials. *Ibid.*, p. 337.

[74] U.S. Industrial Commission, *Report on Trusts and Industrial Combinations*, pp. 410-1, 416, 422-3; David C. Smith, *History of Papermaking in the United States (1691-1969)* (New York: Lockwood Publishing, 1970), pp. 170, 185; Joe S. Bain, *Barriers to New Competition: Their Character and Consequences in Manufacturing Industries* (Cambridge: Harvard University Press, 1956), pp. 154-5; James E. Fell, Jr., *Ores to Metals: The Rocky Mountain Smelting Industry* (Lincoln: University of Nebraska Press, 1979), pp. 225-54; Whitney Eastman, *The History of the Linseed Oil Industry in the United States* (Minneapolis: T. S. Denison & Co., 1968), pp. 173-6; Ellis, "Print Paper Pendulum;" Eichner, *The Emergence of Oligopoly*, pp. 188-95; Richard O. Zerbe, "Monopoly, the Emergence of Oligopoly and the Case

Consolidations experimented with a variety of additional ways of forestalling competition. Extraction of rebates from railroads was the main device the American Sugar Refining Company employed to put rivals at a disadvantage. Others attempted to restrict competitors' access to managerial expertise or skilled labor. When United States Rubber and the Distilling and Cattle Feeding Company acquired firms, they often paid the proprietors to stay out of the business. American Window Glass contracted with the glass-workers union to assure itself a supply of skilled workers. In exchange for a block of window-company stock (par value $0.5 million), the union guaranteed the company (and not its rivals) an adequate supply of scarce skilled labor.[75]

Of course, patents were an important means of restricting competition. For the General Electric Company, they were the primary weapon in the struggle against Westinghouse. Later the two electrical giants pooled their patents and used their control of technology to enforce stable oligopolistic behavior in the industry. Other large firms, such as American Telephone and Telegraph, financed scientific research in order to protect their product lines. By obtaining critical patents, they could prevent substitute goods from being developed.[76]

of Sugar Refining," *Journal of Law and Economics*, XIII (October 1970), p. 512; U.S. Industrial Commission, *Preliminary Report on Trusts and Industrial Combinations*, "Testimony," pp. 852, 875, 888-90; Richard Roe, "The United Shoe Machinery Company," *Journal of Political Economy*, XXI (December 1913), pp. 938-53, and XXII (January 1914), pp. 43-63.

[75] In "Monopoly, the Emergence of Oligopoly and the Case of Sugar Refining" (p. 511), Richard O. Zerbe discounts the importance of railroad rebates to American Sugar, but he presents very little evidence for his claim. See also his "The American Sugar Refinery Company, 1887-1914: The Story of a Monopoly," *Journal of Law and Economics*, XII (October 1969), p. 369. Eichner, *The Emergence of Oligopoly*, pp. 188, 276; Glenn D. Babcock, *History of the United States Rubber Company: A Case Study in Corporate Management* (Bloomington: Indiana University Graduate School of Business, 1966), p. 39; U.S. Industrial Commission, *Preliminary Report on Trusts and Industrial Consolidations*, "Digest of Evidence," pp. 81-4; Pearce Davis, *The Development of the American Glass Industry* (New York: Russell & Russell-Atheneum, 1970), pp. 175-80.

[76] Harold C. Passer, *The Electrical Manufacturers, 1875-1900: A Study in Competition, Entrepreneurship, Technical Change, and Economic Growth* (Cambridge: Harvard University Press, 1953), pp. 321-34; Leonard S. Reich, "Research, Patents, and the Struggle to Control Radio: A Study of Big Business and the Uses of Industrial Research," *Business History Review*, LI (Summer 1977), pp. 208-35; Reich, "Industrial Research and the Pursuit of Corporate Stability: The Early Years of Bell Labs," *Business History Review*, LIV (Winter 1980), pp. 504-29; David F. Noble, *America by Design: Science, Technology, and the Rise of Corporate Capitalism* (Oxford University Press, 1977), pp. 84-109.

Slander was still another means of protecting one's goods from substitutes. Thus, the Royal Baking Powder Company, whose product was manufactured from cream of tartar and soda, widely broadcast its claim that competitors' alum-based powder was poisonous. Similar, though more positive, was the use of advertising to differentiate one's products and promote one's brands. Nabisco, Quaker Oats, American Tobacco, and other large-scale producers of consumer goods funded massive advertising campaigns in the early twentieth century, making it difficult for rivals with smaller financial resources to compete and for new firms to enter the market.[77]

Obviously, some of the devices consolidations employed to restrict competition were doomed to failure from the very beginning. The woodlands of North America were simply too vast for the International Paper Company to control. Likewise, unless protected by patents, contracts to monopolize the output of machinery makers would only stimulate the entry of new producers. But the prevalence of such attempts, whether successful or not, suggests that the consolidations' officers were far less certain about the advantages of vertical integration than Chandler was. Unwilling to trust their company's fate to market forces alone, they experimented with a whole arsenal of anticompetitive weapons with the aim of blocking entry and protecting their positions of dominance.

In the case of many of these weapons, moreover, success or failure depended more than anything else on government policy. This is easy to see in the case of tariffs and patents, but it was also true for many of the other devices described earlier. For example, early federal legislation made extraction of rebates from railroads illegal, and the American Sugar Refining Company was prosecuted and convicted for defying the law. Similarly, tying contracts (agreements that restricted the freedom of buyers and suppliers to deal with competitors) were early ruled illegal. Yet at the same time, vertical integration, which often accomplished precisely the same end, was not. In fact, President Theodore Roosevelt personally approved U.S. Steel's

[77] U.S. Industrial Commission, *Report on Trusts and Industrial Combinations*, pp. lxxxii-iv; Chandler, *The Visible Hand*, pp. 290-9, 334-5; Arthur F. Marquette, *Brands, Trademarks and Good Will: The Story of the Quaker Oats Company* (New York: McGraw-Hill, 1967), pp. 15-83.

acquisition of the Tennessee Coal, Iron and Railroad Company during the Panic of 1907. This purchase, ostensibly a move to shore up a prominent financial house, gave U.S. Steel possession of vast iron-ore reserves in the South. Although this purchase and the Steel Corporation's ore holdings in general were the subject of repeated investigations, nothing ever came of them, and the U.S. Supreme Court ultimately declined to find the consolidation in restraint of trade.[78]

The important point is that most consolidations were unlikely to maintain their dominance over the long run unless they erected barriers to entry, and federal antitrust policy should have been directed toward preventing this from occurring – so long, at least, as the means was not superior efficiency. But the government's response to the great merger movement was a hodgepodge of policies that, as the example of the steel industry indicates, sometimes hindered the combines' efforts, sometimes helped them. The next chapter will explore the reasons why and will then return to the issue of the consolidations' relative efficiencies.

[78] Eichner, *The Emergence of Oligopoly*, pp. 276-82; Robert H. Bork, *The Antitrust Paradox: A Policy at War with Itself* (New York: Basic Books, 1978), pp. 15-49; Gabriel Kolko, *The Triumph of Conservatism: A Reinterpretation of American History, 1900-1916* (Chicago: Quadrangle Paperbacks, 1967), pp. 113-22.

6. The great merger movement and antitrust policy

To a people preternaturally sensitive to the dangers of monopoly, the great merger movement came as a shock. Americans had watched with foreboding the formation of Standard Oil, the first "trust," and with increasing anxiety the imitations that Standard's success spawned in industries as diverse as sugar refining and lead processing. Then, as the merger movement crested, with hundreds of firms vanishing suddenly into horizontal consolidations, it seemed as if the United States had been transformed overnight from a nation of freely competing, individually owned enterprises into a nation dominated by a small number of giant corporations. Very quickly Americans thought they saw their worst fears about such domination confirmed, as consolidations jacked up prices and at the same time moved to secure their monopoly positions by extracting rebates from railroads and restricting competitors' access to raw materials and markets.

As the public outcry mounted, politicians launched investigations at many different levels and in several branches of government. President Theodore Roosevelt resuscitated the Sherman Antitrust Act with his successful prosecution of the Northern Securities holding company in 1904. He and his successor, William Howard Taft, initiated a series of dissolution suits against major consolidations, including Standard Oil, U.S. Steel, and the American Tobacco Company. Finally, under the administration of Woodrow Wilson, Congress supplemented and strengthened the Sherman Act with the passage of the Federal Trade Commission Act and Clayton Antitrust Act in 1914.

Prompt federal action seems to have helped assuage the public's fear and outrage.[1] But whether or not it also protected the competitive structure of American industry has recently been the subject of much debate. To Gabriel Kolko and other "New Left" historians, the reforms of the so-called Progressive period actually represented the

[1] Louis Galambos, *The Public Image of Big Business in America, 1880-1940: A Quantitative Study in Social Change* (Baltimore: Johns Hopkins Press, 1975), pp. 79-114.

"triumph of conservatism." Faced with growing competition, the officers of consolidations had actively sought federal regulation as a means of stabilizing their markets and protecting their positions of dominance. And federal officials had obliged. Dazzled by the equation of bigness and efficiency, sharing business's distaste for "wasteful" competition, they were never much interested in breaking up consolidations. According to Kolko, the trust-busting rhetoric of Roosevelt and other federal officials was insincere, and the few prosecutions they undertook, even when successful, did little to alter the concentration of control in American industry. Rather, most government regulation actually worked in the opposite direction, engineered as it was by, for, and in the interest of the nation's largest corporations.[2]

Since Kolko first published *The Triumph of Conservatism* in 1963, antitrust policy has also come under attack from the right – from legal analysts trained in neoclassical economic theory. Like Kolko, scholars such as Robert H. Bork perceive an enormous gap between the rhetoric and reality of federal policy; however, they disagree with Kolko about why this gap occurred. Rather than questioning the sincerity of public officials, they explain the failure of antitrust policy in terms of the diverse, mutually incompatible legal traditions on which it was based and the confused economic reasoning of the federal judiciary. The result was a policy "at war with itself," an economically irrational set of rules that, in Bork's words, "significantly impair[ed] both competition and the ability of the economy to produce goods and services efficiently."[3]

The key to resolving this debate over federal antitrust policy is the concept of barriers to entry. Most of the consolidations formed dur-

[2] Gabriel Kolko, *The Triumph of Conservatism: A Reinterpretation of American History, 1900-1916* (Chicago: Quadrangle Paperbacks, 1967).
[3] Robert H. Bork, *The Antitrust Paradox: A Policy at War with Itself* (New York: Basic Books, 1978), pp. 4-7, 15-49. See also Richard A. Posner, *Antitrust Law: An Economic Perspective* (University of Chicago Press, 1976); Alan Stone, *Economic Regulation and the Public Interest: The Federal Trade Commission in Theory and Practice* (Ithaca: Cornell University Press, 1977); Peter Temin, "Government and Industry in the Nineteenth Century," paper presented to the Lowell Conference on Industrial History, May 22, 1981. For articles for and against this school of thought, see Eleanor M. Fox and James T. Halverson, editors, *Industrial Concentration and the Market System: Legal, Economic, Social and Political Perspectives* (American Bar Association, 1979).

ing the great merger movement were unlikely to maintain their market power over the long run unless they were able to erect barriers to new competition. Many of the combines, as we have seen, attempted to do just that in the years immediately following their formation. Some of these attempts were doomed to failure from the very beginning, but others depended for their success or failure on government action or inaction, as the case might be. Hence, the key to an assessment of federal policy in this period is the extent to which the government prevented erection of barriers to entry.

At first glance, the government's record on barriers to entry seems oddly mixed. Certainly, federal officials moved quickly in the early twentieth century to proscribe certain "unfair practices" that blocked or retarded entry. But it also failed to curb other activities that had the same effect. For example, the courts ruled early on against tying contracts, agreements that restricted the freedom of buyers and suppliers to deal with competitors. Yet vertical integration, which sometimes accomplished precisely the same purpose, was much more ambiguously treated.

This was not because contemporaries failed to perceive any danger from vertical integration. Quite the contrary. One of the grounds on which the Supreme Court dissolved the American Tobacco Company in 1911 was its acquisition of control over the major part of the tinfoil and licorice produced in the United States. In the words of Justice Edward Douglass White,

We think the conclusion of wrongful purpose and illegal combination is overwhelmingly established by the following considerations: [among them by] the gradual absorption of control over all the elements essential to the successful manufacture of tobacco products, and placing such control in the hands of seemingly independent corporations serving as perpetual barriers to the entry of others into the tobacco trade.[4]

In the American Tobacco case, the Court punished the consolidation for its drive to control the production of tinfoil and licorice, materials that were of secondary importance in the manufacture of tobacco goods and of which no permanent monopoly was possible. By contrast, in dismissing the government's dissolution suit against

---

[4] *United States of America v. American Tobacco*, 221 US 182-3; see also pp. 168-71.

U.S. Steel, the Court discounted what we have seen was the much more serious threat to competition posed by the Steel Corporation's ownership of the best of the nation's iron-ore deposits.[5]

It is this differential treatment that serves as the focus for this chapter. The contradiction cannot, I argue, be accounted for by the influence that big business exerted on government officials (Kolko's theme), although this certainly occurred and undoubtedly affected policy. Nor can it be explained primarily, as Robert Bork would have it, by the contradictory lessons of common-law precedents and the bad economic reasoning of the federal judiciary, though these were admittedly factors too. Rather, the basic problem was structural. Its root was the division of power and authority between the states and the federal government at the turn of the century.

The structural problem

In their efforts to regulate business enterprises and enforce competition in the late nineteenth century, the states had two separate legal traditions on which they could draw. The first was the body of common-law decisions in which judges refused to sanction contracts or conspiracies in restraint of trade or with intent to monopolize. In the 1880s and early 1890s, in response to the spread of the trust and holding company devices, state legislatures passed a series of antitrust laws that codified these decisions in the form of prohibitions and attached criminal penalties to their violation. The second tradition that the states could draw on was their right to charter corporations. This latter heritage was by far the more powerful of the two, as it gave states the authority to determine the very conditions under which incorporated enterprises could do business – to restrict their freedom of contract. At various times and places, states used this power to limit the stock issues and indebtedness of corporations, to delineate the types of businesses in which firms could engage, and even to prohibit mergers. In fact, most antitrust cases initiated by states in the late nineteenth century were prosecuted on the grounds

---

[5] *United States v. United States Steel Corporation et al.*, 251 US 417-66; and 223 Fed 55-179.

that the corporations involved in consolidations had transgressed their charters, had acted *ultra vires*.[6]

The power to charter corporations could also be used to prevent the erection of barriers to entry. The state of Texas, for instance, in 1889 passed an antitrust law that forbade one corporation from owning stock in another. This statute, combined with a general incorporation law that confined firms chartered in the state to one particular line of business, effectively prohibited vertical integration. As Joseph A. Pratt has shown, the enforcement of these laws, however idiosyncratic, prevented the vertically integrated Standard Oil from dominating the Texas petroleum industry and encouraged the entry of new competition, including Gulf, Texaco, and Shell.[7]

The states' authority over corporate charters gave them the legal power to confront the turn-of-the-century consolidations. But their lack of economic power effectively divested this legal authority of any practical significance. With the exception of a few states such as Texas, which possessed vital raw-material resources, states were helpless in the face of corporations whose activities were national in scope. Multiplant giants could respond to prosecution by shifting responsibility for the offending behavior to offices outside the state, by obtaining a charter from a more friendly jurisdiction, or even by closing down their enterprises in the state. As a result, after a brief flurry of antitrust activity in the 1880s and 1890s, state initiatives waned, and the locus of policy shifted of necessity to the federal government.[8]

Yet when the federal government took over responsibility for regulating big business and safeguarding competition, it could draw on only one of the two legal traditions that the states possessed – and the weaker one at that. There was no federal incorporation law giving the national government the same authority as the states to deter-

[6] Charles W. McCurdy, "The *Knight* Sugar Decision of 1895 and the Modernization of American Corporate Law, 1869-1903," *Business History Review*, LIII (Autumn 1979), pp. 304-6, 314-23; Hans B. Thorelli, *The Federal Antitrust Policy: Origination of an American Tradition* (Baltimore: Johns Hopkins Press, 1955), pp. 36-50.
[7] Joseph A. Pratt, "The Petroleum Industry in Transition: Antitrust and the Decline of Monopoly Control in Oil," *Journal of Economic History*, XL (December 1980), pp. 815-37.
[8] McCurdy, "The *Knight* Sugar Decision of 1895," pp. 306-7, 336-40; Thorelli, *The Federal Antitrust Policy*, pp. 235-368.

mine the conditions under which consolidations could do business. All that federal regulators had to draw on were the common-law prohibitions against contracts and combinations "in restraint of trade" or "attempt[ing] to monopolize" that had been embodied in the Sherman Antitrust Act of 1890.[9]

As a result of this weaker legal heritage, it quickly became apparent that the federal government would be much more effective in dealing with combinations involving independent firms, rather than combinations in the form of single corporations, whatever their effect on competition. For example, in the first case prosecuted under the Sherman Act, *Jellico Mountain Coal,* the United States filed suit against a combination of coal-mine owners and coal dealers in Tennessee and Kentucky which, the government claimed, had conspired to raise the price of coal. A federal court found the Nashville Coal Exchange, as the combination was called, in violation of the Sherman Act. Because such "loose" combinations had, under the common law, traditionally been considered in restraint of trade, the case posed no difficulty.[10] The courts, however, were much more cautious in dealing with "tight" combinations, such as the holding companies sanctioned by the incorporation laws of New Jersey and several other states after 1888. The year following the *Jellico* decision, the government failed in several attempts to convince judges to sustain an indictment against the Distilling and Cattle Feeding Company (better known as the Whiskey Trust, but actually a corporation chartered by the state of Illinois). Three judges in three separate proceedings agreed that the corporation could not be held in violation of the Sherman Act simply by the fact of its existence – its size and market share – but only on the basis of evidence showing that its dominance had derived from illegal acts, from restraints it had imposed on the actions of other firms.[11]

That tight combinations were better dealt with by the states using their charter powers than by the federal government under the Sherman Act was explicitly articulated by the Supreme Court in 1895 in

[9] For the common-law origins of the Sherman Act, see William Letwin, *Law and Economic Policy in America: The Evolution of the Sherman Antitrust Act* (New York: Random House, 1965), pp. 18-99.
[10] *Ibid.,* pp. 106-7, 144-5.
[11] *Ibid.,* pp. 111-13, 145-50.

the *E. C. Knight* decision. The case involved a tight combination, the American Sugar Refining Company, a corporation chartered by the state of New Jersey. The government had filed suit under the Sherman Act to force the consolidation to divest itself of the E. C. Knight Company and three other Pennsylvania refineries that it had recently acquired. On the grounds that manufacturing was not commerce, the Supreme Court ruled that the acquisitions did not violate the Sherman Act, notwithstanding the fact that they gave the New Jersey firm a virtual monopoly of the nation's refining capacity. The Court's tortured distinction between manufacturing and commerce has commonly been viewed as an attempt to emasculate the antitrust law. But Charles W. McCurdy has recently reinterpreted the case. As McCurdy has shown, the decision constituted a recognition on the part of the Court that the most effective weapon against tight combinations was the states' charter powers. It also indicated a determination on the part of the Court to preserve the potency of that weapon. It was clear to the majority of justices that the Pennsylvania courts could deal with the *Knight* case as a simple problem in corporation law:

> All four firms that American Sugar had absorbed held Pennsylvania charters, and the laws of the commonwealth conferred no authority on its domestic firms to suscribe to the stock of foreign corporations. Since federal authorities had already collected evidence of the *ultra vires* transactions, the Fuller Court simply assumed that the Pennsylvania attorney general would proceed expeditiously with *quo warranto* suits to invalidate the consolidation.[12]

Furthermore, the majority realized that if the Supreme Court decided against the consolidation, accepting implicitly the Justice Department's argument that manufacturing for interstate distribution was interstate commerce, then states would lose their power to regulate such corporations. This was because the Court had held previously that Congress had the exclusive power to regulate interstate commerce and that, even if Congress did not exercise its power, the states could not fill the gap.[13] In other words, a decision against the American Sugar Refining Company would have fatally weakened the

[12] McCurdy, "The *Knight* Sugar Decision of 1895," pp. 334-5.
[13] *Ibid.*, pp. 328-36. *United States v. E. C. Knight Company*, 156 US 11-12.

states' charter powers, and that the majority of the Court was unwilling to do. In the words of Chief Justice Melville W. Fuller,

> It is vital that the independence of the commercial power and of the police
> power, and the delimitation between them, however sometimes perplexing,
> should always be recognized and observed . . . [A]cknowledged evils, how-
> ever grave and urgent they may appear to be, had better be borne, than the
> risk be run, in the effort to suppress them, of more serious consequences by
> resort to expedients of even doubtful constitutionality.[14]

The Court returned responsibility for oversight of large corporations to the states, but events were not to permit matters to rest
there. The years following the *Knight* decision witnessed the greatest
consolidation movement in the nation's history, and most states
proved economically impotent against the new, giant corporations
operating in national and even world markets. Spurred by a mount-
ing public outcry, the federal government was forced once again to
take up the challenge. In 1902, Roosevelt filed an antitrust suit
against the Northern Securities Company, a holding company
formed to control the Great Northern and Northern Pacific railroads. Pursued with great fanfare by Roosevelt's attorney general,
Philander C. Knox, the case marked the first successful prosecution
of a tight combination under the Sherman Act. In this respect the
Northern Securities decision was a breakthrough, but it was a breakthrough that left unresolved the fundamental issue of the federal
government's power over state-chartered corporations.

The lower court decided the *Northern Securities* case as if it were a
simple extension of the precedents established in a series of earlier
decisions: *United States v. Trans-Missouri Freight Ass'n.* (1897),
United States v. Joint Traffic Ass'n. (1898), and *United States v.
Addyston Pipe & Steel* (1898 and 1899). In those decisions, all of
which involved loose combinations, the Supreme Court had interpreted the Sherman Act literally, as prohibiting every direct restraint of
trade, whether unreasonable or not. In the *Northern Securities* case
this literal interpretation was taken one step further. The railroads,
the court decided, would have violated the Sherman Act if, instead of
creating the Northern Securities holding company, they had trans-

[14] *Ibid.,* p. 13.

ferred control of their business to an association or to an individual. The holding company was simply a more effective way of achieving the same end. Therefore, it, too, had to be considered an illegal combination under the Sherman Act.[15]

This logical extension of precedent was endorsed by the Supreme Court in Justice Harlan's opinion representing four of the five justices in the majority. But literal application of the Sherman Act to tight combinations posed problems that found expression in the dissenting opinions of Justices White and Holmes.[16] There was, as Justice White reminded the Court, an important constitutional issue still to be resolved. In a point reminiscent of Fuller's distinction between commerce and manufacturing in the *E. C. Knight* case, White differentiated commerce from stock ownership. Did Congress have the right, he asked, to regulate the acquisition of stock by and in state-chartered corporations just because they engaged in interstate commerce? In White's opinion the answer was no. Stock ownership did not fit the definition of interstate commerce accepted by the Court since *Gibbons v. Ogden* in 1824. Moreover, the power to regulate what an owner might do with his property did not entail the power to set limits on the amount and nature of the property that might be acquired. The only exception to this rule occurred in the case of corporations, for their acquisitions could be limited by the agency that had chartered them, and whose complete "creatures" they were:

Undoubtedly the States possess power over corporations, created by them, to permit or forbid consolidation, whether accomplished by stock ownership or otherwise, to forbid one corporation from holding stock in another, and to impose on this or other subjects such regulations as may be deemed best. Generally speaking, however, the right to do these things springs alone from the fact that the corporation is created by the States, and holds its rights subject to the conditions attached to the grant, or to such regulations as the creator, the State, may lawfully impose upon its creature, the corporation.[17]

For Congress to regulate the stock ownership of state-chartered corporations would be an unconstitutional usurpation of power from

---

[15] Letwin, *Law and Economic Policy in America*, pp. 218-19.
[16] *Northern Securities Company v. United States*, 193 US 197-411. See also Letwin, *Law and Economic Policy in America*, pp. 218-19.
[17] *Northern Securities v. U.S.*, 193 US 398-9.

the states. Such a usurpation, White believed, would have disastrous consequences, similar to those foretold by Fuller in his *E. C. Knight* opinion. A decision against the Northern Securities Company would mean that Congress had the power to abrogate every railroad charter ever authorized by the states, to break up combinations expressly permitted by the states, and, more ominously, to overturn state laws forbidding railroad consolidations. "No remedy," White concluded, "for any supposed or real infirmity can be afforded by disregarding the Constitution, by destroying the lines which separate state and Federal authority, and by implying the existence of a power which is repugnant to all those fundamental rights of life, liberty and property, upon which just government must rest."[18]

Holmes also predicted that disastrous consequences would follow from the *Northern Securities* decision. Analyzing the language of the Sherman Act, Holmes concluded that the law said nothing whatsoever about maintaining competition. The act simply prohibited contracts, combinations, or conspiracies in restraint of trade – that is, agreements that infringed on the freedom of some economic actor to go about his business in a normal way or to enter the trade of his choosing. The Northern Securities Company, a voluntary union of the stockholders of two companies, imposed no restraints on any party and therefore did not come within the purview of the act. To rule against the Northern Securities Company would be, in effect, to condemn all mergers, whatever their purpose or size, because all mergers (or partnerships or unions of any kind, for that matter) involved some reduction of competition. A ruling against Northern Securities would consign the nation to "the universal disintegration of society into single men, each at war with the rest."[19] It would bring an end to economic growth and technological progress. Such a result, Holmes concluded, could not have been the intent of Congress.

For White and Holmes and the two other justices, Fuller and Peckham, who concurred in their dissent, the application of the Sherman Act to tight combinations still met with insuperable constitutional and logical objections. Yet the justices recognized that horizontal combinations of the kind that the Sherman Act had meant to pro-

[18] *Ibid.*, p. 399.
[19] *Ibid.*, p. 407.

scribe were increasingly taking the form of state-chartered corporations. On what basis could the Court rule against them? The solution to this dilemma was foreshadowed by Justice Brewer's opinion concurring with the majority decision: "Instead of holding that the Anti-Trust Act included all contracts, reasonable or unreasonable, in restraint of interstate trade, the ruling should have been that the contracts were unreasonable restraints of interstate trade, and as such within the scope of the act."[20] In other words, what Brewer was proposing was a "rule of reason" that acknowledged the applicability of the Sherman Act to tight combinations but did not automatically hold them illegal. This was roughly the path the entire Court was ultimately to take, but in the meantime an alternative route seemed possible: The federal government might acquire its own incorporation act.

Fear of economic power and the failure of a federal incorporation law

Support for a federal incorporation law came from two main directions: from the Roosevelt administration and from "progressive" elements in the business community. The latter, recognizing that some form of regulation was inevitable, sought federal incorporation as a means of escaping the confusing welter of state statutes and the uncertainties of the Sherman Act. They also, as Gabriel Kolko has pointed out, saw in federal incorporation a means of gaining sanction for the devices they were using to restrict competition. Roosevelt's commitment to federal incorporation, on the other hand, emerged gradually out of the same concern for efficiency that motivated Holmes's *Northern Securities* dissent. From the beginning of his administration Roosevelt had sought some way of satisfying the public clamor for action against trusts without destroying consolidations that he believed to be furthering economic progress – some way of distinguishing legally between "good" trusts and "bad." The Sherman Act was much too crude a tool for this task, especially given the courts' tendency, exemplified by the *Northern Securities* decision, to

---

[20] *Ibid.*, pp. 360-1.

apply its provisions literally, refusing to take cognizance of the reasonableness of combinations. The only way to prevent the abuse of economic power while simultaneously reaping the benefits of large-scale enterprise, Roosevelt believed, was to grant the federal government (and in particular the federal executive) power to regulate business practices. By 1902, Roosevelt's general support for federal regulation had translated into specific endorsement of a federal incorporation law, to be enforced by a national commission lodged in the executive branch.[21]

Although Roosevelt had urged reform of the Sherman Act from the early years of his presidency, the only significant attempt to secure a bill occurred in 1908, after the Panic of 1907 had exacerbated both the public's fear of big business and big business's fear of instability. Of the more than thirty pieces of antitrust legislation that flooded Congress that session, nearly a third called for some form of federal licensing or incorporation of consolidations engaged in interstate commerce. One of these, introduced in the House in March 1908 by Congressman William P. Hepburn, received serious consideration.[22]

The Hepburn proposal had the status of an administration bill, though Roosevelt never explicitly endorsed it. Actually, the bill derived from a National Civic Federation convention in 1907. Attended by academic, business, labor, and agricultural leaders, the gathering passed resolutions calling for federal licensing or incorporation of firms doing interstate business, as well as an amendment to the Sherman Act that would exempt from prosecution farm organizations, labor unions, and business combinations that were "in the public interest." Shortly after the meeting, a group of National Civic Federation leaders (mainly businessmen) joined together to draft a bill that would embody the spirit of the resolutions.[23]

The resulting Hepburn bill provided for the voluntary registration

[21] Kolko, The Triumph of Conservatism, pp. 61-88, 113-38; Letwin, Law and Economic Policy in America, pp. 195-207, 238-50; Arthur M. Johnson, "Antitrust Policy in Transition, 1908: Ideal and Reality," Mississippi Valley Historical Review, 48 (December 1961), pp. 415-34; Melvin I. Urofsky, "Proposed Federal Incorporation in the Progressive Era," American Journal of Legal History, XXVI (April 1982), pp. 160-83.
[22] Congressional Record, 42 (1908).
[23] Johnson, "Antitrust Policy in Transition," pp. 420-5; Kolko, The Triumph of Conservatism, pp. 131-4; Urofsky, "Proposed Federal Incorporation," pp. 178-9.

with the Commissioner of Corporations (in the Department of Commerce and Labor) of firms involved in interstate commerce. Registration would entail the obligation to submit information about the corporation's organization, proceedings, contracts, and financial condition. Once registered, however, a corporation might bring any proposed contract or combination in restraint of trade before the commissioner for a determination as to its reasonableness. In the event that the commissioner did not within thirty days rule the proposal an unreasonable restraint of trade, the federal government forfeited the right to prosecute the combination. The bill also included a number of supplementary provisions, including a clause designed to protect labor organizations from prosecution under the Sherman Act.[24]

According to Professor Jeremiah Jenks of Cornell, who helped draft the bill, the Hepburn amendment "represent[ed] all the interests in the country, so far as we could arrange it."[25] This was a source of the bill's appeal, but it was also a cause of its failure. The bill had something for everyone, but, whereas everyone regarded their enemies' gains as excessive, no one thought his own gains sufficient. Small businessmen decried the provisions exempting labor organizations from antitrust prosecution; labor spokesmen countered that the law scarcely went beyond recent court decisions. Big businessmen lobbied for amendments that would further weaken antitrust provisions. Their opponents responded that the bill had already compromised enforcement of the Sherman Act. On top of all this conflict, moreover, was a general concern over the increased power the bill would grant the federal executive. Ultimately, the political fallout proved severe enough that Roosevelt moved to dissociate himself from the legislation. The coalition of farm, business, and labor leaders that had originally backed the plan disintegrated. The Hepburn bill failed, and so did the movement for federal incorporation.[26]

Gabriel Kolko has argued that the push for a federal incorporation law in general, and for the Hepburn bill in particular, was led by big

---

[24] For the text of the bill, see U.S. Congress, House, *An Act to Regulate Commerce, Etc.: Hearings on House Bill 19745 before Subcommittee No. 3 of the Committee on the Judiciary*, 60th Cong., 1st Sess., 1908, pp. 3-6.

[25] *Ibid.*, p. 79.

[26] Johnson, "Antitrust Policy in Transition," pp. 426-33.

businessmen seeking immunity from the antitrust laws as they attempted to stabilize their industries. The preceding narrative suggests that there is considerable evidence to support Kolko's position. But there is also evidence that this very support by big business helped to ensure the measure's defeat – both because of the opposition it generated from other interest groups and because of the fear of concentrated economic power it aroused.

Roosevelt had been willing to trade a weakening of Sherman-Act protections for an increase in the power and flexibility of the executive branch in dealing with large-scale enterprises. But many Americans, including congressmen and other policymakers, strongly distrusted all forms of concentrated power – public as well as private. This distrust was apparent in the adverse report issued by the Senate Committee on the Judiciary concerning the Senate's (virtually identical) version of the Hepburn bill. The bulk of the document was devoted to tracing common-law precedents in restraint-of-trade cases to show that the Sherman Act was grounded in a long-standing legal tradition and that, as the embodiment of common-law precedents, the act had grown organically out of the interaction between the American legal system and changing economic circumstances. In contrast to this "model" law, the Hepburn bill threatened to expose the nation to the unfettered power of big business and to concentrate power to a dangerous degree in the executive. The insinuation into the bill of the categories "reasonable" and "unreasonable" restraint of trade constituted a fatal flaw:

> To inject into the act the question of whether an agreement or combination is *reasonable* or *unreasonable* would render the act as a criminal or penal statute indefinite and uncertain, and hence, to that extent, utterly nugatory and void, and would practically amount to a repeal of that part of the act.[27]

As for the sections of the bill providing for registration with the Commissioner of Corporations, the committee could scarcely contain its invective. Drawing on a rhetorical tradition passed down from the time of the American Revolution, the committee compared the Hep-

---

[27] U.S. Congress, Senate, "Amending Antitrust Act: Adverse Report of the Committee on the Judiciary," 60th Cong. 2d Sess, 1909, Rept. 848, p. 10. The House bill never made it out of committee.

burn bill to the usurpations of James I of England: "Shall we confer power upon the mere head of a bureau that the Parliament of England were unwilling to accord to the King, and which they regarded as a menace to their liberties?"[28] In the end, the committee recommended that consideration of the Hepburn bill be postponed indefinitely, in which action the entire Senate concurred.[29]

With all its obvious flaws, the Hepburn bill did not really offer a solution to the dilemma of federal antitrust policy. Nonetheless, its failure was symptomatic of a larger problem. Fear of concentrated economic power lay at the root of the antitrust movement. Yet fear of concentrated political power prevented passage of an incorporation law that would have given the federal government the full arsenal of antitrust weapons that the states possessed. Hence, the basic dilemma remained: How could the federal government control industrial combinations if they took the form of state-chartered corporations?

The rule of reason

With the demise of the Hepburn bill, the issue, by default, reverted to the courts, which in 1911 discovered a solution in "the rule of reason." Propounded by Justice Edward Douglass White in the *Standard Oil* and *American Tobacco* decisions of that year, the rule applied the Sherman Act only to "acts or contracts or agreements or combinations which operated to the prejudice of the public interests by unduly restricting competition or unduly obstructing the due course of trade or which, either because of their inherent nature or effect or because of the evident purpose of the acts, etc., injuriously restrained trade."[30]

The rule of reason has often been interpreted as the judicial version of Roosevelt's distinction between good and bad trusts. But this is a misunderstanding of the Court's intent.[31] Rather, the rule was an

---

[28] *Ibid.*, p. 9.
[29] *Congressional Record*, 43 (1909), Pt. 2, p. 1395. During the House Judiciary Committee hearings, questioning also focused in the main on constitutional issues.
[30] *U.S. v. American Tobacco*, 221 US 179.
[31] White explicitly stated that the rule of reason did not mean that "acts which the statute prohibited could be removed from the control of its prohibitions by a finding that they were reasonable." *Ibid.*, 221 US 179-80. On this point, see Letwin, *Law and Economic Policy in America*, pp. 262-3.

attempt to confront directly the problems created by the *Northern Securities* decision. The great merger movement had proved the necessity of applying the Sherman Act to state-chartered consolidations, but the literal interpretation of the act espoused by Justice Harlan in his majority opinion had threatened to outlaw all consolidations, raising constitutional issues and endangering mergers whose primary purpose was clearly legal. The rule of reason confronted these difficulties by shifting the focus of attention to outcomes (to actions "which operated to the prejudice of the public interests") and by classifying combinations into two distinct categories, for which two different tests of restraint of trade were required. First, there were those contracts or combinations whose "inherent nature or effect" was to restrain trade. This category included combinations involving more than one individual or corporation – that is, loose combinations of the sort that had been ruled illegal since the early 1890s, such as gentlemen's agreements, pools, and other types of cartels. These combinations were illegal per se; that is, the Sherman Act must be applied literally to them. Combinations formed by merger, however, did not fall into the category of agreements that were illegal per se, whose "inherent nature or effect" was to restrain trade. In order to find incorporated combinations in violation of the Sherman Act, the Court would have to have proof that the "evident purpose" of the combination was to restrain trade.[32] Consolidations whose evident purpose was to lower production or distribution costs would not be held in violation of the law. Hence, the problem of efficiency was solved. Moreover, the constitutional issue disappeared as well. A consolidation whose evident purpose was to restrain trade was simply, as the Court had pointed out in the *Northern Securities* case, a more effective way of achieving the same end as a loose combination.

[32] Bork, *The Antitrust Paradox*, pp. 33-41. Bork argues that the rule of reason consisted of three separate tests: the two I have discussed plus a test for "inherent effect," which "White did not define" but which, "almost surely, is the market share of the parties." I can find no evidence for this third test in either the *Standard Oil* or the *American Tobacco* decision. Bork himself admits that "the *Standard Oil* decision turned upon defendants' bad intent. Perhaps it would have gone the same way regardless of their intent because of the 'inherent effect' of the combination – defendants had achieved a 90 percent market share at the refining level largely through the acquisition of rivals – but White did not choose to face that issue" (p. 37).

Like a loose combination, then, it should be considered illegal under the Sherman Act. The fact that the consolidation happened to be a state-chartered corporation was irrelevant, for states did not have the right to charter corporations in violation of federal law.[33]

But, how could government prosecutors establish that the "evident purpose" of a consolidation was to restrain trade? White outlined an answer in his *Standard Oil* decision: "combining . . . so many other corporations, aggregating so vast a capital, gives rise, in and of itself, in the absence of countervailing circumstances, to say the least, to the *prima facie* presumption of intent and purpose to maintain the dominancy over the oil industry, not as a result of normal methods of industrial development, but by new means of combination." But, he continued, a firm could not be held in violation of the Sherman Act by the mere fact of its size. Additional information was needed. The prima facie presumption of intent must be "made conclusive" by examining the conduct of persons and corporations involved in the combination – their actions and the consequences of their deeds.[34] The case would have to be built on the testimony of competitors and customers about abusive, restrictive, or predatory behavior. In other words, it was the consolidation's actions with respect to *other* firms that would count. How little judicial interpretation had evolved since the *Jellico* and Whiskey Trust cases! It was still the relationship *among* corporations that mattered.

Live and let live

This history of the rule of reason explains the government's mixed record on preventing barriers to entry. It was relatively easy to prohibit actions that involved two or more firms, such as railroad rebates or tying contracts. But it was much more difficult to restrict behavior that, like vertical integration, was properly within the bounds of a single corporation. Here the per se prohibitions did not apply. According to the rule of reason, prosecutors had to demonstrate that the corporation had acted with intent to restrain trade and

[33] *Northern Securities v. U.S.*, 193 US 332-3.
[34] *The Standard Oil Company of New Jersey et al. v. the United States*, 221 US 75.

that it had succeeded, or would succeed in the future, in exercising monopoly power.

To make this case in court, prosecutors depended on the testimony of competitors who had been hurt by the dominant firms' actions. Hence, the officers of many consolidations quickly learned that they could avoid prosecution (or at least conviction) by adopting a live-and-let-live posture toward existing rivals and concentrating on erecting barriers to new competition by purely intracorporate means. Judge Gary, U.S. Steel's chairman, was an early master of this strategy. Within four years of U.S. Steel's formation, Gary had abrogated whatever exclusive dealing arrangements had been negotiated by the predecessor consolidations, ordered subsidiaries not to accept rebates from railroads, and pulled U.S. Steel out of the industry's remaining pools. Recognizing that "the worst thing that could happen to [the Steel Corporation] would be to have a monopoly of business," Gary allowed U.S. Steel's share of production to slip at the same time as he pursued a policy of market control through vertical integration. Then, secure against excessive entry, thanks to its domination of ore resources, U.S. Steel set prices at a level that would earn profits for its weaker competitors, but not so high as to antagonize customers.[35] As a result, when the antitrust case against U.S. Steel came to trial, witness after witness stepped forward to testify on behalf of the corporation. The following statement by James A. Campbell, president of the Youngstown Sheet & Tube Company, was typical:

My experience is that [U.S. Steel] is the best competition we have; that they are open and above-board in all of their dealings . . . I think in the early days—I did think in the first two or three years we were in business that there were some things done without the knowledge of the higher officials, that were unfair; but those disappeared promptly, and there has been nothing of that kind—nothing but the fairest competition in every respect for the last seven or eight years.[36]

[35] Actually, customers did not worry so much about the level of prices as their degree of uniformity, lest competitors obtain steel at cheaper rates. They appreciated the stability that U.S. Steel's dominant-firm pricing imposed. U.S. Congress, House, *Hearings before the Committee on Investigation of United States Steel Corporation* (Washington, D.C.: U.S. Government Printing Office, 1912), Vol. I, pp. 177, 224, 248, 372, Vol. III, pp. 1715-19; U.S. Supreme Court, *The United States of America, Appellant v. United States Steel Corporation, et al.: Brief for the United States* (Washington, D.C.: U.S. Government Printing Office, 1917), Vol. II, pp. 192-3.
[36] *Ibid.: Transcript of Record*, Vol. V, pp. 1856-8.

As Justice McKenna pointed out in his opinion for the majority of the Supreme Court rejecting the government's case against U.S. Steel, not only the company's officers but "its competitors and customers, testified that [U.S. Steel's] competition was genuine, direct and vigorous, and was reflected in prices and production. No practical witness was produced by the Government in opposition."[37] The government did call as a witness an economist, who attempted to explain to the Court how U.S. Steel might restrain trade and still manage to maintain friendly relations with all its business partners. But McKenna dismissed his testimony as "speculation:"

We magnify the [economist's] testimony by its consideration. Against it, competitors, dealers and customers of the Corporation testify in multitude that no adventitious interference was employed to either fix or maintain prices and that they were constant or varied according to natural conditions.[38]

Without supporting evidence from competitors or customers, the government failed in its attempt to apply the second test of the rule of reason[39] – to show that the "evident purpose" of the combination was to restrain trade. In the words of Justice McKenna, "it is difficult to see how there can be restraint of trade when there is no restraint of competitors in the trade nor complaints by customers."[40]

[37] *U.S. v. U.S. Steel et al.*, 251 US 447.
[38] *Ibid.*, pp. 447-9.
[39] The government also failed to apply the first test of the rule of reason – that an action's "inherent nature or effect" was to restrain trade. Prosecutors presented evidence that the Steel Corporation had participated in pools and other agreements that were illegal per se. But here again Judge Gary's foresight paid off. The Court concluded that because all such activities had ended before the government brought suit, they were irrelevant to the case at hand. The Court even turned the government's reasoning on its head. U.S. Steel's early participation in pools was taken as evidence that the corporation "did not have power in and of itself, and the control it exerted was only in and by association with its competitors." Therefore, McKenna wrote, "whatever there was of wrong intent could not be executed, whatever there was of evil effect, was discontinued before this suit was brought; and this, we think, determines the decree." *Ibid.*, pp. 441, 452.
[40] *Ibid.*, p. 451. McKenna spoke for Justices White, Holmes, and Devanter. McReynolds and Brandeis took no part in the case. Day dissented, and Justices Pitney and Clarke concurred in Day's dissent. In Day's view, "That the exercise of power may be withheld, or exerted with forbearing benevolence, does not place such combinations beyond the authority of the statute which was intended to prohibit their formation, and when formed to deprive them of the power unlawfully attained." *Ibid.*, pp. 464-5.

A judge-made policy: consequences

When Congress finally reformed the nation's antitrust laws with the passage of the Federal Trade Commission Act and Clayton Act in 1914, it did little more than ratify the pattern of antitrust enforcement developed by the courts in the decade or so following the great merger movement. Congress made no attempt in this legislation to resolve the knotty problem of federal regulation of the internal activities of state-chartered corporations. Although the Federal Trade Commission Act set up a new independent regulatory agency, this body did not have the powers envisioned by Congressman Hepburn or by supporters of federal incorporation. Instead of authority to decide in advance the reasonableness of contracts or combinations in restraint of trade, the commission was given only the right to issue cease and desist orders – that is, to disapprove, not approve, combinations – subject to judicial review. Hence, the final determination still rested with the courts.

Moreover, neither the Clayton Act nor the Federal Trade Commission Act altered the application of the rule of reason. In their substantive provisions, both bills focused, as did the rule of reason, on relations among corporations, rather than on firms' internal activities. The Federal Trade Commission Act simply outlawed "unfair methods of competition," leaving it to the commission and the courts to decide what this meant. The Clayton Act specifically prohibited a number of "unfair" practices, where their effect "may be to substantially lessen competition or tend to create a monopoly in any line of commerce." Not only did this qualifier provide considerable leeway for judicial discretion, but the prohibited practices consisted for the most part of acts (e.g., exclusive dealing arrangements or discriminatory pricing) that were already regarded by the courts as evidence that the "evident purpose" of a combination was to restrain trade.[41]

The Clayton Act and Federal Trade Commission Act notwith-

---

[41] The one section of the Clayton Act that potentially went beyond the rule of reason was the provision prohibiting any corporation from acquiring the stock of other corporations, where the effect was substantially to lessen competition. But this provision was ineffective because it failed to prohibit the acquisition of other firms' assets as well as stock. For the contents of the Clayton Act and Federal Trade Commission Act, see Letwin, *Law and Economic Policy in America*, pp. 273-7.

standing, U.S. antitrust policy was for all practical purposes formulated by judges.[42] Consequently, it is the judicial process that one must understand (in particular the process by which the courts coped with the dilemmas of a federal system of government) in order to comprehend the strengths and limitations of antitrust policy. Neither Bork from the right nor Kolko from the left provides an analytical framework adequate to that task. Certainly, as Bork has suggested, judges were guilty of confused economic reasoning. Sometimes they asserted the goal of antitrust policy to be the prevention of artificial increases in prices; at other times it was the perpetuation of small businesses, although this aim was not always consistent with the first.[43] Protecting small-scale enterprises could be justified by the argument that vigorous competition required large numbers of small independent enterprises, but judges did not hold to this view with any constancy either. Here Kolko was correct when he pointed out the tendency of policymakers (including judges) to equate bigness and efficiency. But what Kolko did not sufficiently appreciate was that the judges' commitment to efficiency was undercut by their distrust of concentrated economic power, apparent even in those decisions in which they found in favor of consolidations.[44]

From the standpoint of economic theory, the decisions issued by the courts from 1890 to 1911 were, as Bork has argued, inconsistent and confusing. But the judges were not attempting primarily to articulate a coherent economic philosophy; they were striving to respond to changes in economic organization and to public demands for action in a way that would be consistent in jurisprudential

[42] This point was made by Morton Keller in "The Pluralist State: American Economic Regulation in Comparative Perspective, 1900-1930," *Regulation in Perspective: Historical Essays*, ed. Thomas K. McCraw (Cambridge: Harvard University Press, 1981), p. 69. See also William R. Cornish, "Legal Control over Cartels and Monopolization, 1880-1914: A Comparison," *Law and the Formation of the Big Enterprises in the 19th and Early 20th Centuries: Studies in the History of Industrialization in Germany, France, Great Britain and the United States*, ed. Norbert Horn and Jürgen Kocka (Göttingen: Vandenhoeck & Ruprecht, 1979), p. 281.

[43] See, for example, Thomas K. McCraw's analysis of Brandeis's writings in "Rethinking the Trust Question," *Regulation in Perspective*, ed. McCraw, pp. 25-55.

[44] For example, in the *E. C. Knight* case Justice Fuller admitted that the sugar trust was an "acknowledged evil" and that the object of its near monopoly of refinery production "was manifestly private gain." 156 US 13-17.

terms.[45] The main problem they faced was structural: how the federal government could fulfill its responsibility to regulate interstate corporations when it did not have the power to charter them. The solution they arrived at was the rule of reason.

The result of this solution was a curious, bifurcated system of law according to which activities that were illegal if undertaken by several firms acting together might be considered legal if performed by a single corporation whose officers did not intend (or could not be proved to have intended) to secure monopoly power thereby. Ironically, though one of the purposes of the solution had been to assuage public fears about large aggregations of capital, it actually had a number of anticompetitive consequences. We have already seen how the rule of reason, with its dependence on competitors' testimony, rendered the government incapable of dealing with a combination such as U.S. Steel, which limited entry through control of ore resources and kept competitors happy with its pricing policy. To make matters worse, the rule of reason also worked to the detriment of firms seeking to challenge giants like U.S. Steel. Small firms could sometimes best compete with large, vertically integrated consolidations by negotiating exclusive dealing arrangements with suppliers and buyers to guarantee themselves a source of raw materials and access to a market. Yet such agreements *among* firms were liable to be found illegal, regardless of their effect on competition. Worse still, dependence on competitors' testimony whenever the per se rules did not apply meant that antitrust suits were least likely to be successful in industries controlled by a dominant firm or a tight oligopoly, and most likely to succeed in competitive industries in which manufacturers were often hard pressed and disgruntled.[46]

But these anticompetitive consequences were not the whole story. Because antitrust suits were henceforth to stand or fall on the basis of competitors' testimony, consolidations were forced to alter their behavior toward their rivals, to relinquish some of their crudest weapons of dominance – railroad rebates, exclusive dealing contracts, se-

---

[45] In the *Northern Securities* decision, Justice Harlan stated explicitly that economic considerations were irrelevant. *Northern Securities v. U.S.*, 193 US 337-8.

[46] Stone, *Economic Regulation and the Public Interest*, pp. 64-9, 78-81.

lective price cutting – weapons that were regarded at the time as "unfair" practices. Consolidations also lost some of their power to discipline rivals by instigating price wars, such as those launched to enforce cartel-like behavior in the steel and newsprint industries after the 1907 Panic. Consolidations were forced henceforth to pursue the dominant-firm strategy more exclusively. After all, the surest way to keep competitors from testifying adversely in antitrust suits was to announce prices in some well-publicized manner and allow competitors to sell as much output as they liked. Moreover, enforcement of the antitrust laws against consolidations spurred them to abandon their wasteful preoccupation with restraining existing competitors and concentrate on improving their competitive positions by putting their own houses in order.

Undoubtedly, such a shift would have occurred to some extent regardless. Recall Chandler's example of the National Biscuit Company, whose officers had by 1901 abandoned their predecessors' policy of controlling competition in favor of focusing their energies "within the company itself." But most consolidations were notoriously slow to make this transition, as the history of the combines formed in the late 1880s and early 1890s (before the Sherman Act was enforced against consolidations) reveals. For example, after its organization in 1890, the Distilling and Cattle Feeding Company spent some $4 million acquiring competitors, only to face new rivals almost immediately. Largely as a result of these futile purchases, the corporation ended up in receivership and was reorganized as the American Spirits Manufacturing Company in 1895. But the new combination only repeated the mistakes of its forerunner. It continued to buy up competitors and financed the organization of an allied consolidation (the Spirits Distributing Company) to take in additional outsiders as well as assume some control of distribution. Again, all to little avail. More competitors entered the industry, and in 1898 American Spirits encouraged the formation of still another combine, the Standard Distilling and Distributing Company, with which it signed a market-sharing agreement. When competition nonetheless continued to grow, the American Spirits Manufacturing Company, the Spirits Distributing Company, Standard Distilling and Distributing, and a fourth combination of Kentucky distillers merged to form the Distilling Company of America. Yet another reorganization followed in 1902.[47]

Similar tales of growing competition and repeated reorganizations could be recounted for the straw-board, starch, linseed-oil, cordage and leather industries.[48] Admittedly, the consolidations in all these industries were notoriously unsuccessful, but the same wasteful pre-occupation with horizontal combination affected successful mergers as well. For instance, three times the American Sugar Refining Company found it necessary to increase its capitalization and buy out competitors in order to maintain its near monopoly of sugar production. Only in the twentieth century did the consolidation change strategy – after its conviction on charges of accepting rebates from railroads. U.S. Rubber bought out competitor after competitor during the depression of the 1890s, only to face a rash of new rivals with the return of prosperity at the turn of the century. Before 1900, Standard Oil acquired a total of more than 200 firms of various types (mostly refineries). About half the acquisitions occurred after 1882, and many important deals were consummated as late as the 1890s. By this means, Standard attempted to maintain its share of oil refining at about 90 percent. Only in the twentieth century did it allow its market share to slip. Finally, the American Tobacco Company provides what is perhaps the most striking example of manu-facturers' obsession with horizontal combination. Its officers were not content simply to control the cigarette business, but poured out vast sums of money to acquire a dominant position in the chewing-tobacco, smoking-tobacco, snuff, stogie, and (most futilely) cigar in-dustries as well. It was this policy that brought about American's court-ordered dissolution.[49]

---

[47] U.S. Industrial Commission, *Preliminary Report on Trusts and Industrial Combina-tions,* 56th Cong., 1st Sess., 1900, House Doc. 476, "Digest of Evidence," pp. 76-9, "Testimony," pp. 176-78; J. W. Jenks, "The Development of the Whisky Trust," *Trusts, Pools and Corporations,* ed. William Z. Ripley (rev. ed.; New York: Ginn & Co., 1916), pp. 34-8.

[48] See Arthur S. Dewing, *Corporate Promotions and Reorganizations* (Cambridge: Harvard University Press, 1914), pp. 16-164; Whitney Eastman, *The History of the Linseed Oil Industry in the United States* (Minneapolis: T. S. Denison & Co., 1968), pp. 31-4. The history of the straw-board combinations can be followed through the pages of the *Paper Trade Journal.*

[49] Richard Zerbe, "The American Sugar Refinery Company, 1887-1914: The Story of a Monopoly," *Journal of Law and Economics,* XII (October 1969), p. 374; Alfred

Antitrust enforcement encouraged consolidations to learn from these examples and develop a live-and-let-live policy toward existing rivals. Of course, there was still the problem of barriers to entry, but the rule of reason constrained behavior in this respect as well. Here again, because of the importance of rivals' testimony, dominant firms were forced to shift to internal means of forestalling additional competition – for example, acquisition of raw-material resources, protection of markets through product differentiation, or increased efficiency by means such as vertical integration to capture economies of speed.

Joe S. Bain's famous 1956 study, *Barriers to New Competition*, suggests that at least some consolidations successfully followed U.S. Steel's lead and protected their market positions by securing control of raw-material resources. How many did this is difficult to say, because Bain studied only a small number of cases. But their ranks were probably limited to the relatively small number of large-scale, mineral-processing industries: copper, lead, nickel, and a few others. Bain's study also indicates that some consolidations returned to the strategy pursued by small firms in the mid-nineteenth century, differentiating their products from competitors' and working to develop strong loyalties for their brands. The number of firms that adopted this tactic was probably greater than the number controlling raw-material resources. Still, as a result of improvements in information and quality control, improvements that reduced buyers' uncertainty about purchasing, this type of barrier was increasingly limited to consumer-goods industries. As for the bulk of the consolidations in producer-goods industries, therefore, success over the long run was probably dependent more than anything else on superior efficiency:

S. Eichner, *The Emergence of Oligopoly: Sugar Refining as a Case Study* (Baltimore: Johns Hopkins Press, 1969), pp. 188-331; Glenn D. Babcock, *History of the United States Rubber Company: A Case Study in Corporate Management* (Bloomington: Indiana University Graduate School of Business, 1966), pp. 26-40, 56; John S. McGee, "Predatory Price Cutting: The Standard Oil (N.J.) Case," *The Competitive Economy: Selected Readings*, ed. Yale Brozen (Morristown, N.J.: General Learning Press, 1975), pp. 380-404; Richard B. Tennant, *The American Cigarette Industry, A Study in Economic Analysis and Public Policy* (New Haven: Yale University Press, 1950), pp. 28-37.

on economies of scale or, as Chandler has suggested, economies of speed.[50]

A full assessment of the economic consequences of the consolidation movement, then, depends on how these different tactics balanced out – their net effect on overall economic efficiency and the relative sizes of the raw-material-processing, producer-goods, and consumer-goods sectors. Unfortunately, the scholarly debate on the relationship between industrial concentration and efficiency has been inconclusive (largely because these same sectoral differences obscure the results of aggregate analysis). Some studies have shown that firms in concentrated industries tend to earn supernormal profits and that part of these profits can be explained by indices of barriers to entry – for example, advertising expenditures per dollar of sales. But other studies have suggested that the reason for the correlation between supernormal profits and industrial concentration is large firms' superior efficiency, which explains both their profit rates and the degree of concentration.[51]

A closer look at one of the most important of these latter studies demonstrates that the evidence is by no means unambiguous. For his article "Industry Structure, Market Rivalry, and Public Policy," Harold Demsetz collected information on rates of return in 1963 for firms of different sizes in industries with varying concentration ratios.[52] The data are reproduced in Table 6.1. Demsetz found that large firms in concentrated industries earned higher rates of return than both their smaller competitors and firms in less concentrated industries, a pattern he concluded was evidence of the large firms'

[50] Except where, as David Noble and Leonard S. Reich have suggested, patents were used to protect market positions. David F. Noble, *America By Design: Science, Technology, and the Rise of Corporate Capitalism* (Oxford University Press, 1977), pp. 84-109; Leonard S. Reich, "Research, Patents, and the Struggle to Control Radio: A Study of Big Business and the Uses of Industrial Research," *Business History Review*, LI (Summer 1977), pp. 208-35; Reich, "Industrial Research and the Pursuit of Corporate Stability: The Early Years of Bell Labs," *Business History Review*, LIV (Winter 1980), pp. 504-29. See Joe S. Bain, *Barriers to New Competition: Their Character and Consequences in Manufacturing Industries* (Cambridge: Harvard University Press, 1956), pp. 53-181.

[51] For an excellent summary of the debate, see F. M. Scherer, *Industrial Market Structure and Economic Performance* (2nd ed.; Chicago: Rand McNally, 1980), pp. 267-95.

[52] Harold Demsetz, "Industry Structure, Market Rivalry, and Public Policy," *Journal of Law and Economics*, XVI (April 1973), pp. 1-9.

Table 6.1. *Rates of return by size of firm and concentration ratio (unweighted averages)*

C^b	No. of industries	$R_1{}^a$	$R_2{}^a$	$R_3{}^a$	$R_4{}^a$	$\bar{R}$
10–20%	14	6.7%	9.0%	10.8%	10.3%	9.2%
20–30%	22	4.5%	9.1%	9.7%	10.4%	8.4%
30–40%	24	5.2%	8.7%	9.9%	11.0%	8.7%
40–50%	21	5.8%	9.0%	9.5%	9.0%	8.3%
50–60%	11	6.7%	9.8%	10.5%	13.4%	10.1%
60%+	3	5.3%	10.1%	11.5%	23.1%	12.5%

$^a R_1$, R_2, R_3, and R_4 are accounting rates of return [(profit + interest)/total assets], calculated using IRS data, for firms with asset values, respectively, of less than $500,000, $500,000 to $5,000,000, $5,000,000 to $50,000,000, and more than $50,000,000.
$^b C$ is the four-firm concentration ratio measured on industry sales for three-digit Standard Industrial Classification categories.
Source: Demsetz, "Industry Structure, Market Rivalry, and Public Policy," p. 6.

superior efficiency. However, Demsetz failed to explore alternative explanations for this pattern. Moreover, as Table 6.1 shows, his results were striking only for the three industries with four-firm concentration ratios greater than 60 percent. In the case of the eleven industries in the 50-60 percent range, the largest size category of firms did only slightly better than their smaller competitors. In the twenty-one industries with concentration ratios of 40-50 percent, firms in the largest size class actually did worse than those in the $5,000,000-to-$50,000,000 category and about the same as those in the $500,000-to-$5,000,000 group. (These results are consistent with our earlier assumption of evenly matched firms.) Moreover, Table 6.1 presents only averages and does not give information on variations in profit rates within size classifications. At the very best, therefore, we can conclude from Demsetz's study that efficiency led to high profits and concentration in some cases, probably in those intermediate-goods industries in which control of raw-material resources was impossible and gains from product differentiation were limited.

In sum, one cannot assess the consequences of the consolidation movement without taking into account the effects of federal antitrust policy on dominant firms' tactics. Fear of concentrated economic power both dictated a strong governmental response to the consolidation movement and limited the form that response could take. Handicapped by the lack of a federal incorporation law which would give the national government effective control over tight combinations, the courts gradually arrived at a policy known as the rule of reason. Henceforth a consolidation was not to be held in violation of the antitrust laws by the mere fact of its existence, but only on the basis of conclusive evidence that its purpose was to monopolize trade. Because such a demonstration required the testimony of competitors about the combine's unfair tactics, antitrust policy forced consolidations to abandon their attempts to restrain existing rivals and instead develop internal means to protect their market positions. In some cases this meant improvements in efficiency. But in others, consolidations with no real advantage in costs were able to maintain their positions by erecting barriers to entry – in the case of U.S. Steel, by controlling vital resources, in other instances perhaps by means of massive advertising. Only an industry-by-industry assessment can determine the net effect of the consolidation movement on economic efficiency.

7. Conclusion

In *The Visible Hand*, Alfred D. Chandler, Jr., argued that the most significant development in the history of the American economy (and indeed the world economy) was the emergence of large, vertically integrated, multiplant enterprises in which, improving on the operation of Adam Smith's invisible hand, professional managers coordinated the flow of product from raw-material sources to finished markets. According to Chandler, some of these large multiplant enterprises developed through a process of internal growth, following out the logic of innovations by key entrepreneurs such as Gustavus Swift or Isaac Merritt Singer and Edward Clark. More frequently, however, they had their beginnings in the very different process of horizontal combination. Formed to escape the severe price competition of the late nineteenth century, many of today's largest industrials originated as consolidations. They survived and prospered, Chandler argued, because their officers then followed the example of companies like Swift and Singer, integrating backward into raw materials and forward into marketing.[1]

Chandler concentrated, for the most part, on the first of these two processes. The second, and in particular the great merger movement, received much less attention from him. My aim in this study has been to fill this gap – to understand why so many firms suddenly merged into horizontal combinations, what the effects of these mergers on competitive behavior were, whether or not the visible hand of the manager was in fact an improvement over the operation of the market.

Consolidations, I have concluded, were by no means an inevitable component of the rise of modern industry, even though so many important firms had their origins in these mergers. Rather, the consolidation movement was the product of a particular conjunction of historical events: the development of capital-intensive, mass-production manufacturing techniques in the late nineteenth century; the

[1] Alfred D. Chandler, Jr., *The Visible Hand: The Managerial Revolution in American Business* (Cambridge: Harvard University Press, 1977), pp. 287-376.

extraordinarily rapid growth that many capital-intensive industries experienced after 1887; and the deep depression that began in 1893. As the examples of the wire-nail, tin-plate, and newsprint industries demonstrated, this conjunction of events gave rise to serious price warfare during the depression of the nineties – price warfare that conventional types of collusion proved incapable of ending. After failing in repeated attempts to halt the decline in prices by means of gentlemen's agreements, selling agencies, and pools, manufacturers in these and many other industries finally organized consolidations.

At the root of this severe competition was the development of capital-intensive, mass-production manufacturing techniques in the late nineteenth century. These techniques raised the proportion of fixed in total costs that firms had to meet. Consequently, whenever a downturn in demand sent prices tumbling below total costs, there was a strong incentive to undersell competitors, with the aim of increasing sales and running full. Many scholars have commented on this incentive. But high fixed costs alone are not sufficient to explain the outbreaks of price warfare during depressions. The temptation to cut prices should have been offset by the firms' recognition of their mutual dependence, of the sureness with which retaliation would follow a cut. An exception to this rule occurred, however, in industries undergoing rapid expansion. There, competitive and marketing relations were already in a state of flux, making retaliation for a cut in prices much less certain. Where new firms were concerned, moreover, fixed costs were typically highest and most pressing; furthermore, some of these enterprises were sure to be undercapitalized. Desperate to realize revenue from sales, they would cut prices aggressively in order to dispose of their output and continue in business.

That consolidations tended to occur in capital-intensive industries that experienced rapid growth on the eve of the Panic of 1893 is confirmed by quantitative data for the manufacturing sector, secondary literature on large-scale industries, and case studies of the steel and paper industries. The same evidence suggests that in the absence of this conjunction of events, the nation's industrial structure would have evolved along different lines. Rather than consolidating, large-scale manufacturing industries would have adjusted gradually to their long-run equilibrium positions, perhaps forming some smaller mergers in the process. As the example of the steel-rail industry demonstrated, where growth was not rapid, price wars were unlikely to be a problem—even though fixed costs were high. In a slowly growing or stagnant industry, firms became accustomed to each other's dealings, came to recognize each other's capabilities and their own interdependence. Regular marketing patterns had time to evolve, making surreptitious price cuts easier to detect, and firms realized that, more often than not, price cutting triggered counter-measures that left everyone worse off than before. Instead of consolidations precipitated by price warfare, competing firms in slowly growing industries established stable oligopolistic relations, reinforced perhaps by some type of cartel-like organization.

If, then, consolidations were not an inevitable aspect of the rise of large-scale manufacturing industries, if the alternative path of development led to stable oligopolistic industry structures, did it matter that so many consolidations were formed at the turn of the century? Certainly, where consolidations adopted dominant-firm pricing their immediate effect was to bring a measure of stability to industries that had suffered years of downward-spiraling price competition. But to what extent did this control persist? Were consolidations able to maintain over the long run their positions of market dominance and, with them, the ability to set prices for their industries?

In most cases the answer is unquestionably no. Whether or not a consolidation maintained its position over the long run depended on its costs of production relative to those of its competitors. If a consolidation's costs were relatively high, it would have to set prices above the so-called limit value, the threshold for stimulating entry into the industry. New competitors would appear, and the consolidation's share of the market would drop. This was the fate of many of the consolidations formed at the turn of the century. Many had acquired at inflated prices large numbers of plants whose equipment was not only old but also badly depreciated as a result of years of severe price competition, years when earnings were not sufficient to finance replacements or improvements out of current revenues, as was the manufacturers' wont. As a result, the combines' production costs were relatively high, and so were the prices they charged for their output. As new competitors equipped with the most up-to-date, efficient machinery rushed into the industry, the consolidations' market shares declined, and their industries reverted to their preconsolidation structure – and ultimately to the alternative development path.

The fact that so many consolidations failed to maintain their positions of dominance suggests that the New Economic Historians – and Chandler – were not so far from the mark in discounting the importance of the great merger movement. But this is not the whole story. Some smaller number of consolidations continued to dominate their industries for years, either by dint of superior efficiency or because they were able to erect barriers to additional competition. Furthermore, the consolidation movement provoked a strong political response, and the antitrust policy that resulted altered the rules of the competitive game for all firms, not just for consolidations.

Erupting as it did among a people for whom fear of concentrated economic power was deep-seated and long-standing, the merger movement generated considerable pressure on the federal government to take action against consolidations. Yet, ironically, this same fear of concentrated power placed constraints on the government's actions that affected its ability to deal with the combines. Most important, distrust of central government power, and the division of power and authority between the states and the federal government to which this distrust had long ago given rise, forced the federal government to assume responsibility for regulating large-scale enterprises with only half the legal arsenal available to the states. Where the states had been able to draw on both their powers of incorporation and their antitrust laws, the federal government had resort only to the latter, weaker weapon. As a result, it was far easier for federal officials to move against loose combinations (i.e., combinations that involved more than one firm) than tight ones (those that took the form of a single corporation and that were increasingly prevalent after 1895).

After two decades of judicial debate on antitrust policy, the Supreme Court finally crafted a solution known as the rule of reason. According to this doctrine, loose combinations in restraint of trade continued to be regarded as illegal per se. Tight combinations might also be held illegal, but prosecutors had to show not only that a combination existed but also that its "evident purpose" was to restrain trade. In order to prove this, they needed to marshal abundant testimony from competitors, suppliers, and customers that the consolidation had engaged in unfair, restrictive, or discriminatory acts – acts that were meant to abridge the freedom of others to go about their business in the normal manner or engage in the trade of their choosing.

This rule of reason solved the basic structural problem created by the division of power and authority between the states and the federal government. At the same time, however, it introduced new irrationalities and inefficiencies into antitrust law. As a result of the dual system embodied in the rule of reason, tight combinations still retained certain options (e.g., control of vital resources through vertical integration) that were the equivalent of acts forbidden to loose combinations (e.g., tying contracts or exclusive dealing arrangements), even though the former might prove more detrimental to competition than the latter. Moreover, the dependence on competitors' testimony in antitrust suits, which the rule of reason required for tight combinations, meant that it was easier to prosecute firms engaged in vigorous competition than those belonging to tight oligopolies.

Here again the viewpoint of the New Economic Historians seems to be borne out – that government, not big business, has done the greatest damage to the competitive system. But again this is not the whole story. Dependence on competitors' testimony in the prosecution of antitrust suits compelled consolidations to shift strategy – to abandon their crudest anticompetitive weapons and protect their market positions by purely internal means. Forced to forbear from tactics regarded at the time as unfair (exclusive dealing arrangements, tying contracts, extraction of rebates from railroads, selective or discriminatory price cutting), they concentrated on enhancing the strengths of their organizations: advertising to differentiate their products from those of competitors, integrating vertically to improve efficiency and sometimes to control raw-material supplies, promoting research and development to improve product efficiency and also to control patents.

Some of these achievements undoubtedly raised the efficiency of the economy as a whole; others probably lowered it. How they balanced out, what their net effect on efficiency has been – whether, as Chandler has argued, the visible hand of management has in fact been an improvement over the invisible hand of the market or simply a means to monopoly power – is impossible to say at this time, given the state of our knowledge. But there is little doubt that the shift in behavior enforced by federal antitrust policy marked an improvement over the wasteful and often futile preoccupation with horizontal control that characterized most giant firms at the time. To see this, one has only to recall the consolidations formed in the late 1880s or early 1890s, which operated for ten to fifteen years under the assumption that mergers were exempt from the Sherman Antitrust Act. One has only to recall the enormous sums these consolidations expended to buy out competitors, the numerous reorganizations they underwent as competition threatened them with bankruptcy, the repeated attempts they made to control production in their own and related industries. Most of this activity was permanently halted by the federal government in the first decade of the twentieth century.

With the abandonment of the strategy of horizontal combination, a new adjustment process began. Consolidations that were hopelessly inefficient or that failed to dominate their markets through control of patents or raw materials or through product differentiation slipped in size and, in a number of cases, actually failed. The rest attained an extraordinary stability. By World War I, as Richard C. Edwards has shown, the adjustment process had for the most part worked itself out. Calculating failure rates for large corporations for the periods 1903 to 1919 and 1919 to 1969, Edwards found that firms disappeared from the list of 100 largest corporations at a rate of three to four per year before 1919, but only one per year from that date on. The difference between the two periods was even more striking when he tested the firms' ability to maintain their assets above a certain minimum level (the constant-dollar value of the assets of the smallest of the 100 firms in the first year of each period). Prior to 1917, an average of two to four firms per year disappeared or dropped below the asset minimum; after 1917, "failures" occurred only once every five years, and most of the latter were due to mergers.[2]

---

[2] Edwards counted firms acquired by other firms as failures. Richard C. Edwards, "Stages in Corporate Stability and the Risks of Corporate Failure," *Journal of Economic History*, XXXV (June 1975), pp. 434-9. For similar results, see Norman R. Collins and Lee E. Preston, "The Size Structure of the Largest Industrial Firms, 1909-1958," *American Economic Review*, LI (December 1961), pp. 986-1003. See also F. M. Scherer, *Industrial Market Structure and Economic Performance* (2nd ed.; Chicago: Rand McNally, 1980), pp. 47-50.

By the 1920s, then, our analysis has come full circle. This study began with a discussion of small firms that pursued a strategy of product differentiation and by that means managed to achieve a high degree of stability. This type of firm had its heyday in the mid-nineteenth century. Then, as transport and communications improvements greatly enlarged the domestic market, the small differentiated firm was increasingly surpassed in importance by a new breed of large-scale, mass-production enterprises. These new firms had priorities fundamentally different from those of their smaller competitors. Aiming for volume production rather than high per-unit margins, they forsook the small firms' concern with price stability, emphasizing instead aggressive cost cutting and price competition to stimulate sales. Not surprisingly, the period in which they operated witnessed the most rapid industrial development in the nation's history.

In the twentieth century, these priorities shifted once again. Whatever their effect on efficiency in a static sense, the consolidation movement and federal antitrust policy brought to power a new generation of business leaders – men who, like Judge Gary, were primarily concerned with stabilizing their industries and developing cooperative relations with their rivals. In many ways, men like Gary were closer to the conservative mindset of the small manufacturers of the mid-nineteenth century than to the aggressive competitors of the 1890s, an affinity that would have significant implications for the economy's subsequent development. In the mid-nineteenth century, the conservatism of business leaders had not much mattered from the standpoint of overall growth and efficiency, because even the firms that most successfully differentiated their products composed only small segments of their industries. There was still plenty of opportunity for innovation elsewhere – plenty of other firms, plenty of experienced entrepreneurs. The pace of technological change was beyond any one firm's control. Today, however, the descendants of some consolidations continue to occupy major shares of their home markets, where they have successfully erected barriers to new competition. In contrast to the mid-nineteenth-century case, the result may actually be to impede the process of technological change. To the extent that stability-minded business leaders are not open to new innovations, or that innovations occur most frequently in new enterprises, where manufacturers are less committed to a particular way of doing things and are more open to new ideas, technological progress will be retarded by barriers to entry. This does not mean that innovation will be completely stifled. Where barriers to entry are highest, the process will simply be forced into external channels: the development of substitute commodities or the growth of new foreign competition. One or both of these responses will ultimately occur; there are no monopolies over the long run. But, where barriers are highest, the long run is likely to be very long indeed, and as a result, technological change may ultimately produce much more serious economic dislocations than normal innovation within an industry itself. The case of today's steel industry, in which foreign competition has forced massive plant closings, serves as a telling example.

Bibliographical essay

The first major study of the consolidation movement was conducted by the U.S. Industrial Commission at the turn of the century. Its two massive volumes of reports and testimony *(Preliminary Report on Trusts and Industrial Combinations,* 56th Cong., 1st Sess., 1900, House Doc. 476; *Report on Trusts and Industrial Combinations,* 57th Cong., 1st Sess., 1901, House Doc. 182) pointed to the conclusion that severe price competition among manufacturers was the primary cause of the consolidation movement. This theme was echoed in the scholarly literature for the next thirty to forty years. For two contemporary surveys of the literature, see Charles J. Bullock, "Trust Literature: A Survey and a Criticism," *Quarterly Journal of Economics,* XV (February 1901), pp. 167-217, and Paul T. Homan, "Industrial Combination as Surveyed in Recent Literature," *Quarterly Journal of Economics,* XLIV (February 1930), pp. 345-75. Much of this scholarship was devoted to explaining the causes of the strident competition of the late nineteenth century. For a clear exposition of one of the most important explanations (what I have called the fixed-cost theory), see Spurgeon Bell, "Fixed Costs and Market Price," *Quarterly Journal of Economics,* XXXII (May 1918), pp. 507-24. Other works employing a similar analytical framework include Arthur Robert Burns, *The Decline of Competition: A Study of the Evolution of American Industry* (New York: McGraw-Hill, 1936); William M. Collier, *The Trusts: What Can We Do with Them? What Can They Do for Us?* (New York: Baker and Taylor, 1900); J. W. Jenks, "The Michigan Salt Association," *Trusts, Pools and Corporations,* ed. William Z. Ripley (rev. ed.; New York: Ginn & Co., 1916), pp. 1-21; Jenks, "The Development of the Whisky Trust," *ibid.,* pp. 22-45; Jenks, *The Trust Problem* (New York: McClure, Phillips and Co., 1900); and Henry R. Seager and Charles A. Gulick, Jr., *Trust and Corporation Problems* (New York: Harper & Brothers, 1929). In "Is Competition in Industry Ruinous?" *Quarterly Journal of Economics,* XXXIV (May 1920), pp. 473-519, Eliot Jones offers a dissenting view. For other important early studies of consolidation, see Jones, *The Trust Problem in the United States* (New York: Macmillan, 1921); John Bates Clark, *The Control of Trusts: An Argument in Favor of Curbing the Power of Monopoly by a Natural Method* (New York: Macmillan, 1905); Richard T. Ely, *Monopolies and Trusts* (New York: Macmillan, 1900); Ernst von Halle, *Trusts or Industrial Combinations in the United States* (New York: Macmillan, 1899); Harry W. Laidler, *Concentration of Control in American Industry* (New York: Thomas Y. Crowell Co., 1931); and Myron W. Watkins, *Industrial Combinations and Public Policy: A Study of Combination, Competition and the Common Welfare* (Boston: Houghton Mifflin, 1927). Later studies that similarly focus on the issue of competition are Joe S. Bain's "Industrial Concentration and Anti-trust Policy," *The Growth of the American Economy*, ed. Harold F. Williamson (2nd ed; Englewood Cliffs, N.J.: Prentice-Hall, 1951), pp. 616-30; Alfred S. Eichner's *The Emergence of Oligopoly: Sugar Refining as a Case Study* (Baltimore: Johns Hopkins Press, 1969); George Bittlingmayer, "Decreasing Average Cost and Competition: A New Look at the Addyston Pipe Case," *Journal of Law and Economics*, XXV (October 1982), pp. 201-79; and Bittlingmayer, "Price Fixing and the Addyston Pipe Case," *Research in Law and Economics*, V (1983), pp. 57-128.

Since World War II, scholars have tended to downplay the importance of escaping competition as a motive for consolidations and to view them instead as the product of a constellation of other factors: an increasingly permissive legal environment, the development of a market for industrial securites, the desire for promoters' profits, the exploitation of economies of scale or speed, and the search for lower-cost sources of financing. Studies in this vein include Ralph L. Nelson, *Merger Movements in American Industry, 1895-1956* (Princeton University Press, 1959); Jesse W. Markham, "Survey of the Evidence and Findings on Mergers," *Business Concentration and Price Policy*, Universities-National Bureau Committee for Economic Research Conference (Princeton University Press, 1955), pp. 141-82; George J. Stigler, "Monopoly and Oligopoly by Merger," *The Organization of Industry* (Homewood, Ill.: Richard D. Irwin, 1968), pp. 95-107; Alfred D. Chandler, Jr., "The Beginnings of 'Big Business' in American Industry," *Business History Review*, XXXIII (Spring 1959), pp. 1-31; Chandler, *The Visible Hand: The Managerial Revolution in American Business* (Cambridge: Harvard University Press, 1977); and Lance Davis, "The Capital Markets and Industrial Concentration: The U.S. and U.K., a Comparative Study," *Economic History Review*, Second Series, XIX (August 1966), pp. 255-72.

As for the case studies, most secondary works on the steel industry focus primarily on pig iron, crude steel, and rail production. The best of these is Peter Temin's *Iron and Steel in Nineteenth-Century America: An Economic Inquiry* (Cambridge: M.I.T. Press, 1964). But see also Kenneth Warren's *The American Steel Industry: A Geographical Interpretation* (Oxford: Clarendon Press, 1973); and, on Carnegie Steel, James Howard Bridge's contemporary account, *The Inside History of the Carnegie Steel Company: A Romance of Millions* (New York: Aldine, 1903); and Harold C. Livesay's recent biography, *Andrew Carnegie and the Rise of Big Business* (Boston: Little, Brown, 1975). For the postconsolidation industry, see Gertrude G. Schroeder's *The Growth of Major Steel Companies, 1900-1950* (Baltimore: Johns Hopkins Press, 1953); as well as the following articles: S. R. Dennison, "Vertical Integration and the Iron and Steel Industry," *Economic Journal*, XLIX (June 1939), pp. 244-58; Richard B. Mancke, "Iron and Steel: A Case Study of the Economic Causes and Consequences of Vertical Integration," *Journal of Industrial Economics*, XX (July 1972), pp. 220-29; Edward Sherwood Meade, "The Genesis of the United States Steel Corporation," *Quarterly Journal of Economics*, XV (August 1901), pp. 517-50; and Donald O. Parsons and Edward John Ray, "The United States Steel Consolidation: The Creation of Market Control," *Journal of Law and Economics*, XVIII (April

1975), pp. 181-219. Useful information on terms, technical developments, and marketing practices is found in W. K. V. Gale, *The Iron and Steel Industry: A Dictionary of Terms* (London: David and Charles, 1971); Stephen L. Goodale, *Chronology of Iron and Steel* (2nd ed.; Cleveland: Penton Publishing, 1931); and B. E. V. Luty, "Iron Ore and Pig Iron," *The Marketing of Metals and Minerals: A Series of Articles by Specialists*, ed. Josiah Edward Spurr and Felix Edgar Wormser (New York: McGraw-Hill, 1925), pp. 82-7. William T. Hogan's *Economic History of the Iron and Steel Industry in the United States* (Lexington, Mass.: Lexington-D. C. Heath, 1971), Vols. I and II, provides much additional detail.

Studies that focus on specific branches of the finished-steel industry are relatively scarce. On tin plate, see D. E. Dunbar, *The Tin-Plate Industry: A Comparative Study of Its Growth in the United States and in Wales* (Boston: Houghton Mifflin, 1915); Thomas William Hundermark, "The Changes in Distribution of Tin Plate Works in Pennsylvania during the Various Stages of Development of the Industry" (unpublished master's thesis, University of Pittsburgh, 1948); and James W. McKie, *Tin Cans and Tin Plate: A Study of Competition in Two Related Markets* (Cambridge: Harvard University Press, 1959). Two books on Wheeling, West Virginia, Earl Chapin May's *Principio to Wheeling, 1715-1945: A Pageant of Iron and Steel* (New York: Harper & Brothers, 1945) and Henry Dickerson Scott's *Iron and Steel in Wheeling* (Toledo: Caslon Company, 1929), treat aspects of both the tin-plate and wire industries. Other works on the wire industry include Charles E. Edgerton, "The Wire-Nail Association of 1895-1896," *Trusts, Pools and Corporations*, ed. Ripley, pp. 46-72; Henry D. and Frances T. McCallum, *The Wire that Fenced the West* (Norman: University of Oklahoma Press, 1965); Joseph M. McFadden, "Monopoly in Barbed Wire: The Formation of the American Steel and Wire Company," *Business History Review*, LII (Winter 1978), pp. 465-89; and Lloyd Wendt and Herman Kogan, *Bet A Million! The Story of John W. Gates* (New York: Bobbs-Merrill, 1948).

Private papers for steel firms that were involved in the merger movement are for the most part either no longer existent or not open to scholars. The only useful collection I found consisted of the records of firms that merged into the American Steel & Wire Company. This collection, located at Harvard University's Baker Library (Baker Mss. 596), consists mainly of papers of the Washburn & Moen Manufacturing Company, but there are also scattered records from some of the other constituents.

An important collection of public documents is the records of the Federal Trade Commission's World War I investigation of the steel industry, stored in the National Archives Building in Washington, Record Group 122, File 8900. This collection contains actual monthly cost sheets for each of U.S. Steel's plants for the period October 1917 to the end of the war, as well as similar documentation for many of U.S. Steel's competitors. For the commission's own analysis of these documents, see U.S. Federal Trade Commission, *War-Time Profits and Costs of the Steel Industry* (Washington, D.C.: U.S. Government Printing Office, 1925).

The primary sources I found most useful for this study were publications by the industry's trade associations. The American Iron and Steel Association's *Bulletin* collected data on individual market transactions of pig iron and steel billets in the 1880s and 1890s. AISA's *Directory to the Iron and Steel Works of the United States* enabled me to keep track of the many entrances and exits of firms to and from the industry, and its *Statistics of the American and Foreign Iron Trades: Annual Report of the Secretary* contained much valuable information on prices and production, sometimes broken down by months. The industry's most important trade journal was *Iron Age*. Published weekly, it reported data on market conditions as well as newsworthy items about the doings of individual firms. Other trade journals I found informative were the *American Metal Market and Daily Iron and Steel Report*, the *American Manufacturer and Iron World*, and the *Metal Worker, Plumber and Steam Fitter*. For financial details about individual firms I consulted the *Commercial and Financial Chronicle, Moody's Manual of Industrial and Miscellaneous Securities*, and *Chicago Securities*.

After publications by trade associations, the sources I found most helpful were government documents. Tariff hearings contain voluminous information on industry prices, production costs, and trade conditions. See U.S. Congress, Senate, *Testimony Taken by the Subcommittee on the Tariff of the Senate Committee on Finance, 1887-1888*, 50th Cong., 1st Sess., 1888, Rept. 2332; U.S. Congress, House, *Tariff Hearings before the Committee on Ways and Means, 1896-1897*, 54th Cong., 2d Sess., 1897, Doc. 338; U.S. Congress, House, *Tariff Hearings before the Committee on Ways and Means, 1908-1909*, 60th Cong., 2d Sess., 1909, Doc. 1505. U.S. Congress, Senate, *Replies to Tariff Inquiries*, 53d Cong., 2d Sess., 1894 (various report numbers), contains manufacturers' responses to a Senate questionnaire about prices and production levels after the Panic of 1893. For additional information on production costs, see U.S. Commissioner of Labor, *Sixth Annual Report, 1890: Cost of Production: Iron, Steel, Coal, Etc.* (Washington, D.C.: U.S. Government Printing Office, 1891).

Of the many government investigations of the United States Steel combination, the most useful are U.S. Congress, House, *Hearings before the Committee on Investigation of United States Steel Corporation* (Washington, D.C.: U.S. Government Printing Office, 1912), and U.S. Commissioner of Corporations, *Report on the Steel Industry, Part I: Organization, Investment, Profits, and Position of the United States Steel Corporation* and *Part III, Cost of Production* (Washington, D.C.: U.S. Government Printing Office, 1911 and 1913). Another invaluable source consists of the many volumes of briefs and testimony compiled during the federal government's dissolution suit against U.S. Steel: U.S. Supreme Court, *The United States of America, Appellant v. United States Steel Corporation, et al.* (Washington, D.C.: U.S. Government Printing Office, 1917). These are stored in the law division of the Library of Congress.

On the paper industry, the major secondary works are David C. Smith, *History of Papermaking in the United States (1691-1969)* (New York: Lockwood Publishing, 1970); Lyman Horace Weeks, *A History of Paper-Manufacturing in the United States, 1690-1916* (New York: Lockwood Trade Journal

Co., 1916); Constance McLaughlin Green, *Holyoke, Massachusetts: A Case History of the Industrial Revolution in America* (New Haven: Yale University Press, 1939); and L. Ethan Ellis, *Newsprint: Producers, Publishers, Political Pressures* (New Brunswick: Rutgers University Press, 1960). More restricted in focus are David C. Smith's "Wood Pulp and Newspapers, 1867-1900," *Business History Review*, XXXVIII (Autumn 1964), pp. 328-45, and Trevor J. O. Dick's "Canadian Newsprint, 1913-1930: National Policies and the North American Economy," *Journal of Economic History*, XLII (September 1982), pp. 659-87. For technical information about the industry's development and manufacturing techniques, see R. H. Clapperton, *The Paper-making Machine: Its Invention, Evolution and Development* (Oxford: Pergamon Press, 1967); John A. Guthrie, *The Economics of Pulp and Paper* (Pullman: State College of Washington Press, 1950); Royal S. Kellogg, *Pulpwood and Wood Pulp in North America* (New York: McGraw-Hill, 1923); and Louis Tillotson Stevenson, *The Background and Economics of American Papermaking* (New York: Harper & Brothers, 1940).

As in the case of the steel industry, my most important primary sources were trade publications, especially the *Paper Trade Journal* and *Paper World*. *Lockwood's Directory of the Paper, Stationery and Allied Trades* enabled me to trace technological developments in the industry as well as track firm entrances and exits. One collection of private papers, the Knowlton Bros., 1813-964, Collection 2877 at Cornell University's Regional History Archives, offered some insight into the management of the Ontario Paper Company, a small but highly competitive newsprint manufacturer. Again, I supplemented these primary sources with government documents, which provided a wealth of information about costs, prices, and conditions in the industry. In addition to the tariff hearings listed earlier, the most valuable documents were the House's multivolume *Pulp and Paper Investigation Hearings*, 60th Cong., 2d Sess., 1909, Doc. 1502, and the accompanying *Pulp and Paper Investigation Report*, 60th Cong., 1st Sess., 1908, Rept. 1786. But see also U.S. Federal Trade Commission, *Newsprint Paper Industry*, 65th Cong., 1st Sess., 1917, Senate Doc. 49; and U.S. Census Office, "Paper and Wood Pulp," *Census of Manufactures: 1905*, Bulletin 80.

Quantitative information on the manufacturing sector as a whole came from U.S. Census Office, *Twelfth Census: Manufactures* (Washington, D.C.: U.S. Government Printing Office, 1902). For additional information on aggregate trends and on the behavior of manufacturing firms in general, I consulted Richard P. Brief, "Nineteenth Century Accounting Error," *Journal of Accounting Research*, III (Spring 1965), pp. 12-31; Brief, "The Origin and Evolution of Nineteenth-Century Asset Accounting," *Business History Review*, XL (Spring 1966), pp. 1-23; Victor S. Clark, *History of Manufacturing in the United States* (1929 ed.; New York: Peter Smith, 1949), Vol. III; Norman R. Collins and Lee E. Preston, "The Size Structure of the Largest Industrial Firms, 1909-1958," *American Economic Review*, LI (December 1961), pp. 986-1003; Richard C. Edwards, "Stages in Corporate Stability and the Risks of Corporate Failure," *Journal of Economic History*, XXXV (June 1975), pp. 428-57; Shaw Livermore, "The Success of Industrial

Mergers," *Quarterly Journal of Economics,* L (November 1935), pp. 68-96; Harold C. Livesay and Patrick G. Porter, "Vertical Integration in American Manufacturing, 1899-1948," *Journal of Economic History,* XXIX (September 1969), pp. 494-500; John Moody, *The Truth About Trusts: A Description and Analysis of the American Trust Movement* (New York: Moody Publishing, 1904); Thomas R. Navin and Marian V. Sears, "The Rise of a Market for Industrial Securities, 1887-1902," *Business History Review,* XXIX (June 1955), pp. 105-38; and G. Warren Nutter and Henry Adler Einhorn, *Enterprise Monopoly in the United States, 1899-1958* (New York: Columbia University Press, 1969).

Qualitative data on the competitive behavior of individual manufacturing firms were culled from a variety of industry studies: Glenn D. Babcock, *History of the United States Rubber Company: A Case Study in Corporate Management* (Bloomington: Indiana University Graduate School of Business, 1966); Stanley Baron, *Brewed in America: A History of Beer and Ale in the United States* (Boston: Little, Brown, 1962); William H. Becker, "American Wholesale Hardware Trade Associations, 1870-1900," *Business History Review,* XLV (Summer 1971), pp. 179-200; Wallace E. Belcher, "Industrial Pooling Agreements," *Quarterly Journal of Economics,* XIX (November 1904), pp. 111-23; Arthur Harrison Cole, *The American Wool Manufacture* (Cambridge: Harvard University Press, 1926), Vol. II; Pearce Davis, *The Development of the American Glass Industry* (New York: Russell & Russell-Atheneum, 1970); Arthur S. Dewing, *Corporate Promotions and Reorganizations* (Cambridge: Harvard University Press, 1914); Whitney Eastman, *The History of the Linseed Oil Industry in the United States* (Minneapolis: T. S. Denison & Co., 1968); James E. Fell, Jr., *Ores to Metals: The Rocky Mountain Smelting Industry* (Lincoln: University of Nebraska Press, 1979); M. J. Fields, "The International Steam Pump Company: An Episode in American Corporate History," *Journal of Economic and Business History,* IV (1931-2), pp. 637-64; Louis Galambos, *Competition & Cooperation: The Emergence of a National Trade Association* (Baltimore: Johns Hopkins Press, 1966); Williams Haynes, *American Chemical Industry, Vol. I: Background and Beginnings,* and *Vol. VI: The Chemical Companies* (New York: D. Van Nostrand, 1954 and 1949); Orris C. Herfindahl, *Copper Costs and Prices: 1870-1957* (Baltimore: Johns Hopkins Press, 1959); Theodore J. Kreps, *The Economics of the Sulfuric Acid Industry* (Stanford University Press, 1938); William G. Lathrop, *The Brass Industry in the United States: A Study of the Origin and the Development of the Brass Industry in the Naugatuck Valley and Its Subsequent Extension over the Nation* (Mount Carmel, Conn.: William G. Lathrop, 1926); John S. McGee, "Predatory Price Cutting: The Standard Oil (N.J.) Case," *The Competitive Economy: Selected Readings,* ed. Yale Brozen (Morristown, N.J.: General Learning Press, 1975), pp. 380-404; Randall Mariger, "Predatory Price Cutting: The Standard Oil of New Jersey Case Revisited," *Explorations in Economic History,* 15 (October 1978), pp. 341-67; Arthur F. Marquette, *Brands, Trademarks and Good Will: The Story of the Quaker Oats Company* (New York: McGraw-Hill, 1967); David F. Noble, *America by Design: Science, Technol-*

ogy, and the Rise of Corporate Capitalism (Oxford University Press, 1977); Harold C. Passer, *The Electrical Manufacturers, 1875-1900: A Study in Competition, Entrepreneurship, Technical Change, and Economic Growth* (Cambridge: Harvard University Press, 1953); Joseph A. Pratt, "The Petroleum Industry in Transition: Antitrust and the Decline of Monopoly Control in Oil," *Journal of Economic History*, XL (December 1980), pp. 815-37; Leonard S. Reich, "Research, Patents, and the Struggle to Control Radio: A Study of Big Business and the Uses of Industrial Research," *Business History Review*, LI (Summer 1977), pp. 208-35; Reich, "Industrial Research and the Pursuit of Corporate Stability: The Early Years of Bell Labs," *Business History Review*, LIV (Winter 1980), pp. 504-29; William Z. Ripley, editor, *Trusts, Pools and Corporations;* Richard Roe, "The United Shoe Machinery Company," *Journal of Political Economy*, XXI (December 1913), pp. 938-53, and XXII (January 1914), pp. 43-63; Herman Steen, *Flour Milling in America* (Minneapolis: T. S. Denison & Co., 1963); Richard B. Tennant, *The American Cigarette Industry, A Study in Economic Analysis and Public Policy* (New Haven: Yale University Press, 1950); Harold F. Williamson and Arnold R. Daum, *The American Petroleum Industry: The Age of Illumination, 1859-1899* (Evanston, Ill.: Northwestern University Press, 1959); Richard Zerbe,"The American Sugar Refinery Company, 1887-1914: The Story of a Monopoly," *Journal of Law and Economics*, XII (October 1969), pp. 339-75; Zerbe, "Monopoly, the Emergence of Oligopoly and the Case of Sugar Refining," *Journal of Law and Economics*, XIII (October 1970), pp. 501-15.

In analyzing theoretically the behavior of firms in these industries I drew most heavily on F. M. Scherer's monumental *Industrial Market Structure and Economic Performance* (2nd ed.; Chicago: Rand McNally, 1980). I also consulted Joe S. Bain, *Barriers to New Competition: Their Character and Consequences in Manufacturing Industries* (Cambridge: Harvard University Press, 1956); Yale Brozen, editor, *The Competitive Economy: Selected Readings;* Harold Demsetz, "Industry Structure, Market Rivalry, and Public Policy," *Journal of Law and Economics*, XVI (April 1973), pp. 1-9; Eleanor M. Fox and James T. Halverson, editors, *Industrial Concentration and the Market System: Legal, Economic, Social and Political Perspectives* (American Bar Association, 1979); Darius W. Gaskins, Jr., "Dynamic Limit Pricing: Optimal Pricing under Threat of Entry," *Journal of Economic Theory*, III (1971), pp. 306-22; N. J. Ireland, "Concentration and the Growth of Market Demand: A Comment on Gaskins' Limit Pricing Model," *Journal of Economic Theory*, V (1972), pp. 303-5; Don Patinkin, "Multiple-Plant Firms, Cartels, and Imperfect Competition," *Quarterly Journal of Economics*, LXI (February 1947), pp. 173-205; Almarin Phillips, *Market Structure, Organization and Performance: An Essay on Price Fixing and Combinations in Restraint of Trade* (Cambridge: Harvard University Press, 1962); George J. Stigler, "The Dominant Firm and the Inverted Umbrella," *The Organization of Industry*, pp. 108-12; Stigler, "The Economies of Scale," *ibid.*, pp. 71-94. Many additional theoretical insights were embodied in other works I have already mentioned.

On the specific subject of antitrust policy, the best general study is William Letwin's *Law and Economic Policy in America: The Evolution of the Sherman Antitrust Act* (New York: Random House, 1965). Stimulating but more polemical are Robert H. Bork, *The Antitrust Paradox: A Policy at War with Itself* (New York: Basic Books, 1978); Gabriel Kolko, *The Triumph of Conservatism: A Reinterpretation of American History, 1900-1916* (Chicago: Quadrangle Paperbacks, 1967); Thomas K. McCraw, "Rethinking the Trust Question," *Regulation in Perspective: Historical Essays* (Cambridge: Harvard University Press, 1981), pp. 1-55; Richard A. Posner, *Antitrust Law: An Economic Perspective* (University of Chicago Press, 1976); and Peter Temin, "Government and Industry in the Nineteenth Century," paper presented to the Lowell Conference on Industrial History, May 22, 1981. Other useful studies include William R. Cornish, "Legal Control over Cartels and Monopolization, 1880-1914: A Comparison," *Law and the Formation of the Big Enterprises in the 19th and Early 20th Centuries: Studies in the History of Industrialization in Germany, France, Great Britain and the United States*, ed. Norbert Horn and Jürgen Kocka (Göttingen: Vandenhoeck & Ruprecht, 1979), pp. 280-303; Morton Keller, "The Pluralist State: American Economic Regulation in Comparative Perspective, 1900-1930," *Regulation in Perspective*, ed. McCraw, pp. 56-94; Alan Stone, *Economic Regulation and the Public Interest: The Federal Trade Commission in Theory and Practice* (Ithaca: Cornell University Press, 1977); Hans B. Thorelli, *The Federal Antitrust Policy: Origination of an American Tradition* (Baltimore: Johns Hopkins Press, 1955).

My greatest intellectual debt in the chapter on antitrust is to Charles W. McCurdy's "The *Knight* Sugar Decision of 1895 and the Modernization of American Corporate Law, 1869-1903," *Business History Review*, LIII (Autumn 1979), pp. 304-42. I tested the ideas suggested by this provocative article against close readings of the following cases: *United States v. E. C. Knight Company*, 156 US 1-46; *Northern Securities Company v. United States*, 193 US 197-411; *The Standard Oil Company of New Jersey et al. v. the United States*, 221 US 1-106; *United States of America v. American Tobacco*, 221 US 106-93; *United States v. United States Steel Corporation et al.*, 223 Fed 55-179; *United States v. United States Steel Corporation el al.*, 251 US 417-66. On the subject of federal incorporation I found Arthur M. Johnson's "Antitrust Policy in Transition, 1908: Ideal and Reality," *Mississippi Valley Historical Review*, 48 (December 1961), pp. 415-34, and Melvin I. Urofsky's "Proposed Federal Incorporation in the Progressive Era," *American Journal of Legal History*, XXVI (April 1982), pp. 160-83, illuminating guides to the policy debate. I also followed the controversy in the *Congressional Record* and in the following related documents: U.S. Congress, House, *An Act to Regulate Commerce, Etc: Hearings on House Bill 19745 before Subcommittee No. 3 of the Committee on the Judiciary*, 60th Cong., 1st Sess., 1908; U.S. Congress, Senate, *Amending Antitrust Act: Adverse Report of the Committee on the Judiciary*, 60th Cong., 2d Sess., 1909, Rept. 848.

Index

Adelman, M. A., 93
Addyston Pipe and Steel combination, 100
Addyston Pipe and Steel decision, 109, 166
Amalgamated Association of Iron, Steel, and Tin Workers, 40
American Agricultural Chemical Company, 98
American Bicycle Company, 98
American Bridge Company, 84, 97
American Cereal Company, 36, 98, 102, 157
American Hide and Leather Company, 141
American Linseed Company, 155
American Malting Company, 141
American Sheet Steel Company, 83, 97
American Smelting and Refining Company, 155
American Steel and Wire Company of Illinois, 67n, 74–5, 76
American Steel and Wire Company of New Jersey, 58, 76, 83, 84, 134–5
American Steel Hoop Company, 83–4, 97
American Straw Board Company, 98
American Sugar Refining Company, 99, 123, 155, 156, 157, 165, 182
American Telephone and Telegraph Company, 156
American Thread Company, 141
American Tin Plate Company, 24, 41, 83, 104–5, 115, 134, 135, 155
American Tin Plate Company of Indiana, 14, 37, 40n, 41
American Tobacco Company, 114n, 157, 182
American Tobacco decision, 159, 161, 173, 182

American Window Glass Company, 141, 156
American Wire Nail Company, 67
American Woolen Company, 98
Anaconda Copper Company, 155
antitrust laws, federal, *see* Clayton Antitrust Act; Sherman Antitrust Act
antitrust laws, state, 162–3, 169
Association of Tin Plate Makers of the United States, 14, 41

Baackes, Michael, 63
Baackes Wire Nail Company, 64, 66n, 67
Bain, Joe S., 111n, 183
Baltimore Iron, Steel, and Tinplate Company, 41n
barriers to entry, 37, 142, 145, 153, 160, 190, 194
  early attempts to erect, 155–7
  extent of problem, 183–6
  government policy toward, 157–8, 161–2, 163, 175–6
  see also United States Steel Corporation
Becker, William H., 27
Berlin Mills Paper Company, 127, 130–1, 132, 138, 140
Bethlehem Steel (Iron) Company, 57, 77n, 82, 83
bicycle industry, 28, 98, 102
Bork, Robert H., 160, 162, 174n, 179
Brewer, David J., 169
Brief, Richard P., 53–4
Brittan, Lewis, 75
Bullock, Charles J., 5–6
Burns, Arthur R., 52–3

Cambria Steel (Iron) Company, 57, 58, 77n, 82, 83
Campbell, James A., 176

capital-output ratio, 29, 30–1, 88–9, 90–1, 94–6, 112
Carnegie, Andrew, 11, 34, 37, 38, 64, 66n, 67, 77, 78n, 80, 83
Carnegie Company of New Jersey, 57n, 83, 84
Carnegie Steel Company, Ltd., 57, 58, 82
cast-iron pipe industry, 99, 101
Census of Manufactures, 29, 88–93
Chandler, Alfred D., Jr., 7, 8, 32, 92, 102, 153–5, 157, 181, 187, 190, 191
chemical industry, 101
Chisholm, Hugh J., 89n, 114
Cincinnati Barbed Wire Fence Company, 76
Clark, Edward, 187
Clarke, Charles C., 123
Clayton Antitrust Act, 159, 178
Cleveland Rolling Mill Company, 70, 75, 80n
Cliff Paper Company, 56, 138, 140
collusion, 15–16, 24–5, 27, 45, 52–3, 107, 109, 116, 188, 189
    examples of, 14, 25–7, 41, 69–71, 78–81, 82–3, 85–6, 100–1, 118–9, 127–9, 135, 136–7, 138
    outlawed, 109, 162, 164, 166–7, 174, 178, 180, 190–1
Colorado Fuel and Iron Company, 77, 78, 80n, 83
Consolidated Steel and Wire Company, 67n, 73, 74, 81
consolidation movement, *see* merger movement, great
cordage industry, 100, 182
Cowles, David S., 31n, 89n
Crowell, Henry Parsons, 19
cut-nail industry, 63

Daniels, F. H., 75
Davis, Lance, 8
Demsetz, Harold, 184–5
difference-of-means test, 89–94
discriminant analysis, 90n, 112–4
Distilling and Cattle Feeding Company, 99, 141, 156, 164, 175, 181–2

dominant-firm strategy, 120–6, 129–31, 133–4, 135–6, 141, 152–3, 181, 189–90

E. C. Knight decision, 109, 165–6, 167, 168, 179n
Eastern Pig Iron Association, 24, 33n
economies of speed, 32–3, 92, 145, 153, 183, 184
Edwards, Richard C., 192
Empire Iron and Steel Company, 96

Federal Steel Company, 83, 84
Federal Trade Commission Act, 159, 178
Felton, E. C., 33
fertilizer industry, 98, 101
fixed-cost theory, 50–2, 99–100, 188
    criticized, 52–9
    modified, 59–62, 86, 87, 103, 116, 187–9
    modified version tested, 87–96, 112–14
fixed costs
    effect of age of firm on, 59, 60, 139, 189
    estimated, 88–9, 140
    failure to account adequately for, 53–4, 103–6
    as incentive to run full, 31–2, 50–2, 84, 99–100, 126, 188–9
    proportion in total costs, 30–1
    urgency of, 55–9
Flambeau Paper Company, 55
Frick, Henry Clay, 57, 83
Fuller, Melville W., 166, 167, 168, 179n

Gary, Elbert H., 118, 137, 146n, 153, 176, 177n, 193
Gary dinners, 118, 136, 138
Gates, John W., 11, 34, 73, 75, 76, 81
General Electric Company, 156
glass industry, 98, 100, 101, 103, 122
glucose industry, 28, 98
Glucose Sugar Refining Company, 98, 141
Gould Paper Company, 138, 140

Grand Crossing Tack Company, 67n
Great Northern Paper Company, 55,
  127, 129, 130, 131, 138, 140
Greer, George, 104
Griffiths, W. H., 104
Gunpowder Trade Association, 101n

H. P. Nail Company, 64, 67n, 74
hardware industry, 27
Harlan, John M., 167, 174, 180n
Hastings, Arthur C., 56, 89n
Hepburn, William P., 170, 178
Hepburn bill, 170–3
Herkimer Paper Company, 106–7
Hill, James J., 146
Holmes, Oliver Wendell, Jr., 167, 168,
  169, 177n

I. M. Singer Company, 8, 187
Illinois Steel Company, 34, 57, 67n,
  77n, 80, 81, 83, 134–5
incorporation power, federal, 169–73,
  178, 186, 190
incorporation power, state, 162–9, 190
Ingram, William A., 33n
International Paper Company, 44, 54,
  106, 114–15, 135, 136, 155, 157
  competitive strategy, 127–34
  market share, 126–7, 130–1, 132–3,
  141
  and monopoly power, 119, 127–9,
  138
  motives for formation, 105–7
  production costs, 139–41
  profits, 130n, 133, 142
International Silver Company, 110, 141

Jay Paper Company, 107
Jellico Mountain Coal decision, 164,
  175
Jenks, Jeremiah W., 6n, 110n, 171
John Hamilton and Company, 19, 22
Johnson Steel Company, 80n, 82
Joint Traffic decision, 166

Kennedy, Julian, 33, 39, 97
Knowlton, G. W., 32, 56, 60

Kolko, Gabriel, 159–60, 162, 169, 171,
  179

L. L. Brown Paper Company, 35
Lackawanna Iron and Steel Company,
  57, 58, 77n, 82, 83
leather industry, 100, 101, 182
Lee, Susan Previant, 9
linseed-oil industry, 29, 101, 182
Lisbon Falls Fibre Company, 138, 140
Livermore, Shaw, 141–2
Livesay, Harold C., 29
logit analysis, 94–6, 113n

McCurdy, Charles W., 165
McElwain, J. S., 28
McKenna, Joseph, 177
McNair, Clarence I., 56
malt industry, 101
Mariger, Randall, 121–2
Markham, Jesse W., 2n, 7–8, 88n, 108
Martin, Frederick Roy, 131
Maryland Steel Company, 80n
meatpacking industry, 28
merger movement, great, 1–5, 159, 166
  effect on competition, 116–17, 119–
  21, 133–4, 136, 138–9, 152–3, 157–
  8, 180–1, 183–6, 189–90, 191, 193–4
  explanations of, 6–8, 45, 87, 103–4,
  105, 107–14, 116, 187–9
  and industrial concentration, 2–5,
  124, 126–7, 133, 134–5, 139, 141–2,
  149–52, 153, 189–90
  quantitative analysis of, 87–96, 112–
  14, 141–2, 154–5
  reaction to, 5, 159, 166, 186, 190
  role of promoters in, 107–8, 114–16
Meurer Brothers Company, 19, 22–3
Moody, John, 2n, 102
Moore, William H., 41, 115
Morgan, J. P., 73

N. and G. Taylor Company, 19, 22–3
National Biscuit Company, 115, 154,
  157, 181
National Civic Federation, 170
National Cordage Company, 141, 155

National Starch Manufacturing Company, 99
National Steel Company, 58, 83, 84, 96
National Tube Company, 84, 97
Nelson, Ralph L., 7, 87, 88n, 109–11
New Castle Wire Nail Company, 67, 74, 75
New Economic History, 9–10, 190, 191
New York Times, The, 129, 131–2
newsprint industry, 18, 31, 45, 46, 47, 60, 114–15, 118, 138, 152, 188
    collusion, 119, 127–9, 134, 138
    competition, 44–5, 105–7, 126, 130–4
    economies of scale, 42–3
    economies of speed, 32
    failures, 44, 105–7
    firms evenly matched, 41–5
    growth of, 41–2, 126–7, 128, 130
    methods of finance, 55–6
    prices, 26, 126, 131–2
    production costs, 140
    profits, 105–7, 132
    running full, 32, 56, 106
    technological developments, 28, 41, 43, 97, 139–40
    vertical integration, 31, 32, 44
non-ferrous metals industry, 29, 100, 155, 159, 183
Norris, John, 32n, 61n, 106
Northern Securities Company, 159, 166, 168
Northern Securities decision, 166–9, 174, 180n
Northwest Paper Company, 55

oatmeal industry, 18, 36, 98, 100, 102
Ohio Steel Company, 80n, 82
Oliver Wire Company (Oliver and Roberts), 67, 74
Ontario Paper Company, 60
Oswego Falls Pulp and Paper Company, 127

Parks, John H., 69
Parsons Paper Company, 17, 26, 28
Passell, Peter, 9
Pejebscot Paper Company, 126, 138, 140

Pennsylvania Steel Company, 33, 57, 77n, 82, 83
petroleum industry, 17, 29
Piercefield Paper and Mining Company, 107
pig-iron industry, 32–3, 84, 144, 149
    collusion, 24, 27
    prices, 19–22, 24
    product differentiation, 17, 19–22, 23–4, 34–5
    shutdowns and curtailments, 23
Pitcairn, John, 103, 122
Pittsburgh Plate Glass Company, 98, 103, 122
Pittsburgh Wire Company, 67, 70, 74, 75, 76
Plummer, John D., 131
Pope, A. A., 102
Porter, Patrick G., 29
Pratt, Joseph A., 163
Premier Steel Company, 40n, 80n
product differentiation, 16–27, 34–7, 154, 157, 183, 191, 193

Quaker Oats Company, see American Cereal Company

Rail Association, 78, 80–1, 85
Reid, Daniel G., 14, 104, 115
Remington-Martin Paper Company, 55, 138, 140
Republic Iron and Steel Company, 96
Roosevelt, Theodore, 157–8, 159, 160, 166, 169–70, 171, 172
Royal Baking Powder Company, 157
rubber industry, 100, 101
rule of reason, 173–5, 178, 180, 183, 186, 190–1
Rumford Falls Paper Company, 105–6

St. Regis Paper Company, 55, 127, 132, 138, 140
Salem Wire Nail Company, 67n, 73–4
salt industry, 54, 101
Schroeder, Gertrude, 147
Schumacher, Ferdinand, 36, 98, 102
Schwab, Charles M., 146–7

Sherman Antitrust Act, 107, 109, 159, 164, 165, 166, 167, 168, 169, 170, 171, 172, 174, 175, 181, 192
Singer, Isaac Merritt, 187
Smith, Adam, 15, 25, 187
Standard Oil Company, 122, 159, 163, 182
Standard Oil decision, 159, 173, 175
starch industry, 17, 18, 99, 182
steam-pump industry, 101
steel industry (crude), 28, 38, 52, 62, 87, 96, 97, 149, 194
  collusion, 38, 78, 80, 82–3, 84–6, 118, 136–7, 176, 189
  competition, 80–2, 85–6
  economies of speed, 32–3, 84
  growth of, 76–7, 85
  methods of finance, 56–8
  prices, 78–9
  production costs, 143–4
  running full, 33–4, 84
  vertical integration, 32–3, 38, 83, 84, 144–7
steel-rail industry, *see* steel industry (crude)
steel-wire industry, 62, 67n, 86, 87, 107, 188
  absence of economies of speed, 84
  collusion, 69–71, 85, 118, 135, 136–7
  competition, 66–9, 71–6, 85, 135–6
  concentration, 74–5, 76, 134–5, 152
  failures, 64, 150–1
  firms evenly matched in, 67n
  growth of, 63, 64, 70, 73, 85, 134–5, 150–1
  prices, 63–5, 68, 69, 71, 72, 74–6, 118, 137, 148
  production costs, 68, 72, 143–4
  profits, 72–3, 75–6
  running full, 66–8, 71, 84
  technological developments, 28, 62–3, 97
  vertical integration, 63, 84
Steele, George F., 89n
Stevenson, John, Jr., 75, 105
Stigler, George J., 42, 121–2
straw-board industry, 98, 182

sugar industry, 36, 99, 100, 101, 102, 123, 159, 165–6
survivor test, 42
Susquehanna Iron and Steel Company, 96
Swift, Gustavus, 187
Swift and Company, 8, 187

Taft, William Howard, 159
Taylor, Nathan, 35
Tennessee Coal, Iron and Railroad Company, 147n, 158
textile industry, 98, 100, 101
Thomas Iron Company, 23, 24
Thurber, F. B., 123
tin-plate industry, 27, 47, 107, 188
  absence of economies of scale, 39
  collusion, 14–15, 24, 27, 118, 136–7
  competition, 14–15, 41, 60–1, 105, 115, 135–6
  concentration, 115, 134, 152
  failures, 41, 151
  firms evenly matched in, 39–41, 42
  growth of, 39, 134, 150–1
  prices, 14–15, 19, 118, 137, 148
  product differentiation, 19, 22–3, 36–7
  production costs, 143–4
  profits, 104, 115
  running full, 45, 105
  shutdowns and curtailments, 22, 41, 135
  tariffs, 29, 39, 97
  technological developments, 40
  vertical integration, 39, 147, 149
Tin Plate Manufacturers' Association, 14, 24, 41
tobacco industry, 28, 114n, 182
Trans-Missouri Freight decision, 166

Union Bag and Paper Company, 130
United Shoe Machinery Company, 155
U.S. Cast Iron Pipe and Foundry Company, 100
United States Envelope Company, 141
United States Leather Company, 141
United States Rubber Company, 156, 182

United States Steel Corporation, 96,
    104–5, 138, 153
  barriers to entry, 145, 149–51, 153,
    176, 186
  collusion, 118, 135, 136–7, 176, 177n
  competitive strategy, 121, 135–7,
    176, 180
  control of raw materials, 145–9, 153,
    158, 162, 176, 180, 186
  dissolution suit, 158, 159, 161–2,
    176–7, 180
  market shares, 134–5, 152, 176
  organization of, 83–4
  production costs, 142–4
  profits, 149
  vertical integration, 144–5, 176
United States Steel decision, 158, 159,
    161–2

vertical integration, 29–30, 32, 91–93,
    94n, 153–5, 157, 161–2, 175, 183,
    191
  see also newsprint industry; steel in-
    dustry (crude); steel-wire industry; tin-
    plate industry; United States Steel
    Corporation
Virginia-Carolina Chemical Company,
    98

Virginia Iron, Coal and Coke Company,
    96

Warwick Iron Company, 23
Washburn and Moen Manufacturing
    Company, 70, 74, 75–6
Washington Steel and Tin Plate Mills,
    104
Westinghouse Electric Company, 156
Weston, Byron, 35
whiskey industry, 17, 99, 100, 101, 123
White, Edward Douglass, 161, 167–8,
    173–5, 177n
Williamson, Jeffrey G., 9–10
Wilson, Woodrow, 159
wire-nail industry, see steel-wire industry
Wire-Nail Association, 69–71, 100
Wolff, R. H., 72n
writing-paper industry (including ledger
    paper)
  collusion, 25–7
  failures, 26
  prices, 17–18, 26
  product differentiation, 16–18, 19, 35
  shutdowns and curtailments, 25–6, 27

Youngstown Sheet and Tube Company,
    176